The Quest for a General Theory of Leadership

NEW HORIZONS IN LEADERSHIP STUDIES

Series Editor: Joanne B. Ciulla
Professor and Coston Family Chair in Leadership and Ethics,
Jepson School of Leadership Studies, University of Richmond, USA

This important series is designed to make a significant contribution to the development of leadership studies. This field has expanded dramatically in recent years and the series provides an invaluable forum for the publication of high quality works of scholarship and shows the diversity of leadership issues and practices around the world.

The main emphasis of the series is on the development and application of new and original ideas in leadership studies. It pays particular attention to leadership in business, economics and public policy and incorporates the wide range of disciplines which are now part of the field. Global in its approach, it includes some of the best theoretical and empirical work with contributions to fundamental principles, rigorous evaluations of existing concepts and competing theories, historical surveys and future visions.

Titles in the series include:

The Quest for a General Theory of Leadership

Edited by

George R. Goethals

E. Claiborne Robins Distinguished Professor of Leadership Studies, Jepson School of Leadership Studies, University of Richmond, USA

Georgia L.J. Sorenson

Research Professor and Founder, James MacGregor Burns Academy of Leadership, University of of Maryland, College Park, USA and Chair and Professor of Transformation, US Army

NEW HORIZONS IN LEADERSHIP STUDIES

Edward Elgar
Cheltenham, UK • Northampton, MA, USA

Published by
Edward Elgar Publishing Limited
The Lypiatts
15 Lansdown Road
Cheltenham
Glos GL50 2JA
UK

Edward Elgar Publishing, Inc.
William Pratt House
9 Dewey Court
Northampton
Massachusetts 01060
USA

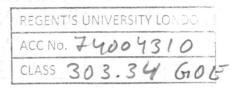

Paperback edition 2007
Paperback edition reprinted 2014

A catalogue record for this book
is available from the British Library

Library of Congress Cataloguing in Publication Data
The quest for a general theory of leadership / edited by George R. Goethals,
Georgia L.J. Sorenson.
    p. cm. -- (New horizons in leadership studies series)
    Includes bibliographical references and index.
    1. Leadership. 2. Leadership--Philosophy. I. Goethals, George R. II.
Sorenson, Georgia Jones. III. New horizons in leadership studies.
    HM1261Q47 2006
    303.3'401--dc22
                                    2006004803

MIX
Paper from
responsible sources
FSC
www.fsc.org FSC® C021018

ISBN 978 1 84542 541 8 (cased)
      978 1 84720 324 3 (paperback)

Typeset by Manton Typesetters, Louth, Lincolnshire, UK
Printed in Great Britain by Berforts Information Press Ltd

To the Leadership and Legacy of
James MacGregor Burns

Contents

Figures and tables

FIGURES

TABLES

Contributors

James MacGregor Burns is Professor Emeritus of Political Science at Williams College. He teaches at the Academy of Leadership at the University of Maryland and has taught at the Jepson School of Leadership Studies at the University of Richmond, Virginia. He is the winner of the Pulitzer Prize and National Book Award for his biography of Franklin Roosevelt. Author of the seminal book, *Leadership*, in 1978, and senior editor of the *Encyclopedia of Leadership*, he is a pioneer in the field of leadership studies. A political scientist and past president of the American Political Science Association and the International Society of Political Psychology, he received his education from Williams College, Harvard University and the London School of Economics.

Joanne B. Ciulla is Professor and Coston Family Chair in Leadership and Ethics at the Jepson School of Leadership Studies, the University of Richmond, Virginia, where she was one of the founding faculty members. A BA, MA and PhD in philosophy, her books include *The Working Life: The Promise and Betrayal of Modern Work*; *Ethics, The Heart of Leadership*; *The Ethics of Leadership*; *Honest Work*; *A Business Ethics Reader* (co-authored); and *The Quest for Moral Leaders* (co-edited). Ciulla is associate editor of the *Leadership Quarterly* and is on the editorial boards of *Leadership* and the *Business Ethics Quarterly*.

Richard A. Couto helped found the Antioch PhD program in Leadership and Change as well as the Jepson School of Leadership Studies at the University of Richmond, Virginia. He held the Modlin Chair in the latter and is currently Professor in the former. His recent books focus on community leadership, *To Give Their Gifts*; democratic theory and practice, *Making Democracy Work Better*; and higher education, *Courses in Courage*. His contribution to this book permitted him the twin opportunities of detailing both an increasingly visible incident of the civil rights movement and leadership as causality. He grew up in Lawrence, Massachusetts. Being a Boston Red Sox fan, since birth, has helped him to maintain hope in the face of disappointment. Thus, he still trusts in leadership for the democratic prospect.

Elizabeth Faier directs the Sheikha Fatima bint Mubarak Program for Leadership at Zayed University in the United Arab Emirates and was previously a member of the Jepson School of Leadership Studies at the University of Richmond, Virginia. She holds an AB from Cornell University and MA and PhD degrees from Indiana University, all in the discipline of anthropology. Dr Faier's early research focuses on emergent leadership and identity among Palestinian activists in nongovernmental organizations. Her other research addresses leadership in urban spaces, focusing on the ways in which leadership and social relations are spatialized and made concrete within the built environment. She is the author of *Organizations, Gender, and the Culture of Palestinian Activism in Haifa, Israel* (Routledge, 2005).

George R. 'Al' Goethals is E. Claiborne Robins Distinguished Professor of Leadership Studies at the University of Richmond, Virginia. He was on the faculty of Williams College for 36 years where he served as chair of the department of psychology, founding chair of the program in leadership studies, acting dean of the faculty, and provost. His recent scholarship has explored peer influences on academic achievement, image-making in presidential debates, presidential leadership, and the presidency of Ulysses S. Grant.

Michael Harvey is Chair of the Department of Business Management at Washington College, Maryland. He has a PhD in government from Cornell University and a master's in international business from the University of Wisconsin-Milwaukee. He has written on Machiavelli and on leadership, literature, and imagination. He is also interested in how leaders communicate, and is the author of *The Nuts and Bolts of College Writing*.

Gill Robinson Hickman is currently a Professor in the Jepson School of Leadership Studies at the University of Richmond, Virginia. She has held positions as dean, professor of public administration and human resource director. Her books include *Leading Organizations: Perspectives for a New Era*, and *Managing Personnel in the Public Sector: A Shared Responsibility* (with Dalton Lee). She is currently working on a forthcoming book titled, *Leading Change in Multiple Contexts: Connecting Purpose, Concepts and Practices*.

Douglas A. Hicks, PhD is Associate Professor of Leadership Studies and Religion at the Jepson School of Leadership Studies of the University of Richmond and Director of the University's Bonner Center for Civic Engagement. He is author of two books, *Inequality and Christian Ethics* (2000) and *Religion and the Workplace* (2003), both published by Cambridge University Press. He is an editor, with J. Thomas Wren and Terry L. Price, of the three-volume reference work *The International Library of Leadership* (2004). He has held a visiting faculty position at Harvard Divinity School and has received summer research support from the National Endowment for the Humanities.

Crystal L. Hoyt is an Assistant Professor of Leadership Studies at the Jepson School of Leadership Studies at the University of Richmond, Virginia. She completed her doctorate in social psychology at the University of California at Santa Barbara. Her research and curricular interests include social behavior, leadership and group dynamics, research methodology in the social sciences, examining the effects of stereotypes and discrimination on women and minority leaders, leader perception, and the role of confidence in shaping group leadership. Her research has appeared in journals including *Psychological Inquiry, Group Dynamics, Small Group Research, Journal of Leadership and Organizational Studies, Presence*, and *Leadership Review.*

Sonia Ospina, is an Associate Professor of Public Management and Policy and Codirector of the Research Center for Leadership in Action at the Robert F. Wagner School of Public Service, New York University. Her research interests include organizational and management theory; leadership in public contexts; and public management reform, governance, and collaborative problem solving in public service in the USA and in Latin America. She currently directs the Research and Documentation Component of the Leadership for a Changing World Program.

Terry L. Price is Associate Professor at the Jepson School of Leadership Studies at the University of Richmond, Virginia. He has degrees in philosophy, politics, and psychology from the University of North Carolina at Chapel Hill and the University of Oxford, and he completed his doctorate in philosophy at the University of Arizona. His work has been published in outlets such as *American Philosophical Quarterly, Encyclopedia of Leadership, Journal of Political Philosophy, Journal of Value Inquiry, Leadership and Organization Development Journal*, and *Leadership Quarterly*. He is co-editor of the three-volume reference set *The International Library of Leadership* and of *The Quest for Moral Leaders: Essays in Leadership Ethics*. He is also author of *Understanding Ethical Failures in Leadership* (Cambridge University Press, 2006).

Ronald E. Riggio, PhD is the Henry R. Kravis Professor of Leadership and Organizational Psychology and Director of the Kravis Leadership Institute at Claremont McKenna College. Professor Riggio is the author of over 100 books, book chapters, and research articles in the areas of leadership, assessment centers, organizational psychology and social psychology. His research work has included published studies on the role of social skills and emotions in leadership potential and leadership success, empathy, social intelligence, emotional skill and charisma. He is an associate editor of the *Leadership Quarterly* and is on the editorial boards of *Leadership, Journal of Nonverbal Behavior,* and *Leadership Review.*

Georgia L.J. Sorenson, PhD is Chair and Professor of Transformation of the US Army at the Army War College, Pennsylvania, and Research Professor at the James MacGregor Burns Academy of Leadership at the University of Maryland. She is founder of the Academy as well as a founder of the International Leadership Association. She was visiting senior scholar from 2002–2004 at the Jepson School of Leadership Studies. Sorenson is co-editor (with George Goethals and James MacGregor Burns) of the four-volume *Encyclopedia of Leadership* (Sage, 2004), and co-author of *Dead Center: Clinton–Gore Leadership and the Perils of Moderation* (Scribner's) with James MacGregor Burns. Sorenson serves as editor or associate editor of several leadership studies journals including *Leadership*, *Leadership Quarterly*, and *Leadership Review* and is on the board of numerous organizations devoted to leadership studies. Email: gsorenson@academy.umd.edu

Mark C. Walker is currently an Assistant Professor of International Relations at American University in Washington, DC. He is the author of *The Strategic Use of Referendums: Power, Legitimacy, and Democracy* (Palgrave, 2003); his article on the role of morality, self-interest, and leaders in international affairs was published in *Leadership Quarterly* in 2006. His research agenda is based broadly upon the individual decision-maker – singly and in aggregate – and the methodology of conducting leadership studies. He has applied his analytical framework to international and domestic politics comparatively with a recent attempt to understand the determining factor that affects decision-making in the US national security council. He earned his MA and PhD in political science from the University of California at Berkeley and his BS in political science from the Massachusetts Institute of Technology. Email: mcwalker@alum.mit.edu.

J. Thomas Wren is Professor and Interim Dean at the Jepson School of Leadership Studies at the University of Richmond, Virginia. He received his BA from Denison University. He has an MA and PhD in history from the College of William and Mary, an MA in public policy from George Washington University, and a JD from the University of Virginia. He is the co-editor of the three-volume *International Library of Leadership* (Edward Elgar, 2004), and editor of *The Leader's Companion: Insights on Leadership through the Ages* (Free Press, 1995).

Acknowledgements

The editors wish to thank all of those – family, friends, and colleagues – who made this scholarly venture possible. First, we want to express our special appreciation to our friend and mentor James MacGregor Burns for initially challenging us take up the task of creating a general theory of leadership. We hope this book justifies his faith in the project.

A special note of appreciation must be extended to the three institutions that initially supported our efforts, namely, the Program in Leadership Studies at Williams College, the James MacGregor Burns Academy of Leadership at the University of Maryland, and the Jepson School of Leadership Studies at the University of Richmond, Virginia. Kenneth Ruscio, Dean of the Jepson School, has been particularly helpful and supportive, and we are grateful.

We wish to thank the scholars who pushed us onward in our journey – chapter authors as well as others who weighed in from time to time, namely, Bruce Avolio, Zachary Green, John L. Johnson, Jean Lipman-Blumen, Deborah Meehan, Ronald Walters, and Gary Yukl.

Deborah Meehan of the Leadership Learning Community provided an early grant to support the initial phases of our efforts. This support, in conjunction with that of Shelly Wilsey, allowed several lively sessions focused on our project at the International Leadership Association meetings in 2002, 2003, and 2004. Support from Williams College allowed us to use the beautiful facilities at Mount Hope in Williamstown, Massachusetts for our extended planning retreat in 2002. Lisa Carey Moore worked tirelessly with great skill and diplomacy on all retreat arrangements. We wish to thank Michael Cassin and the Clark Art Institute for an after-hours tour of the Clark's superb collection, an experience that enlivened considerably our creative thinking during our retreat.

We want to thank Joanne Ciulla for encouraging us to publish this volume in her series on New Horizons in Leadership Studies. Her support for the project, and her own contributions to it, are greatly appreciated. Cassie King helped edit several of the book's chapters and we are deeply grateful for her talented assistance. We want also to thank Alan Sturmer at Edward Elgar for his encouragement, patience, and wise counsel.

Nothing would be possible without the support of our families. To Marion Goethals, Olive Sorenson Jones, and Suzanna Strasburg we owe more than can be said simply here. Thank you.

Introduction

The chapters in this book tell the story of an intellectual journey of nearly five years' duration. Early in the year 2001 James MacGregor Burns, to whom this book is dedicated, asked the two of us, first Georgia Sorenson and then Al Goethals, whether we would like to join him and others in writing an integrative theory of leadership. We accepted the challenge, knowing that the chances of any group of scholars actually producing such a theory were, quite frankly, low. There were two difficulties. One, coming up with an integrative, or what we came to call a general, theory was daunting in itself. Few if any intellectual disciplines or fields have a widely accepted overarching theory. There are highly influential theories in many disciplines, such as plate tectonics in the geosciences, but few comprehensive models. Two, trying to get a group of scholars from different disciplines to come up with a single theoretical statement of any kind, or quality, seemed foolhardy. Theories are not generally formualted by groups. Nor are most essays, stories, novels, treatises or briefs. One might argue that parts of some of the founding documents of the United States of American were produced by groups, but we may judge that the better parts were largely produced by individuals, such as Thomas Jefferson and James Madison. Nevertheless, we proceeded, and through a process described in the opening chapter of the present volume, we engaged a stellar group of scholars to work on the project.

Since we began, the composition of our working group (eventually termed GTOL for general theory of leadership) has expanded. But the authors of the chapters in this book have been consistently engaged. All or most of us have met on eight separate occasions, for up to five days at a time. The collaborative experience has been extremely stimulating, both personally and intellectually. Although we did not accomplish exactly what we set out to accomplish, we are very pleased with this book. It reveals process as well as product. We have learned as much about leadership from working together as from producing our individual chapters. The scholarly community still awaits a general theory of leadership, but we have taken the first steps toward the goal of creating one.

The story of our quest is summarized in Tom Wren's superb chapter detailing the intellectual obstacles that we faced at the beginning of our journey. It reveals that we let spirit and excitement perhaps overrule judgment in undertaking our quest in the first place. That we got as far as we did is clearly attributable to the deft and sometimes subtle leadership of our common mentor, James MacGregor

Burns. Wren tells the story of getting to that place in thorough and compelling fashion. As he explains, as our group thought about how we might ever understand leadership, we realized that we needed to come to terms with some basic aspects of the human condition. It turned out that coming to terms was not the same as coming to agreement. Coming to terms, in the end, meant agreeing to disagree about some fundamental issues. The various conclusions that several of us reached are quite eloquently discussed in Chapter 2, Michael Harvey's essay on the human condition.

We also decided near the beginning of our undertaking that we needed to confront the nature of theory. If we were to construct a general theory, it was important to consider what a theory was and was not, and what it could do and not do. This point of view was articulated persistently and ultimately persuasively by our late colleague, Fred Jablin. Mark Walker graciously bowed to the group's pressure to write about the nature of theory as it applied to our project. His very useful paper constitutes Chapter 3 in this volume.

With the three above-mentioned chapters providing some foundation, we then took on the task of composing chapters that dealt with what we early identified as the fundamental aspects of leadership that any overarching theory must address. These were power and motivation, leader–follower relations, ethics and values, change and causality, meaning making, and historical and cultural context. The next three chapters deal with the first three of these topics. Michael Harvey provides an erudite discussion of the faces of power, as they have been described in various literatures, from Shakespeare to social psychology to Foucault. As Harvey (Chapter 4) explains, power can be quite subtle, or it can be very direct. It can be mutual, lodged in interdependence, or it can be largely asymmetric, wielded almost totally by only one party in an interaction. Our challenge is to see how the many different kinds of power are employed in leadership, and in followership. In Chapter 5, Crystal Hoyt, Al Goethals and Ron Riggio discuss social psychological aspects of group dynamics and the leader–follower relationship that are crucial to understanding the perils and potentials of leadership. It is clear from their analysis that the results of group dynamics and leadership can be constructive or destructive, ethical or unethical, and that the outcome is largely dependent on the methods and morals of leaders. We turn next to Terry Price and Doug Hicks's (Chapter 6) consideration of perhaps the most universal, though largely unquestioned, philosophical question in leadership – namely, the apparent and sometimes real role differentiation (and inequality) in the leader–follower relationship. The GTOL group returned with regularity over our years working together to issues of inequality and justice. Price and Hicks constructively take up these questions as they discuss trait, situational, transactional, and transformational approaches to inequality as well as traditional and modern philosophical attempts to comprehend the dilemmas inherent in this central human relationship.

The philosophical tension apparent in the search for equality brings us squarely into the realm of mindful action, the purview of the concluding chapters. While most people agree that there is a great need for better leadership in all circumstances, our group came to see that the understanding and practice of sound leadership has a crucial role in addressing inequality and its consequences – unequal distribution of wealth, power, opportunity, and dignity. Gill Hickman and Dick Couto (Chapter 7) bring issues of leadership and inequality to center stage by examining a key but largely unknown leadership event during the US civil rights movement: the effort to desegregate schools in Prince Edward County, Virginia. Hickman and Couto take issue with the 'Newtonian, mechanistic and old science' view of a leader or leaders initiating change and instead offer a complex net of co-arising historical, economic, group and environmental factors that ebb and flow, push and pull, to collectively birth change. Using a constructionist approach as opposed to an essentialist one, they deftly demonstrate the interpenetrating and complex nature of leadership in action. Sonia Ospina and Georgia Sorenson (Chapter 8) deepen this analysis by intensifying the constructionist illume. They assert that a leadership event 'happens when a community develops and uses, over time, shared agreements to create results that have collective value.' Understanding the meaning-making process in groups helps us to be cognizant of understanding leadership and change from the essential actors' point of view, and not from our own formulations. Leadership, they conclude, is thus relational – oft times invisible – emergent and contextually rooted in community.

Much of the work of the general theory scholars was not coming to conclusion but rather coming to conversation. Over the years there had been wide-ranging debate in our group about whether a general theory of leadership could be a-historical and a-contextual. Could there be a universal theory which would apply across cultures and times – to drill down into the essence of the elemental nature of human leadership? Our final chapter – prior to the Commentary chapter and the Afterword, fittingly a conversation – is about context in leadership. Scholars Tom Wren and Liz Faier, elucidate the differences in the understanding of context from their own disciplinary perspectives (Chapter 9). Historian Wren perceives context as the environment in which leadership takes place while anthropologist Faier considers context more abstractly, as a space constructed and named by those participating in events. Thus Wren and Faier return to the old familiar mind and matter terrain. Does consciousness precede being, as politician and philosopher-playwright Václav Havel suggested? This deliciously metaphysical question and chapter provides a fitting transition to the two concluding pieces of our volume.

Joanne Ciulla contributes a thoughtful Commentary (Chapter 10), examining the book's central themes and the connections between each of the chapters. A 'synthesis' is probably impossible, but Ciulla's commentary usefully distills much of what we have discussed. Finally, James MacGregor Burns contributes an Afterword, the story of his own struggles with understanding leadership and building the foundation for the field of leadership studies. On that foundation, those who follow Jim's leadership can continue to transform the field. We wish them well as they carry forward the quest and question of a general theory of leadership.

George R. Goethals,
Georgia L.J. Sorenson

1. A quest for a grand theory of leadership

J. Thomas Wren

What happens when a collection of scholars from differing disciplines comes together to create a grand theory of leadership? This is the question philosopher Joanne B. Ciulla came to identify as particularly intriguing as a group of academics assembled to attempt precisely that. Although the substantive challenges of creating a grand theory of leadership had always been the group's focus, it gradually dawned on the participants that *how* they were going about the task of coming together across disciplines to create an integrated product was as significant as *what* they were creating. Political scientist Georgia Sorenson noted that 'there is a *process* and a *product* here. We need to write about the reflective process' as well.[1] Similarly, in the throes of a particularly difficult debate over foundational assumptions, Joanne Ciulla commented: 'Perhaps we could show what it's like to be in a group of people trying to do this and what it is like to do it: to watch people struggling with this intellectual [challenge].'[2] Or, as Ciulla later phrased it, 'A paper on what happened when leadership scholars tried to create a unified theory might be more interesting and useful to the field than one on [the] unified theory [itself].'[3] The substantive output of the academics engaged in this initiative is an important contribution, and is presented in this volume. This opening chapter, however, purports to trace the challenges and achievements of the process itself. In doing so, it also illustrates the pitfalls and potential of a multidisciplinary field such as leadership studies.

BEGINNINGS: CALL AND RESPONSE

In November, 2001, Pulitzer Prize-winning leadership scholar James MacGregor Burns convened an interdisciplinary group of leadership scholars at the Jepson School of Leadership Studies at the University of Richmond, Virginia. The academics hailed from three universities with established leadership programs: the University of Richmond, the University of Maryland at College Park, and Williams College. Disciplines represented included political science, psychology, philosophy, communications studies, history, public administration, anthropology, and religion. Since that beginning the group has expanded significantly, and currently numbers 25 scholars and practitioners from a dozen institutions.[4]

At that November meeting, Burns outlined his vision. In the description provided by the *Chronicle of Higher Education* in a later article on the venture, Burns expressed his desire to 'provide people studying or practicing leadership with a general guide or orientation – a set of principles that are universal which can be then adapted to different situations.'[5] In short, Burns desired, in his term, a 'general theory of leadership.' He also articulated a related objective, which was to 'legitimize a field that some skeptics still dismiss as lightweight and ill-defined... . We are intent,' said Burns, 'on making [leadership studies] an intellectually responsible discipline.'[6]

Two fellow scholars joined Burns in launching the project: George 'Al' Goethals of Williams College and Georgia Sorenson of the University of Maryland and the Jepson School. These three became the governing 'troika' of the group, and project leaders. Their first task was to establish the parameters of the project. Sorenson expanded upon both the need for the project and the proposed approach the group should take. 'I believe we urgently need to understand and to communicate what we know about leadership,' she began. She cited leadership scholar Jerry Hunt, who stated: 'What is missing, in addition to quantity of theoretical formulations or models is a "grand" or generalized theory of leader–subordinate relationships – if such a theoretical development is possible.' Likewise, Sorenson quoted Ralph Stodgill's assertion that 'the endless accumulation of empirical data has not produced an integrated understanding of leadership.'[7] Sorenson remarked with confidence that 'in time, there will be a general theory of leadership,' citing the successful examples of the general theory of relativity and successes in the fields of economics and criminology. 'But whether this is possible or not,' she concluded her charge to the assembled scholars, 'it is certainly incumbent upon us to better integrate what we already know.'[8]

Sorenson coupled her call for a general theory with a vision as to how the scholars might go about achieving it. 'A General Theory of Leadership Project,' she elaborated, 'would have, for me, features of the Genome Project – a "hot group" whose task is a careful construction of what is known, an identification of what is not known and needs to be known, an accounting of ideas/variables that are in dispute or contradictory, and some hard thinking about how it all hangs together. In short, we would be building a leadership DNA.' Sorenson also called for a second group to conduct meta-analyses of existing literature to feed to the Leadership Genome Group.[9] In the tradition of the 'hot group,' she envisioned the creation of 'a group that will hole up in a place for a long time until we come up with a general theory.'[10]

With Burns, Goethals, and Sorenson having given the call for the construction of a general theory of leadership, the next several months were given over to the responses of the scholars, in the form of an exchange of papers. As might be predicted from a group of academics, particularly one as multidisciplinary as this, the rejoinders were widely disparate and sometimes contradictory, but each represented a reasoned response to this notion of a general theory that was to extend beyond disciplines to structure an entire field of academic endeavor. Approaching these position papers with analytical care, it is possible to identify several key issues that would continue to engage the group over the coming months and years. These initial debates among group members reveal both the challenges and the possibilities of such multidisciplinary undertakings.

To be sure, the very idea of a general theory met with some skepticism. 'I find the idea of a general theory of leadership Quixotic,' wrote philosopher Ciulla. 'I have no inclination to work on developing one, but I am curious about why some of my distinguished colleagues think we should.'[11] All the scholars who had reservations, however – including Ciulla – presented cogent reasoning to buttress their concerns, often with specific recommendations for ways to circumvent the perceived difficulty. The ensuing debate energized the initiative. It is worthwhile, then, to parse out the issues upon which the academics seemed to divide.

One of the foundational issues was the very idea of an integrative theory. Although by their very participation in the project all members were committed to the possibility of integration at some level, there was debate among those who favored integration along the lines of the Burns/Goethals/Sorenson vision and those who advocated the advantages of retaining the 'let a thousand flowers bloom' approach more characteristic of the current multidisciplinary field of leadership studies. This tension between an integrated, unitary articulation of leadership and an approach that argued for a more diverse conceptualization would become one of the permanent fault lines of the project, and presaged what could very roughly be labeled a divide between the approaches of the humanities and the social sciences. The remarkable thing was not that there were such divisions, which were predictable and perhaps inevitable, but that the scholars determined to persevere despite the differences. That is part of this tale. First, however, it is important to stake out the concerns.

Douglas A. Hicks, a scholar whose work spans the disciplines of religious studies and economics, made the case for a more inclusive approach by citing the experiences of those two disciplines. In the field of economics 'there exists one predominant general theory of economic systems and behavior,' posited Hicks. That general theory is 'the standard neo-classical model ... [that] largely corresponds to the practice of free-market capitalism.' This unitary capitalistic paradigm excludes all competing conceptualizations. In contrast to the '"true way" in economics,' continued Hicks, 'there is no one clear methodology or general theory in the study of religion... . Approaches vary widely; sometimes they are complementary and sometimes contradictory.' Hicks then made a specific application of his argument to the matter at hand: 'It should be clear by now,' he wrote, 'that debates about the meaning of prevailing methodologies, or general theories of a field are not exclusive to leadership studies.' Given the present state of the field of leadership studies, he concluded, 'it does not seem either possible or preferable to design a general theory of leadership that determines who is out and who is within a discipline – as has happened in economics. Rather, the religious studies model of emphasizing disciplinary approaches – and how they can be incorporated in a boundary-crossing conversation – seems the more promising way to go.' Hicks went on to propose a better approach: 'I recommend that we consider proceeding in terms of mapping parallel disciplinary approaches to leadership... . This does not require denying that common elements of leadership processes exist across contexts,' he conceded, 'but it does not settle the question before we start. It also takes an inclusive view of who can fit in the tent of leadership studies and it invites us to move beyond the definitional questions to substantive matters.'[12]

As Hicks's final comments made clear, there was nothing in this criticism that implied that the efforts of the group were of little worth; quite the contrary. Joanne Ciulla took a similar tack, and elaborated upon the rationale for a more inclusive and diverse approach. Drawing upon her knowledge of the philosophy of science, she cited the writings of Inre Lakatos, who had opposed Thomas Kuhn's rather linear conceptualization of scientific revolutions. According to Lakatos, 'a field of knowledge does not need everyone working under one paradigm to advance... . There is nothing wrong with a field has a number of research projects going on that work from differing paradigms.'[13] Somewhat similar to Hicks, Ciulla proposed a different approach. 'I don't think we should be developing a theory, but rather looking at what we already have and thinking about how to put the pieces together.' What is needed is 'a serious discussion of the state of the field and how we might help pull it together, not under one theory, but as a web of approaches and perspectives and problems that constitute leadership studies.'[14]

Other scholars evinced concern for anything that tended to reinforce the dispersed state of the field. James MacGregor Burns lamented the fact that 'the study of leadership has become fragmented and some would say even trivialized.' The proposal to create a general theory of leadership is 'an attempt to bring some sort of order to the field.'[15] Others applauded the effort to achieve some sort of synthesis. Richard A. Couto agreed that 'as the field of leadership studies develops, some scholarship will have to devote effort to a synthesis of theories,'[16] while Burns suggested that 'for some time now students of leadership have been working toward a theory of leadership that is more integrated and inclusive and yet applicable and "practical," without sacrificing rigor and depth.'[17] The 'General Theory of Leadership Project' [GTOL], as it came to be called, was merely an extension of this salutary development.

In reflecting upon this series of exchanges, the ultimate tension was not a matter of clear-cut support or opposition to a general theory of leadership so much as it was a debate over the impact of setting boundaries. As anthropologist Elizabeth A. Faier phrased it, 'We have some boundary issues [that involve the question] "what counts as leadership?"' In making integrative decisions, some ideas and approaches will inevitably be excluded. 'What are we going to exclude?' was, to Faier, the troubling question.[18] Philosopher Terry L. Price expanded upon the essence of the concern. In his initial reaction to the project, Price thought 'that an integrated theory of leadership was an interesting, but, ultimately doomed project. Because particular disciplines are not themselves integrated,' he continued, 'any effort to integrate work on leadership from the various disciplines would involve assuming away important substantive questions... . Accordingly, parties to the project would be at risk of sacrificing the intellectual value of truth to the intellectual value of integration.'[19]

This did not mean that a resolution of the tension was not possible. Price, who had posed perhaps the most cogent rationale against integration, eventually converted to a more optimistic stance. 'I begin with a confession,' he wrote in the second round of papers. 'Since writing for the last set of papers, I've changed my basic view of the endeavor.' His earlier concerns about the dangers of integration had not disappeared, but 'although I still think this risk exists, our discussions have led me to believe that it is significantly less threatening than I originally thought.' Price thought that it might indeed be possible to integrate the insights of multiple disciplines, although the result could be 'we might end up with more than one reasonable, internally consistent theory of leadership.' But 'this need not strike us as a problematic outcome.'[20] Price, in essence, was able to perceive a result that allowed integration yet still respected differences. Douglas A. Hicks reached his own truce with the issue by envisioning a broad model of leadership. 'Leadership is richest when we create space, instead of setting boundaries,' he said. '[We] need a theory that allows for conflict; that creates space for it.'[21] Thus, out of this foundational conflict came what would become one of the strengths of the project: a theoretical conceptualization that aspired to embrace a multitude of approaches to leadership. Although these tensions remain and have not been fully resolved, progress has been made.

A somewhat parallel foundational discussion centered on the nature of theory, a discussion that elucidated some of the contrasting disciplinary approaches and assumptions of social scientists and humanists. Indeed, the term 'theory,' and in particular the term 'general theory' – even though that became a part of the moniker of the group – occasioned no little debate and even some consternation. From the very outset, then, there was some ambiguity regarding the nature of the ultimate product of the group.

In her opening presentation to the group, project leader Georgia Sorenson posed the challenge in traditional theoretical terms. In a section entitled 'A Brief

Reminder of the Parameters of Theory,' Sorenson, quoting social scientists Chester Schriesheim and Steven Kerr, noted that, 'at least from a social science perspective, "a theory should first have internal consistency; that is, its propositions should be free from contradiction. Second, a theory should have external consistency; that is, it should be consistent with observations. Third, it must be … stated so that its predictions can be verified. Finally a practical theory should have the attribute of scientific parsimony."' Elaborating further, Sorenson defined a 'general theory' as 'a metaview – one in which theories and their parts are imbedded.'[22]

On the other hand, James MacGregor Burns, although he selected the term 'general theory of leadership' as the group's objective, made statements that appeared to belie a strict reading of the term. In his opening communication to the scholars, he expressed interest in exploring 'the analytical possibilities of the study of leadership that could [at] least provide "principles of leadership" for a leadership 101 class, just as one expects to learn the principles of physics or chemistry in an introductory course.' He appeared to acknowledge that the efforts of the group might 'only be a preface to more integrated theories of leadership. As we work toward that goal,' he continued, 'we can at least try to work out some generalizations on leadership.'[23]

This ambiguity as to desired outcome continued through the ensuing discussions. For their part, the academic participants differed concerning what the term 'theory' might mean for purposes of this project. In an early discussion, this notion of theory engendered uncertainty as to whether it meant, for the group, a traditional social science perspective, or some more 'Proustian' approach. As the philosopher Terry Price pointed out, 'This raises a deeper question to begin with: in the end, we come from our own disciplines. The question of *what is theory* is determined by this.'[24] Political scientist Richard Couto added, 'the importance of theory varies among the disciplines that contribute to the study of leadership, and the nature of theory varies among the disciplines that hold it to be important.'[25] And so it proved.

Predictably perhaps, social scientists and humanists viewed both the nature of theory and its value differently. Couto outlined the essential nature of the social science approach when he wrote that 'in general, the social sciences hold steadfastly to hopes of theories that, like those of the natural sciences, will explain phenomena and enable social scientists to predict them as well.'[26] And Frederic M. Jablin, a scholar in communication studies, was close to his social scientific roots when he urged the group to be precise in its approach. 'Although I am hopeful as to our ability to develop an integrative theory,' he wrote, 'I do have concerns … about our work. First, I am still unsure as to whether or not we have a common understanding of "theory" (e.g., axiomatic theory, grounded theory, mid-range theories)… .'[27] Jablin went so far as to suggest that if the group was serious about constructing a legitimate theory, it should hire a consultant to 'present a primer on theory building to help frame what theory looks like.'[28]

Others in the group, primarily humanists, resisted the social science perspective. Joanne B. Ciulla, a philosopher, remarked: 'Perhaps I have been misinterpreting the phrase "general theory of leadership." To my ears it sounds restrictive and unrealistic, given the nature of leadership as a phenomena.... Leadership, unlike physics, is about human behavior, which does not lend itself to deductions from a theoretical system.'[29] Another suggested in the initial discussion that 'solutions may come from other than traditional ways of looking at theory.'[30]

Again, the challenge the group faced was how to reconcile a difference in perspective. And again, the members of the group demonstrated a willingness to make the attempt. Social scientist Frederic M. Jablin, for instance, had initially questioned 'whether or not what we are shooting for as an outcome is a "theory" or something else.' However, he also went on to say 'I'm OK with "something else," but I would like for us all to have a common understanding of that outcome.'[31] Unfortunately, Jablin's call for a specific resolution of the nature of theory for purposes of the group's work was not heeded. Subsequent group activities suggest, however, that the resolution has been in favor of a broader, more humanistic approach.

The discussion of the nature of theory generated also a critique by some members of the group of the assumptions that apparently underlay the project. Specifically, these scholars questioned the validity of the assumption of linearity that seemed to undergird the theoretical discussion. This line of criticism seemed to stem from two distinct rationales. The first simply argued that the process of leadership was too complex to capture in any sort of linear model or theory. This usually took the form of advocacy for some sort of systems approach. Joanne Ciulla was one who championed this sort of approach. Early on, she posed the question: 'Can we look at it from a systems perspective?' This might capture subtleties that 'theories exclude.' 'If we look at it from systems theory,' she reasoned, 'we can learn a great deal about how to make connections and inferences.'[32] This criticism of traditional theoretical approaches, it would seem, was not particularly devastating to the project. As Frederic Jablin noted, while a systems approach is nonlinear, it remains a process model of leadership.[33] In any event, James MacGregor Burns seemed amenable to proceeding along these lines, if it suited the will of the group. 'Leadership,' he said, 'lends itself to a systems approach.'[34]

Other members of the group posed a more fundamental critique of traditional notions of theory as framing an understanding of the world, one that struck at the heart of the idea of an *a priori* theoretical framework. Anthropologist Elizabeth Faier articulated this position most forcefully. To Faier, the very idea of some universal theory of leadership was problematic. To begin with, there was a difficulty with any conceptualization of universalism. While admitting 'we

[must] seek out ways to "make sense" ... ,' nevertheless 'to fully understand the ways in which leadership unfolds means that we have to recognize the limitations and positionality of "making sense."' Moreover, in addition to the fallacy that there is only one, unitary, perspective to be had, Faier also rejected the notion that the leadership relation could ever be conceived of as static. To Faier, 'leadership ... is a process wholly dependent on human action, local problems, social structures, history, and systems of beliefs, values, and symbols... . [E]mbracing static models obscures the changes that occur within cultural systems, individual acts of agency, and social practices of leadership... .' Finally, Faier argued, traditional theory does not allow for the dynamics of identity formation. 'Leadership,' she suggested, 'stems from and plays into identity formation. ... Bypassing the impact of the multiple, overlapping, and competing levels of leader and follower identities (age, gender, race, nation, community, etc.) ignores fundamental elements of the human tradition.'[35]

Richard Couto also depicted a postmodern conceptualization of theory. Having explained the rational and scientific approaches of social scientists, he described other scholars who 'distance themselves from an effort to "reduce" human events to science altogether or to outdated paradigms of the natural sciences. Among the latter group of post-modern [scholars],' Couto asserted, 'the effort to find a general theory of leadership smacks of a quixotic Enlightenment-era quest promoted by a Newtonian scientific view of a mechanical universe. Some members of this group,' he continued, 'would assert that if there is a general theory of leadership, it will flow from new post-Newtonian natural scenarios, which emphasize systems and probability.' Even that may be asking too much of some, for 'the group divides along the line of whether or not general theories are possible.'[36]

For his part, Couto set about the task of suggesting how such an approach might look. He began with a traditional 'Analytical Framework of Leadership,' complete with matrix. But this was clearly insufficient. 'If only the study and conduct of leadership were as easy or neat as a set of straight lines and boxes!' Couto wrote. He then transformed it into a 'Dynamic Model of Leadership,' but, as he explained it, 'moving leadership from the straight lines of the printed page to actual day to day experience means moving to a dynamic system of interrelated parts and subsystems of constant change without clear boundaries – a fractal, not a chart... .' Thus, 'all the elements of leadership and their components swirl in interrelated activity and in ever-changing patterns of all the factors of the framework, analogous to the activity at the subatomic level of matter.' This model was sufficiently complex that it 'unfortunately cannot be placed on paper,' although the reader was given a link to 'An Animated Model of Quantum Leadership.'[37]

Clearly, the above critiques of linearity in thinking about leadership, if accepted, have varying degrees of impact upon the group's output. As suggested above, systems thinking, while an important departure, can still be more or less incorporated into traditional ways of thinking about leadership. The epistemic and constructivist criticisms, and certainly the quantum view of leadership theory, are less easy to reconcile. Ultimately, the GTOL group has not passed judgment one way or the other; one will find elements of the competing views in subsequent chapters of this volume. Tensions such as this have generated some argument for substituting multiple narratives of leadership for an integrated approach. The nature of this debate within the group will be addressed later in this chapter.

Although the above analysis has identified the most serious challenges to a general theory of leadership that the responding academics posed, it does not exhaust the cautions and concerns that various scholars expressed. These can be treated more briefly.

Related to the earlier discussion of integration is the 'is/ought' paradox; that is, the tension between descriptive approaches to theory and prescriptive or normative ones. Philosopher Terry Price identified this concern. According to Price, 'pure descriptivists of the empiricist ilk might claim that there is nothing on the other side of the divide.' On the other hand, while 'pure prescriptivists will hardly deny the place of the descriptive enterprise, ... they might fail to acknowledge its relevance to the task they have set for themselves, viz., discovering how leaders and followers should behave.' It is possible, argued Price, that the 'is/ought gap' is just too great for a general theory to straddle. 'Unfortunately,' he went on, 'what we understand to be the nature of their interaction may ultimately depend on our pre-theoretical assumptions ... about the interface of descriptive and prescriptive considerations.' If true, this could have serious consequences for the project. 'My guess, then,' continued Price, 'is that the nature of interplay between the prescriptive and descriptive components of leadership is significantly more complex than much of the literature lets on. This does not bode particularly well for a general theory of leadership,' because 'insofar as the project of coming up with a general theory of leadership takes for granted that real integration is warranted, it unjustifiably privileges some pre-theoretical options over others.' Price saw only one solution. 'To do justice to important intellectual values in addition to the value of integration, our general theory will have to make room for the full range of pre-theoretical positions with respect to the interface between the descriptive and ... prescriptive sides of the subject of inquiry.'[38]

While Price concerned himself with pre-theoretical assumptions, Frederic Jablin weighed in with concerns about the levels of analysis to be employed. 'I hope that as we proceed we consider the applicability of our work in terms of "micro" (e.g., dyadic, interactional) as well as "macro" (e.g., culture and structures) levels of analysis and in terms of everyday/mundane as well as extraordinary contexts and processes. ... I fear we lean toward the macro and the extraordinary in our discussions of leadership and do not fully consider that our ideas need to translate to lower levels of analysis (dyads, groups) as well as to "ordinary"/mundane leadership contexts.'[39]

Still others had more general cautions to convey. Elizabeth Faier, an anthropologist, was concerned that non-Western perspectives might get short shrift.[40] She urged the group members to 'move ... beyond simplistic categorical and definitive notions of leadership that are not applicable to non-Western contexts.' Similarly, Faier cautioned that 'Leadership theorized within different cultural and historical venues must take difference and change into account; I have doubts,' she concluded, 'as to whether an integrative theory could make room not only for group variance but such changes in cultural systems.'[41] In another vein, Price urged the group to recognize also that its theorizing about leadership would inevitably 'raise important ethical questions.' Creating a leadership theory will necessarily involve a prescriptive aspect, Price argued, and this 'focus on moral leadership, and its analysis, will tell us something about not only what ends ought to be pursued but also what constitutes their ethical pursuit.'[42]

There were, then, a number of important concerns. caveats, and cautions voiced by the scholars in response to Burns, Goethals, and Sorenson's call for an integrated theory of leadership. In the ensuing months and years (as we shall see), some were addressed and resolved, others rejected, and still others simply ignored. But before we continue the narration of this quest for a general theory of leadership, it is important to acknowledge that the response to the initial call for such a theory yielded more than skepticism. Several scholars embraced the challenge, and produced initial papers that sought to move the enterprise forward. A summary of these, and their implications for the project, is in order.

Not surprisingly, several of the scholars looked to their own disciplines for insight. Social psychologist Zachary Green sought to explain leadership as a part of a group phenomenon. 'Leadership,' he argued, 'is a function of the group. Beyond person or process, leadership is an expression of the actions or intentions of a human collective. Without the group, leadership remains in the realm of the potential... .'[43] Another psychologist, Al Goethals, asserted that 'perhaps the most important argument is to place more focus on the emotional and psychological bonds between leaders and followers, and to understand how these dynamics combine with other factors, especially cognitive factors, to produce leadership.'[44] He proceeded to cite classic psychological studies such as those by Sigmund Freud and by French and Raven, as well as studies of the persuasion process and cognitive dissonance theory.

Elizabeth Faier also turned to her home discipline of anthropology for insight, but with considerable caution. She acknowledged that traditional anthropological studies had much to offer the understanding of leadership. 'Anthropology studies leadership,' she wrote, 'as social structure, social practice, and a component of culturally specific phenomena such as kinship, authority and power, prestige, legal and economic systems, symbols, culture change, and identity formation.' But there were also significant difficulties posed by the anthropological approach. For one thing, 'one characteristic of anthropological research is that data drive theory rather than data prove a hypothesis – this obviously poses a great challenge to the incorporation of anthropology into an integrative theory.' Moreover, as was discussed earlier in Faier's challenge to a linear theory of leadership, modern anthropology tends to take a constructivist approach to knowledge. As Faier put it, 'anthropologists are not only intimately involved with the collection of data but also with its construction.' Still and all, Faier argued that an anthropological approach holds out great hopes for the better understanding of leadership. 'I would like to suggest,' she concluded, 'that anthropology's contribution extends beyond case studies into ways we can theorize the relationship among leadership, social practice, and cultural logic. Moreover, linking leadership to broader questions of how people negotiate structure and agency or to the relationship between the individual and society would enable a "thicker" examination of leadership processes... .'[45]

It is useful to pause here and consider the implications of these disciplinary references. By grounding their papers in their respective disciplines, these scholars implicitly adopted the stance of advocating the development of leadership theory from a multidisciplinary perspective. It was, in a sense, a reprise of the earlier debate about the risks of attempting to achieve an integrative theory. There, it will be recalled, some group members argued that too much would be lost by integration or, as some phrased it, drawing boundaries. Douglas A. Hicks, whose arguments were cited in the earlier analysis, made the strongest statement for this multidisciplinary approach. Drawing upon his specialty of religious studies, Hicks noted that 'the field of religious studies is divided [much like leadership studies] along methodological, even disciplinary lines. The phenomena of religion are studied via anthropological, historical, sociological, philosophical, theological, and even literary-critical methodologies.' Given this state of affairs, Hicks reflected upon his probable response if just such an integrative task were presented to his home academic field. 'If I, as a scholar of religion,' he wrote, 'were called upon to produce a General Theory of Religion, I would think first in terms of these disciplinary approaches. I would refuse to prioritize some universal theory... . While there are points of tension and possible contradiction among such views, they illuminate different dimensions... .'[46]

Yet despite the strong arguments of those among the group who supported a multidisciplinary approach, there proved to be undoubted complications arising from the fact that scholars from many disciplines were involved. Because this became a reality with which the group would consistently struggle, it is worthy of brief mention here. As Richard Couto put it, 'the problem is not with inclusiveness but with the conflicting nature of disciplines in interdisciplinary study and of clashing paradigms within disciplines.'[47] Although it oversimplifies the matter, it is useful to think of the problem in terms of two camps: the social scientists and the humanists. Joanne Ciulla framed this debate well. She cited C.P. Snow's comment that there are 'two cultures' of scholars. 'In Snow's day,' Ciulla explained, 'they were the humanities and the natural sciences. Today the split is between the humanities and the social sciences.' Returning to Snow's remarks, he noted that these two categories of scholars represented 'two groups – comparable in intelligence, identical in race ... who had ceased to communicate.'[48] Ciulla went on to cite also 'the philosopher Carl Hempel [who] offers insight into why it is so difficult to fit together research from different disciplines.' Hempel focused not on methodology so much as he did the differing contributions provided by the scholarly camps. Hempel 'argues that the role of empirical science is to describe the world, but we also need to explain and understand it.' Ciulla then provided her own typology of the scholarly world: 'Description is generally done by social scientists, explanation by historians, anthropologists, religious scholars, etc., and critical analysis by philosophers.'[49]

The collection of insights set out above reveals the Gordian knot set out before the assembled scholars. As Ciulla makes clear, all the tribes of the scholarly community have something important to offer this bold attempt to portray leadership. On the other hand, as Snow and several of the debates outlined above suggest, there are real and substantive differences among scholars in terms of assumptions, focus, and methodology. Fortunately, the GTOL group never reached the stage of non-communication perceived by Snow. Indeed, the entire process has been marked by remarkable openness among the participants. Nonetheless, the differences among the disciplines have remained among the most intractable of the challenges facing those seeking a general theory of leadership.

Finally, in our analytical tour of the responses by the academicians to the call for a general theory of leadership, some of the group members responded to the initial charge by submitting proposed models or narratives of leadership intended to serve as the first step toward the creation of a grand theory. These scholars accepted the call for a general theory as a valid – albeit intimidating – task for a group of interdisciplinary scholars to undertake.

J. Thomas Wren, for example, first created a 'Periodic Table of Leadership,' in which he attempted to locate and classify 'as many approaches to leadership,' said Wren, 'as I could recollect.' (See Figure 1.1 as an example of this integrative approach).This typology, he wrote, 'goes beyond ... leadership theory per se, and seeks to include what might be called the "liberal arts" approaches to leadership, as well as some of the more recent qualitative models.' Having attempted to portray the universe of leadership studies in an organized way, Wren proceeded to outline what he called a 'Process Model' of leadership that began with an 'initiating event,' followed by 'constituent response,' and so on through

I CONTEXTUAL

Hi Historical Approaches	
Cu Cultural Approaches	
Cc Cross-cultural	
Di Diversity Approaches	
Od Organizational Design	
Gr Gender Approaches	

II INDIVIDUAL

A. Trait	**Tt** Trait Theory	**Ps** Personality Approaches			
B. Behavioral	**Bv** Behavior Theory	**Ob** Organizational Behavior	**Mo** Motivation Theory	**Py** Psychological Approaches	
C. Cognitive	**Im** Implicit Theory	**At** Attribution Theory	**Ch** Charismatic Theory	**Ld** Leader Development	**Sf** Self Leadership
	F Follower Approaches	**Ro** Role Theory			

III PROCESS

A. Contingency	**Cy** Contingency Theory	**Si** Situational Theory	**De** Decision Theory	**Pg** Path-Goal Theory				
B. Transactional	**Ic** Idiosyncasy Credits	**Lm** Leader/Member Exchange	**Tr** Transactional Leadership					
	Po Power Approaches	**Co** Communication Theory	**In** Influence Approaches	**Gp** Group Process	**De** Democratic Theory	**Sy** Systems Theory	**Cr** Conflict Resolution	**Au** Authority Issues
	Ls Leader Substitutes	**St** Strategic Approaches	**Tm** Team LDSF	**Vi** Vision Approaches			**Pr** Participatory Approaches	**Aw** Adaptive Work

IV NORMATIVE

Ci Citizen Leader	**Il** Instrumental Approaches
Sr Servant Leader	**Tl** Transformational Leadership
E Ethical Theory	**Tg** Transforming Leadership
Va Values Approaches	**Cg** Change Theory
Rv Revolutionary Approaches	

V METHOD

Qu Quantitative Method
Ql Qualitative Method
Pb Problem-Based
Ar Action Research

Figure 1.1   Periodic table of leadership studies

leader emergence, policy debate, outcome, implementation, and feedback loop. Wren then placed upon a diagram of his model 'the abbreviations from the Periodic Table to suggest some of the approaches to leadership that might be most relevant to each particular stage of the model.' Whether the model itself was valid was less important to Wren than the fact that he had attempted to create 'a model of the leadership process demonstrating how the disparate approaches to leadership might be integrated into a coherent intellectual structure.' From that, believed Wren, could come a coherent theory of leadership.[50]

Gill Robinson Hickman, a scholar of public administration, similarly articulated a model of the leadership process that began with a need for action, followed by a recognition of purpose, communication, concurrence and willingness to participate, and, finally, collective action.[51] So, too, did political scientist Richard Couto propose a model of leadership. 'The field of leadership studies,' he asserted, 'has work to do to create models of direct and deliberate democratic leadership. This paper explains how this might be done within a synthesis of recent leadership scholarship that amounts to a general theory of leadership.' Then, drawing from the works of James MacGregor Burns, Howard Gardner, and Ronald Heifetz, Couto discussed the role of narratives in leadership, the range of values in democratic discourse, and the concept of adaptive work.[52]

Finally, James MacGregor Burns himself contributed an elegant narrative of leadership 'As a process leadership begins, in my view, with palpable human wants and needs that can be broadly generalized. Potential leaders … respond to these wants and legitimize them as *needs* deserving of recognition and response… . Conflict arises out of the competition of people for economic and psychological satisfactions.' Then, 'as basic needs for food and shelter are met, people develop hope for the satisfaction of "higher" needs.' As Burns summed it up, 'the clues to the mystery of leadership lie … in a powerful equation: embattled values grounded in real wants, invigorated by conflict, empower leaders and activated followers to fashion deep and comprehensive change in the lives of people.' To this process 'leaders bring their own resources, including their skills, into play as they reflect the underlying forces. They recognize and articulate the wants and needs, mobilize supporters, sharpen conflict, fashion new agreements among participants, innovate creative outcomes that transcend the original parameters of conflict and – always – strengthen and elevate the whole process by bringing to bear the most exacting moral criteria.'[53]

Faced with such a plethora of responses to the call for the creation of a general theory of leadership, the group considered several possible alternatives. The first and most obvious one was to throw in the towel, write the experience off as a 'learning' one, and proclaim that the time was not yet ripe – if ever it would be – for the creation of a general theory of leadership. It is a testament to the group's goodwill and dedication to the mutual endeavor that no one seriously put this possibility forward. A second alternative, one quite familiar to academics, was to continue to argue over the issues, imitating Grant, who once said 'I am pre-pared to fight along this line if it takes all summer.' This would have led to many fascinating discussions, but would, in all probability, have proved fruitless. The General Theory of Leadership group chose a third alternative, one suggested by project leader Georgia Sorenson. Referring to her observations of university politics, Sorenson noted that members of academe often adopt a fiction. 'Some universities operate as ... an "as if" organization. As faculty, we participate *as if* students and learning are paramount, *as if* faculty had a voice, and *as if* ad-ministrators are not judged by capital campaigns.'[54] This became known to the group as the *as if condition*. As Terry Price articulated it, 'Our modus operandi [should] be one of acting "as if." That is to say that we should act as if it were possible to integrate what the various disciplines have to say about leadership.'[55] In sum, the assembled scholars agreed to put aside their quite real reservations and differences on some of the fundamental issues, and to move forward together in a continuing discussion of leadership, with open minds and willing attitudes. And so the work on a general theory of leadership continued.

A considerable amount of space has been devoted to a portrayal of the amal-gam of skepticism, fundamental differences in approach, and positive proposals for going forward that greeted the initial proposal that a group of scholars from multiple disciplines should create a general theory of leadership. This level of detail appears justified in a chapter which seeks to portray the intellectual chal-lenges of the creation of such a grand theory. The analysis of the ensuing stages of the work of the GTOL group can be somewhat more condensed, as the schol-ars, for the most part, adhered to the *as if condition* and suppressed the sort of fundamental criticisms that characterized the first stage of the process. Still and all, the group's continuing efforts revealed both remarkable progress toward a unified understanding of leadership and underlying tensions in the process which threatened the ultimate success of the undertaking. It is to the narration of that story that this analysis now turns.

The collection of academicians that had come to be known as the GTOL group continued to meet and exchange papers on a regular basis. For purposes of analytical coherence, the remainder of this chapter will be divided into seg-ments linked to the gatherings of the group that produced key moments or turning points in the process.

RICHMOND: DETERMINING THE SCOPE OF THE PROJECT

Following the initial meeting with James MacGregor Burns, Al Goethals, and Georgia Sorenson in November 2001 and an exchange of papers in early 2002, the participants in the General Theory of Leadership project met again at the

Jepson School of Leadership Studies in Richmond for three days in March. This represented their first face-to-face, substantive meeting of the participating scholars. As might be anticipated from a gathering of a dozen scholars from multiple disciplines who had been called together to address such a complex and amorphous topic, the ensuing discussion was freewheeling and somewhat undisciplined [at one point in the midst of a rambling exchange, James Mac-Gregor Burns, in near despair, reminded the group of the 'need to re-focus'].[56] For purposes of coherence in the narration, if not perfect chronological accuracy, the following analysis will impose more order upon the discourse than was apparent at the time. For example, many of the reservations and differences of opinion regarding the notion of a general theory of leadership discussed in the preceding section of this chapter were addressed in the March meeting, but for purposes of this chapter, the relevant commentary has been folded into the earlier discussion, *supra*. With this caveat regarding editorial license, we can turn to the insights of the Richmond meeting.

Because this is a chapter dedicated to exploring the intellectual challenges posed by the attempt to create a multidisciplinary general theory of leadership more than it is a report on substantive outcomes, a detailed report on the content of the Richmond deliberations is unnecessary here. However, one of the things that made the Richmond meeting important to the ongoing process was the general tenor and scope of those substantive discussions. That is to say, as the assembled scholars undertook the consideration of one topic after another, there emerged a consistent pattern regarding the group's level of analysis and what it found to be important. More specifically, this particular gathering of scholars, drawn from both the humanities and the social sciences, chose to discuss the phenomenon of leadership at a rather high level of abstraction, usually in 'macro' terms, and with a perceptible concern for the normative consequences of the leadership relation. Thus this initial discussion, although many of its precise conclusions would not have a large impact upon later deliberations, nevertheless was an important stage in the group's progress toward its intended goal. In sum, the Richmond meeting helped to frame the general outlines of the group's approach to a general theory of leadership.

Upon convening in Richmond, one of the first orders of business was to consider how to begin the discussions in an organized fashion. Al Goethals, who with Burns and Sorenson formed the troika who managed the project, suggested that 'a problem-oriented approach may be useful.' He went on to propose that the group look to specific cases, such as '9/11' or school shootings, and attempt to deduce insights into leadership. From such analysis could come insights into such leadership issues as the role of leaders, decision-making, sense-making, and organizational structures.[57] In the end, however, it was the agenda offered by James MacGregor Burns that carried the day. Burns proposed that the group could begin to move toward an integrated understanding of leadership by discussing what he considered to be the key 'elements' of leadership: power, motivation, leader–follower relations, and values. Once the scholars had parsed these constructs from the perspectives of their respective areas of expertise, thought Burns, the group could then begin the ultimate task of attempting some sort of integration. The scholars acceded to this proposal, and the effort toward constructing a general theory of leadership began in earnest.[58]

The group's examination of the construct of 'power' provides a good example of the expansive parameters of the approach taken toward leadership. The discussion began in a rather traditional fashion. Acknowledging that 'power is one thing that distinguishes the leadership relation,' it was suggested that one way to pursue the analysis would be to consider (a) a definition of power, (b) the sources of power, (c) the use of power, and (d) the ethics of its use. Beginning along this path, the initial definitions of power tracked traditional social science conceptualizations such as 'the capacity to influence.' At this point, however, the discussion took a turn. The definition of power moved into a postmodernist conceptualization. Citing Foucault's notion that 'power is in the system; ... it is imbedded in social relations and institutions,' some argued that 'power is a relationship,' often an unequal one. In another metaphor, power was depicted as a 'conversation' which 'is always going on – it is fluid.' This soon morphed into a consideration of the consequences of power, particularly for notions of human agency and capacity.[59]

This willingness to consider one of the central constructs of leadership in its broadest reaches would become typical for the group. Moreover, this was joined by an attempt to make linkages to a wide range of related constructs. This latter tendency of the group became manifest in the discussion when Gill Robinson Hickman and Douglas Hicks proposed consideration of an extreme case – that of slavery, with its seeming exercise of absolute power by one side and the total denial of human agency to the other. From that limiting case, Hickman and Hicks derived separate portrayals of the dynamics of the operation of power.

Hickman explained her depiction: 'One way to elucidate the workings of power in leadership,' she said, 'is to look at three related continua, involving power, motivation, and action.' Power, when applied in an individual situation such as slavery, is characterized by individual power-wielding and inequality. At the other end of the spectrum is power-sharing among a collective, which is more egalitarian. Motivation in the case of slavery is mere desperation, while in the collaborative case there is trust and the possibility of sustainability. Likewise, when one looks to action, unequal power-wielding results in no individual agency, while the sharing of power yields full agency. Hickman's model, in the words of one observer, represents a 'move from parsimony to complexity,' and George Goethals suggested that 'leadership' may be the transitioning from the limiting ends of the continua to that of a more collective, egalitarian allocation of power and full agency on the part of the participants.[60]

Doug Hicks, building upon Hickman's initial insight and Goethal's comment, constructed his own continuum, characterized as 'Domination' at one extreme and 'Leadership' at the other. At the 'Domination' end, one finds 'power wielded by individuals or systems, coercion, desperation, no agency, and unequals'; under 'Leadership,' there is 'power distributed fairly amongst persons and systems, freedom, sustainability, full agency and human potential, and moral equals.'[61]

The discussion of power, then, began with traditional views of the construct, moved to more relational and postmodern conceptions, and ended with a deep discussion of human agency and the role of leadership in unleashing it. This was typical of the group's discussion, and of the richness of pursuing a multidisciplinary approach to the topic.

A similar pattern can be detected in the discussions of the other constructs postulated by Burns. The consideration of motivation, for example, began with a rather prosaic discussion of the social science approach, with mention of process theories, modeling, and intrinsic motivation. This quickly moved – in a development typical of that richness created by having multiple disciplines in the room – to a more fundamental discussion of the human condition, and its implications for motivation. The scholars cited Kant, Mill, Smith, and Aristotle, and notions of *homo oeconomicus, homo individualus,* and *homo politicus.* This, in turn, led to an erudite discussion of the term 'happiness' as the essential motivation of humans, and a consideration of the conceptions of that term from the ancient Greeks through the Enlightenment. Other scholars brought in differing cultural interpretations of the term, including non-Western ones.[62]

When discussion turned to the dynamics of leader–follower relations, the group's predilections again surfaced. After desultory initial conversation, attention, as was the group's wont, turned to a discussion of a fundamental underlying issue. As the initial conversation progressed, some of the humanists in the room proclaimed their sense that the mainstream approaches to leader–follower relations in the leadership literature were too mundane. What was needed, they proclaimed, was a careful look at the 'initiating conditions of leader–follower relations, which is, after all, an exploration of the human condition.' Philosopher Terry Price framed the issue. The only way to really understand the nature of the leader–follower relation is to investigate its roots: 'What is there about the human condition that makes us need leadership?' he asked. 'This leads us,' he continued, 'to notions of justice, of agency. It leads to questions about the universal human condition [is it collaborative?]; also to questions of what motivates us [an unmet need?]; and it also brings up the sense of self.' Only the consideration of such deep and complex matters could bring real understanding to this issue.[63]

The final construct on the group's agenda – values – was in actuality a continuing topic throughout the three-day conference. As Joanne Ciulla noted, 'values should not be ghettoized; they are a subset of every part of leadership.' This was demonstrated in the discussion of J. Thomas Wren's 'Process Model' of leadership. Although the model as portrayed by Wren (and then applied to the case study of Franklin Delano Roosevelt by James MacGregor Burns) appeared straightforward enough, observers noted that 'values surround the Process Model [such as assumptions of linearity] that some do not share.'[64] The same universality was true for the ethics of leadership. As Ciulla said, 'Ethics is the set of all human relationships. Leadership is a subset of human relationships.' Ergo, it is 'really impossible to separate issues of ethics out as independent; we are *always* talking about ethics when we talk about leadership.' This led to a discussion, spreading across two days, of the role of values – and ethics – in leadership.[65] The precise arguments presented in the ensuing debate need not detain us here; suffice it to say that there were debates over everything from definitions to applications. What is important to take from the discussion, however, was the group's commitment to engage in an affirmative and overt consideration of these matters as the discussions of a grand theory progressed.

In all of these examples, the assembled scholars chose to focus upon the larger, humanistic approach to leadership, in opposition to the more circumscribed approach demanded by traditional notions of theory. Thus the Richmond meeting was as important for its seeming resolution of the question of scope and focus of the project as it was for any of its substantive conclusions regarding the specific elements of leadership. The General Theory of Leadership group was to build upon this at its next important gathering.

MOUNT HOPE: FOUNDATIONAL ASSUMPTIONS

The next scheduled meeting of the GTOL group – and the next major intellectual turning point for its deliberations – was a three-day retreat in June, 2002, at an estate owned by Williams College and located in the countryside outside of Williamstown, Massachusetts. Appropriately or inappropriately for the future of the project, this estate is known as Mount Hope. In any event, it was at Mount Hope that the project's eventual product began to take form. In addition to an illuminating session with special guest scholar Gary Yukl, the group got down to the real business of considering a general theory. In terms of the intellectual process we are detailing in this paper, Mount Hope is important for two things: First, it represented a confirmation that the approach of the group was to be largely humanistic in nature; namely, to be an exploration of leadership as part and parcel of the human condition in the broadest sense. Second, the multiple narrations of leadership that emerged from the Mount Hope deliberations helped to pose the issue that was to shape all subsequent interactions of the group; that is, whether a truly integrative approach was possible, or whether it is best to acknowledge 'multiple truths' in the characterization and understanding of leadership.

Prior to the Mount Hope meeting, participants engaged in another exchange of papers, designed both to reflect upon the outcomes of the Richmond session and to look ahead to the retreat in Williamstown. Not surprisingly, the subject matter of those papers ranged over most of the myriad issues discussed in Richmond. Their content, to the extent it became central to the group's deliberations, will be included elsewhere in this chapter. One noteworthy development that emerged from this round of papers, however, involved the ongoing dynamic of expectations among members of the group. In something of an ironic twist, these expectations appeared to be somewhat fluid. Terry L. Price had initially 'thought … that an integrated theory of leadership was an interesting but, ultimately, doomed project,' but opened his paper thusly: 'I begin with a confession. Since writing for the last set of papers, I've changed my basic view of this endeavor… . [O]ur discussions have led me to believe that it is [more achievable] … than I originally thought.'[66] J. Thomas Wren, on the other hand, who had initially embraced the possibility of an integrated theory, was now more circumspect. 'The challenges to our endeavor that were suggested by our individual papers,' he wrote, 'were confirmed by our discussions.' After detailing the principal points of contention, Wren noted that they were 'sufficient to create [a] cloud of foreboding' concerning the future of the project.[67] For his part, James MacGregor Burns, the inspiration for the project, was unwavering in his belief in ultimate success. 'Based on our early meetings and exchanges, and on the recent submissions,' he said, 'I am all the more confidant that we have the intellectual resources and determination to tackle our great objective, of a general or at least integrated theory of leadership,' albeit 'we are all also well aware of the problems and difficulties and are approaching the project, I think, in a realistic way.'[68] These underlying expectations would become crucial when the group later confronted strategic issues concerning the ultimate product of its work.

One of the intriguing dynamics of the gathering at Mount Hope involved how the membership of the group re-shaped the initial agenda proposed by the project directors to conform more closely to the thrust of the Richmond meeting. A pre-conference communication by host Al Goethals had proposed 'a possible schedule for the meetings. We wanted to observe the principles of having smaller groups work on the topics we identified in March… . We propose having each subgroup discuss the three topics that were agreed in March, and the fourth that was discussed but not agreed on. These are values, leader/follower dynamics, motivation and power, and culture and context.'[69] Equally important, at least to James MacGregor Burns, was the need for creating some kind of work product. 'We have,' he informed the group, 'our three-day Mt Hope conference where it is vitally important, in my view, that we develop written materials… . It will be imperative for us to produce actual *drafts*, in whatever form, at the Mt. Hope meeting. We will never have such a great opportunity both to discuss our subject further but also to break down into group or individual activities where we produce written documents.'[70]

The academicians who assembled at Mount Hope in June had no objections to Burns's call for written product, but they did question a return to a discussion of the 'elements' of leadership that had been the focus of the Richmond meeting. Elizabeth Faier, for example, observed that 'categories ... of leadership ... might not encapsulate its essence ... . Some of March's frustrating moments stem [from] containing our conversation to a discussion of parts when leadership itself is a process, ... something greater than the aggregate of its parts... .'[71] Similarly, Joanne Ciulla chafed at the division of the discussion according to the discrete elements of leadership. 'This looks nice and neat,' she admitted, 'but we also noticed in our discussions that these areas all tended to spill over into each other. It seemed that every boundary bled into the next area. I have come to the conclusion that discussing the parts in isolation from each other [e.g., power, motivation, ethics, leader–follower] would not be useful... . From our last discussion the variety came, not from the elements of leadership itself, but how people put these elements together.'[72]

'So where does this leave us in terms of Mt. Hope discussions?' Faier appropriately asked. Several participants came up with similar answers. Faier herself responded: 'I hope we can expand our discussion ... [in such a way as to] free us from over-defining components, fitting them into a mosaic-like model, and thus limiting ourselves to a theory that combines highly bounded pieces rather than focuses ... on process.'[73] Ciulla was more specific. 'Here is what I propose we do at Mt. Hope ... . [We should] give each group the basic pieces of the leadership puzzle and see how they put it together. Then we can get together as a whole and see what the pictures look like.'[74] J. Thomas Wren proposed a similar idea, and suggested how it could contribute to the group's objectives. 'Because I believe that we are neither ready (or in some cases, willing) to proceed with traditional theory-building activities, I propose an alternative approach... .' This charged each group with the task of 'constructing a narrative of how leadership works... . When we reconvene with our three separate narratives, we can look for any commonalities or "family resemblances." From these might come some generalizations, and ultimately, some propositions that might someday form the basis for a general theory.'[75]

It remained, however, to determine how to frame the narrative task of the respective groups. It was here that other members of the group harked back to the larger themes about the human condition that had consistently drawn the interest of the scholars in Richmond. It was Terry Price who put it best. Thinking back to Richmond, he observed that 'on the first day of the last set of meetings, [Al Goethals] made a claim to the effect that we have to understand the human condition in order to understand the nature of leadership. The humanist in me finds this a very attractive way of framing our enterprise. It roots the study of leadership in the liberal arts and sees it as a broader feature of the human experience.' Price was not naïve, however. 'Of course, the downside is that a general theory of leadership that takes this framing as its starting point has its work cut out for it. The theory must glean insights from a few thousand years of literature, philosophy, and history and couple them with the findings of a hundred or so years of social science research.'[76]

Fortunately for the sanity of the group, Price posed another possibility. 'An alternative interpretation of the claim that we have to understand the human condition in order to understand leadership takes it to mean that we have to think about what makes leadership necessary and what makes it possible if we are to understand the phenomena itself... .' Price elaborated: To build on this ... , we might consider the preconditions for leadership. First, what is it about the human condition that makes leadership necessary? Is it, say, that social, political and organizational life brings with it problems that can only be solved or, at least, best be solved by leadership? Second, what must be true of humans if we are to exercise leadership as a viable response to these problems?' Price suggested that 'if we could answer these two main questions, our answers would go a long way toward an understanding of the ends of leadership [as] well as the means for achieving these ends. Put simply,' he concluded, 'on this approach to theory building, the current stage of intellectual endeavor in which we are engaged would be understood as articulating the foundations of the study of leadership.'[77]

Taking its cue from Price and the others, each team was sent away to its caucus site with the following questions in hand: (1) *What is it about the human condition that makes leadership necessary?* (2) *What makes it possible?* Finally, once those foundational questions were answered, the groups were directed to turn to a third: (3) *What processes or conditions characterize the emergence, maintenance, or transformation of leadership?*

The teams were formed in such a way as to balance disciplinary approaches and the demographics of the group, and named, respectively, Red, Purple, and Gold (after the school colors of founding institutions Williams College, the University of Maryland, and the University of Richmond).[78] Following several intensive discussion and drafting sessions, each produced a document that contained at least the beginnings of a response to the designated questions. A detailed portrayal of the content of each can be found in the next chapter of this volume, an attempt at synthesis by Michael Harvey, who joined the group at the Mount Hope meeting.[79] For purposes of this analysis, it is sufficient to sketch in broad outline the contents of the resulting papers. Of more importance to this analysis are the consequences of these multiple narrations of the foundations of leadership.

The Red team responded to the question of *What is it about the human condition that makes leadership necessary and possible?* by creating what they called a 'leadership creation parable.' In that parable, they made several assertions about the human condition and the environment in which leadership initially came into being. The Red team painted a rather bleak portrait of surrounding conditions. It was a world of perceived disorder and entropy, where there was material scarcity, a lack of knowledge, and a sense of insecurity. The nature of the human condition that confronted that world was one of inequality: there was considerable variability in individuals' abilities, desires, and needs. Then, too, there was an 'inner tension' between 'the individual's desire for both self-sufficiency and dependency.' Humans also are torn between a desire for order and an attraction to mystery. In sum, says the Red team, 'These are the original conditions – disorder, variability, the tensions of our desires for sociability and self-sufficiency. Out of this comes a need for leadership.'[80]

The Purple team's narrative of the foundational conditions for leadership tended to track that of the Red team. Purple, too, envisioned a world of 'perceived challenges and shortcomings,' which call forth leadership in response. Moreover, 'the assumption of the Purple team is that inequality and dependence are an inherent part of the leadership relation. Variability in competence and access to power leads to differentiated roles and dependencies among the actors, a relationship which [under normal conditions] must be negotiated... . As a result of such negotiations,' Purple argued, 'the leadership relation can be seen to be a product of "consent,"' although 'this notion of consent has an ethical overlay.' Once the leadership relation is in place, 'leaders initiate narratives and framings to help the group understand the world, themselves, and other groups, as well as suggest solutions to external problems... . In addition, followers contribute elements in an evolving, negotiated narrative about group roles, group identity, group history, and the world.'[81]

The Gold team created a different sort of narrative, one that appeared to take a more positive and more constructivist approach. Gold acknowledged that humans differ in their capabilities, and that 'leadership arises from physiological and social needs and the human desire for expression.' That being said, Gold, more than Red or Purple, championed leadership as the act of constructing meaning. 'Being human involves having imagination and creative capacity, ability to be self-reflective, and ability to use language to create and communicate meaning with each other.' Moreover, 'being human involves social interaction through which humans construct reality.' This notion of 'constructing reality' was the nub of leadership. Indeed, 'leadership ... helps to construct or create ... human needs and wants... . Leadership is a creative act – literally bringing new realities into being.' For Gold, being human, and leadership, and even power are 'a matter of social relationships. Leadership must not be analyzed in terms of individual actors alone. Actors come into leadership relationships in the context of larger social terrains of meaning,' and is a result of both constructing reality and negotiating roles within that reality.[82]

With the production of the Red, Purple, and Gold papers, the General Theory of Leadership group finally had what James MacGregor Burns had been seeking: some written product from the group's efforts, however tentative and preliminary. Moreover, that product was consistent with the priorities of a group that had chosen to focus upon the larger, humanistic aspects of leadership. It must be noted, however, that these three preliminary essays essentially begged the question of what would come next; i.e., whether the same type of narrative would be extended to such matters as leader emergence and group processes, or whether there would be any attempt to derive from these prose accounts of leadership any propositions that could form the basis of a theory satisfactory to the social scientists.

In the meantime, a more foundational issue came to occupy the GTOL project: the question of the extent to which some form of true integration is possible. This issue was brought front-and-center by the three Mount Hope papers. Some preliminary discussions occurred during and immediately after the Mount Hope sessions, and the matter received more substantial attention subsequently.

The debate revolved around the question of whether the group should create one integrated document from the Mount Hope papers, or be content with multiple narratives of the leadership relation, each differing in both its foundational assumptions and in its particulars. From the beginning, there were supporters of both schools, and, as the ensuing chapters in this volume indicate, the group has been content to move along parallel tracks, keeping open the possibility of either, or both, options.

The possibility – or probability – of conflicting analyses was manifest as soon as the decision was made to work in multiple small groups at Mount Hope. In a memorandum prior to the meeting, Burns wrote: 'What I am more concerned about – and this is simply to get this on the agenda for the planning conference the first day at Mt. Hope – is how we will plan to put together what I expect will be a multiplicity of drafts on specific aspects of the subject dealt with in small groups.'[83] Terry Price had anticipated something similar. 'Admittedly,' he wrote in a pre-conference submission, 'at the end of our meetings, we might wind up with more than one reasonable, internally consistent theory of leadership.'[84]

So, too, were the two possible responses to this reality previewed prior to the meeting. Burns demonstrated his unwavering commitment to an integrated product. 'It was agreed,' he acknowledged, 'as I recall, at the March meeting that we would break down into smaller groups [at Mt. Hope], because of the obvious likelihood that the larger group could not do any drafting... . I agreed with this, but then the question is ... through what process do we integrate these findings into a group-endorsed document. I could imagine the different subgroups coming up with totally or considerably different drafts, which would make the integration quite fruitful but also very difficult.' And, in a separate communication, Burns urged the group to consider 'how these discussions can … be transformed into an overall agreed-upon document.'[85] Price, on the other hand, while envisioning multiple, conflicting documents, did not fear that result. 'This,' he said, 'need not strike us as a problematic outcome.' If the group did decide to prioritize one interpretation over another, Price simply advocated that the group make this decision consciously, and be transparent in its rationale.[86]

The resolution of the integration/multiple perspectives debate was postponed pending further reflection and exchanges among the scholars. In the meantime, a few of the participants suggested that an appropriate first step would be to isolate and identify the central assumptions underpinning each narrative. Such an analysis could form the basis for further consideration of the likelihood and desirability of creating an integrated theory. In the concluding discussions at Mount Hope, Elizabeth Faier observed that 'different cosmological views will lead to different reasons for leadership,' and suggested as examples assumptions about the nature of man, the role of inequality, and the extent to which the leadership process itself is negotiated or proceeds along some more predictable pattern.[87] Others contributed additional potential points of contention, but it was left to J. Thomas Wren to address the issue most thoroughly.

In a paper entitled 'The Mt. Hope Disaccords: Reflections on Varying Assumptions,' Wren set forth his task. 'Given our aspirations to create a unified depiction (I will not call it theory) of the leadership process,' he argued, 'first among our remaining challenges is to identify and address the underlying assumptions…. If we do not lay out our differing starting points, in order to debate them and to make necessary linkages between our premises and our conclusions, we can never hope to create a product (or products) worthy of taking forward to a jury of our peers, and certainly never harbor aspirations of constructing a unified approach to leadership.'[88] Wren proceeded to analyze the Red and Gold papers from Mount Hope.

His first focus was on epistemology. 'The various approaches to leadership theory raise important epistemological issues,' he argued. 'Theoretical approaches with differing understandings of how one comes to know and relate to perceived reality can yield dramatically contrasting views of the leadership relation.' Turning to the Gold and Red papers, he found 'a discrepancy that … requires illumination. The Gold team,' he went on, 'quite explicitly takes a stand concerning how they perceive the acquisition of knowledge in the world,' which is 'constructed.' This 'approach to making sense of the world,' observes Wren, has important theoretical consequences. 'On the positive side, the Gold approach appears well suited to a complex and interdependent world. On the other hand, it promises to set us adrift in a postmodern sea of uncertainty and immobility … . This does not mean that one adopting the Gold team's perspective can say nothing about leadership; indeed, a rather elegant description of how leaders and followers interact (e.g., the utility of storytelling, etc.) can be set forth. However, aspirations to propose any causative relationships become suspect.' The Red paper, on the other hand, 'takes a more linear approach' regarding cause and effect, 'to include a defined and accepted beginning point [to leadership] that leads (seemingly inevitably) to a predictable response.' In sum, Wren concludes on this point, 'each perspective is likely to yield a substantially differing depiction of the leadership process.'[89]

Likewise, says Wren, the groups differ in their perception of the nature of man. 'Gold places a stress upon the fact that "humans are social beings." Much of Gold's depiction of group behavior and meaning-making is premised upon a shared experience among members of the group. For Red,' on the other hand, 'the assumptions about the social nature of man appear to be … different… . Red appears to view man in more individualistic terms.' To illustrate Wren cites the Red treatment of trust: '"one cannot easily depend upon others when it is not clear what one has in common with them."' Again, these 'differing assumptions regarding the role of the individual vis-à-vis society' are 'profound and difficult to bridge.'[90]

So, too, is the perception of the leadership challenge different for the two groups. This flows naturally from their earlier assumptions. As Wren put it, 'The two groups' conceptualization of the external world and the challenges it poses are predictably different, given their epistemological distinctions. If men, according to Gold, "construct many aspects of their reality," the Gold view of the world and the challenges it poses are likewise socially constructed.' In contrast, 'the Red approach has quite a different view of the world and the leadership challenges it poses.' Red's narration of a world characterized by disorder and entropy 'has the air of universality; a sense that leadership always emerges in response to perceived threats to survival. The Gold approach appears more fluid and open.'[91]

If the perceived leadership challenge is different, so too is the response, or as Wren phrased it, 'the underlying assumption about what it is that the leadership relation is trying to accomplish,' or to put it yet another way, the differing assumptions about the purpose of leadership. Given Red's portrayal of a disorderly world, the goal of leadership is '*control*… . For Gold, on the other hand, leadership is less about control than the mutual management of meaning. Again, Wren concludes, 'the Red approach appears more linear, while the Gold version is more fluid and open.'[92]

Finally, Wren turned to an issue that was less obvious. 'Imbedded in the respective accounts of the two groups,' he argued, 'but nowhere adequately articulated for purposes of challenge and discussion, is an implicit hierarchy of values.' The value that received most of his attention was that of '*equality*… . The Gold Team … values equality as both the means and end of leadership.' In contrast, 'for the Red Team, inequality is at the heart of leadership.' Wren paused to consider the implications. 'The implications for leadership are profound,' Wren intimated. 'At the most obvious level, a theory grounded in assumptions of inequality ... is quite distinct from one that sees inequality as an evil to be superseded, with the inequalities themselves subject to negotiation and definition.' For Red, then, 'the actual process of leadership is portrayed as "compliance-gaining processes," rather than Gold's more egalitarian "negotiations."' 'More subtly,' he continued, 'the matter goes to the heart of the leadership relation.' For Red, 'inequality is not only real, but good and necessary. Perhaps some people (leaders) *are* better able to perceive and act than others. The Red group appears to be open to this possibility; the Gold group, with its embrace of "group social construction," seems to reject this notion. At the least' concluded Wren, 'this seems a central matter as we approach a theory of leadership. Indeed, I suspect that our attempts at synthesis may founder on the shoals of inequality before anything else.'[93]

In his conclusion, Wren did not reject the idea of an integrated theory, but asserted that 'it is important that we confront and debate our assumptions.' He acknowledged that, 'in the end, the fundamental differences in our premises [may] make it impossible to come up with an acceptable synthesis.' This did not daunt him. 'If so, we should accept this,' he reasoned, 'and do our best to move forward with multiple "narrations" of the leadership process, each buttressed by a clear account of its founding assumptions.'[94] Wren's analysis of the output of the Mount Hope meeting has received no little attention here, but this seems justified, in light of the fact that such matters prefigured the next stage of the General Theory of Leadership group's process.

GUADALAJARA: INTEGRATED THEORY VS. ALTERNATIVE OUTCOMES

The final segment of the GTOL group's work that will be the focus of our attention is not as chronologically defined as were the earlier sections of this chapter. The developments chronicled here extended across an 18-month period from June 2002 to November 2003, and included a session with fellow scholars and practitioners at the International Leadership Association meeting in Seattle in November, 2002, and another session at the Jepson School in April, 2003. The focal point, however – because it was the moment when the next stage of the process crystallized – is a presentation and discussion conducted at the International Leadership Association meeting in Guadalajara, Mexico, in November, 2003.

During that 18-month span, the GTOL project added several new participants. A consequence of having the new contributors was that the group perforce revisited some of the issues detailed earlier in this analysis. Although there was at times a sense of drift, the return to the fundamental issues that inevitably surround an attempt to create a general theory of leadership ultimately spurred the group out of its brief doldrums and gave the project fresh energy.

Although many issues were addressed, the most important developments were undoubtedly a re-invigorated discussion concerning the ultimate product of the group's efforts, together with more sophisticated attempts at a synthesis of the group's work. Certainly the most important matter that remained under discussion was the long-standing one of whether (and how) to create an integrated result, as opposed to pursuing some other, more constrained, product of the group's efforts. The scholars, rather than coming to final conclusions regarding this essential issue, were content to pursue both tracks. That is to say, they continued to experiment with various formulations of an integrated depiction of leadership, while at the same time contemplating various alternative formulations that recognize the difficulties inherent in an integrated approach.

Certainly one of the two parallel tracks the GTOL group has followed since Mount Hope has been one toward some sort of integration. The most important of these was a paper by James MacGregor Burns, the most forceful proponent of integration throughout. Burns drafted his paper following a session at the International Leadership Association conference in Seattle, held in November, 2002. At that session, the members of the group presented a status report on their deliberations, and then engaged in a productive dialogue among the panelists and an audience of scholars and practitioners. Later, drawing upon his initial essay on leadership created in February as a starting point and interpolating insights from the Mount Hope and Seattle discussions, Burns crafted a statement of leadership.

He began with 'a definition of leadership that appeared to emerge from the Seattle conference,' which was 'leadership as an influence process, both visible and invisible, in a society inherited, constructed, and perceived as the interaction of persons in ... conditions of inequality – an interaction measured by ethical and moral values and by the degrees of realization of intended, comprehensive and durable change.'[95] Burns then proceeded to outline the dynamics of this process.

He turned first to 'the human conditions of wants and needs among masses of people.' Unfortunately, 'they lack ... knowledge as to how to gain these things.' This creates the need for leadership. 'It is the job of leadership,' he explained, 'not only to legitimate certain wants ... but to educate and instruct and guide the victims toward solutions. This creates a leader–follower relationship.'[96] 'In the emerging leader–follower relationship,' Burns continued, 'the first – but by no means the only – task of leadership is interaction with followership in meeting the priority of order. But,' he went on to note, 'order in itself is hopelessly inadequate unless it is employed to protect high values, such as freedom, justice, ... equality of opportunity or condition, or ultimately happiness.'[97]

Burns went on to explore the dynamics of the leadership process, in particular the 'functions of values and conflict.' These are inseparable. 'Values are not just static or [integrated] entities;' he argued, 'they are very much in conflict.' Thus 'conflict is ... [a] crucial aspect or element of leadership; ... strong leadership ... does not reject conflict – it thrives on it.' In turn, 'the functions of values and conflict cannot be separated from the causal role of *power*.' 'Power,' according to Burns, 'is complex, despite all the simplistic accounts that impute vast and permanent authority and supremacy to various leaders and rulers. Power is not only quantitative, measured by dollars or guns or votes.' In addition, power is 'qualitative and subjective, measured by leaders' and followers' wants and feelings and attitudes.' These dynamics culminate in the real purpose of leadership. To Burns, 'all of the above ultimately leads to the transcending question of grand change – change that is intended, comprehensive, durable, and grounded in values.'[98]

Having created his own effort toward an integrated depiction of leadership, Burns ended his paper with a plea to his fellow members of the GTOL group. Having cited historical examples of FDR and the Montgomery bus boycott to demonstrate his points, he used them to encourage the group to coalesce behind this effort at an integrated approach to leadership. 'If those activists could integrate the complex processes and elements of leadership in *practice*, in *reality*,' he reasoned, 'should we not be able to do so in *theory*?'[99]

Meanwhile, other dynamics within the GTOL group militated against this. Consequently, at the same time that efforts at integration continued, there was also energy devoted to the other of the parallel tracks; that is, toward acknowledging the fundamental divisions among the members of the group, and developing a product that recognized and honored these differences. This effort gained traction as a result of yet another meeting of the group, at the Jepson School in Richmond in April, 2003.

There, the group welcomed several new members to the conversation: scholars Bruce Avolio from the University of Nebraska, Sonia Ospina from the Wagner School at NYU, Ron Riggio from Claremont McKenna, and Mark Walker from American University, plus Deborah Meehan representing the Leadership Learning Community and practitioner John L. Johnson. The addition of the new voices occasioned another of the group's long tradition of insightful discussions. At the same time, these newcomers inevitably posed many of the same issues that had been raised by the initial call for a general theory of leadership, concerns that had been placed aside by the *as if condition*.

For example, social psychologist Ron Riggio articulated many of the same concerns as had been voiced by social scientist Fred Jablin at the outset of the process: the need for rigor in definitions, and for a theoretical design that can become the basis for replicable research. Sonia Ospina, on the other hand, presented a cogent argument for taking a constructivist position, drawing upon arguments that had previously been voiced by anthropologist Elizabeth Faier. She questioned the value of positivist theory, suggesting that meaning is jointly constructed by participants, and that theories, at best, provide only partial views of their objects, since it is impossible to capture a single reality. These differences in premises and approach, so evident in the group's early debates but put to the side by the 'as if condition' [that is, the willingness of the participants to ignore their differences for the moment, and to proceed *as if* a successful resolution could be achieved], now could no longer be ignored.

In response to this development, the group turned to its next great initiative. Group members were given a rather formidable task to complete prior to the group's next meeting at the International Leadership Association's conference in Guadalajara, Mexico, in November, 2003. The details of this assignment are relatively important, since they structured the ensuing discussion.

In a communication drafted by Mark Walker and J. Thomas Wren, the coordinators of this phase of the project, the authors began by acknowledging that 'we continue to confront two fundamental challenges to our aspirations of producing some form of integrated view of leadership.'[100] These are worth quoting in their entirety:

1. First, there continues to exist real skepticism about the entire endeavor. In part, this is due to a discomfort with the notion of creating a 'general theory.' Scholars disagree as to what is meant by, and what is encompassed within, the term. Much of the disagreement appears to stem from the differing perspectives taken by social scientists and humanists, or by positivists and constructivists (etc.). Recognizing that the entire endeavor could run aground upon these shoals at the very outset, participants agreed to set aside their respective concerns, and to proceed 'as if' the endeavor could succeed. Now, as we push toward the creation of some publishable output, such concerns can no longer be ignored.
2. Second, although each meeting of the group has resulted in hours of intellectually stimulating debate over a plethora of critical issues relating to leadership, our attempts to integrate these insights into a coherent whole have not advanced far. Our closest approximation has been the Mt. Hope narratives of the Red, Gold, and Purple teams. If this project is going to be successful (at some level), we need to consider how, if at all, we might create some way of bringing together our disparate insights.[101]

Given the dual challenges of divergent premises and difficulties in integration, the assignment given the group was two-fold, each part designed to address one of the identified issues.

The first assignment was to 'create a matrix of fundamental issues and perspectives.' It was 'designed to address the "as if" problem above,' by asking the scholars to identify with some precision the divisions or differences among the members. More specifically, group members were asked 'to create your own analytical matrix of leadership studies.' The top (horizontal part) of the matrix should consist of 'the differing perspectives that you believe are most central to our understanding of leadership.' Thus, this portion of the matrix might list the differing disciplines, or perhaps 'epistemological approaches' such as 'social scientific/humanistic' or 'positivist/constructivist.' Once having identified the source of the disagreements, the side (vertical aspect) of the matrix should 'identify the central issues upon which those perspectives tend to disagree.' With the matrix thus organized, the process of 'fill[ing] in the cells ... provides a comparison of the differing conclusions from each perspective.'[102]

Although seemingly complex at first blush, the assignment had the serious objective of identifying the various points of contention. 'Our goal,' wrote Walker and Wren, 'is to utilize these matrices ... to begin to address in a substantive fashion the very real concerns and disputes among us. We should not expect to resolve those disputes' – at least in the near term, and, 'in some ways that might be detrimental' – 'but ... to create a framework that allows us to perceive where we differ and how.'[103] Only with the group's differences out in the open could there be hope of addressing them productively.

The second assignment given to the group was less structured, and was 'designed to help us with our challenge of integration.' As Walker and Wren explained it, 'During our discussions, we often noted how we needed to bring things together (probably in some format far short of a "theory").' Thus, 'the second, unstructured part of your assignment is to create your own metaphor, model, narration, or ... theory ... that identifies what are, for you, the central aspects of leadership and how they fit together.' Walker and Wren concluded: 'Hopefully, at our next session, our consideration of the various responses to this assignment may generate some insights as to how we might ultimately present our conclusions in a way that is inclusive of our differences, yet integrative in terms of our understanding of leadership.'[104]

The sharing and presentation of the responses to this assignment was to take place the following November (2003) in Guadalajara. In point of fact, only a few of the group members actually contributed either a matrix, model, or metaphor, but the submissions that were received were sufficient to form the foundations for an important dialogue. This was undoubtedly due to the fact that the smattering of contributions was so diverse as to encompass most of the central issues attendant to the process of creating a general theory of leadership. Four individuals submitted matrices, one submitted a proposed integrative model of leadership, and yet another proposed a metaphor intended to bring insight to the leadership studies community without forcing upon it any unjustifiable integration of dissimilar approaches. A brief summary of this varied body of work is therefore justified.

The first matrix was by Mark Clarence Walker, entitled 'Schools of Thought in the Study of Leadership' (see Table 3.2). Its purport was to delineate the differences in assumptions among several of the key theories of leadership. Walker thus identified on his horizontal axis Great man theory, behavioral theory, contingency theory, cognitive theory, moral leadership theories, and strategic leadership theory as the primary theoretical approaches. He distinguished them (vertical axis) according to their 'key component; relative role of leader and followers; related theories and concepts; and theorists.' In creating a matrix of this nature, Walker carefully denoted some key distinctions among the mainstream (primarily social science) approaches to leadership.[105]

J. Thomas Wren took a broader approach with his matrix. Labeling it a 'theoretical matrix,' Wren created three essential divisions among those who approach the task of creating a theory of leadership: social scientists (or 'positivists'), humanists, whom he labels 'interpretavists,' and postmodernists, also called 'constructivists.' Each of these categories of scholars differs, Wren suggested, in their answers to five key questions: How is the problem defined? What type of information/data is used in seeking an answer? What method is used? How does one judge the validity of the outcome? How should the outcome be applied? By 'filling in the cells' with the answers to those questions for each group, Wren created a way to readily identify some central differences in premises that have hampered the efforts of the group to come to some integrated result.[106] (See Table 3.3 as an example of this 'matrix' approach to identifying areas of tension).

Gill Robinson Hickman took a somewhat similar approach with her matrix. Her horizontal row identified the 'Leadership Perspectives' of humanism, essentialism (positivism), social constructivism, environmentalism, feminism, and pluralism (see Table 3.4). The matrix's vertical column contained a listing of issues upon which those perspectives differ. The issues included human nature, mobilizing forces, the purpose of leadership, ethics, context, participants, power, and level of action and analysis. The scope of her matrix, then, was broader than Wren's, but it, too, provided important insights into the source of differences among those addressing the phenomenon of leadership.[107]

A final matrix, by Terry Price, was devoted not so much to differences in approach but more to underlying similarities across seemingly disparate approaches. In a somewhat more complex approach, Price created two categories of 'fields' or 'disciplines,' the first of which he called 'descriptive/explanatory,' such as organizational leadership (see Table 3.5). The second he labeled 'prescriptive/justificatory,' which embraced such approaches as social and political philosophy. The two categories of 'field' or 'discipline' – and Price invited the inclusion of others – he suggested, address similar questions, albeit in differing ways. Price identified four characterizations of leadership (across the top of his matrix), and indicated how the two identified categories of scholarship approach each by providing examples in his cells. Thus, under 'leadership as personal characteristics,' organizational leadership draws upon 'trait theories,' while social and political philosophy look to such sources as Plato's *Republic*. Price went on to provide a similar analysis for the characterizations of leadership as 'situational response', as 'transaction', and as 'transformation'. With his matrix, Price revealed the extent to which broadly differing approaches often seek answers to identical questions.[108]

Joining the four matrices submitted was one integrative model of leadership. This was the work of Gill Robinson Hickman. Her complex model depicted four 'dimensions' of leadership: 'mobilizing forces, levels of leadership action and analysis, perspective, and effect or outcome' (see Figure 3.1). Across those dimensions, Hickman arrayed the 'perspectives on leadership' from her matrix; i.e., humanism, essentialism, social constructivism, environmentalism, feminism, and pluralism. The dynamics of her model were displayed by means of arrows depicting 'participant, process, conflict, change, ethics, and power.' Further sophistication was added by including levels of analysis such as individuals, dyads, groups, and collectives. Hickman admitted that her two-dimensional portrayal really needed to be more of a three-dimensional holograph in order to capture adequately its complexity. Nevertheless, she succeeded in including in one all-encompassing representation most of the matters of contention that had occupied the GTOL group during the two years of its existence.[109]

Finally, Joanne Ciulla contributed a metaphor that might productively occupy the group's next stage of deliberations. Ciulla advocated that the group 'map the territory'; that is, create an intellectual (perhaps even literal) cartographic representation of the various approaches to leadership. This, argued Ciulla, might be the most feasible possible outcome of the group's effort, and at the same time would prove quite useful.[110]

The discussion surrounding these contributions in the open session at the Guadalajara conference, occurring before a standing-room-only congregation of fellow scholars and practitioners, was remarkably rich and varied. Indeed, Georgia Sorenson, who had been unable to attend, but had received considerable feedback from members of the audience, later wrote: 'It sounded like it was a fantastic session... . I have had so many people tell me it was by far the best session they ever attended on leadership.'[111] The reason for such kudos was almost certainly not the innate brilliance of the contributions, but more due to the fact that those in attendance had the rare opportunity to witness scholars struggling with such intractable issues, and had a chance to offer constructive ideas and criticisms. That has also been the objective of this chapter, and volume. In this sense, just as in many ways the Guadalajara session marked a high water mark of the GTOL process, it also caused the group to contemplate its final product.

WASHINGTON: EPILOGUE AS PROLOGUE

In two meetings following the Guadalajara conference, one at the Jepson School in Richmond, and one at the International Leadership Association conference in Washington, DC in November 2004, the GTOL group considered the next steps. In those meetings, the member scholars determined that the results of three full years of dialogue concerning the development of a 'general theory' had advanced sufficiently to publish the various resulting insights. The lingering issues of the tensions among approaches to leadership, temporarily masked by the 'as if condition,' were to be left unresolved. So, too, did the group decline to take a final stand on the issue of the possibility and advisability of the ultimate creation of an integrated theory, as opposed to taking some more diverse and inclusive approach. Instead, the members of the group decided that the most productive way to proceed was to create a volume of essays designed to capture, to the best of our ability, the nuances of three years of scholarly debate and discussion. This volume is the result.

The determination not to finally resolve the fundamental tensions that had been an inherent part of the project was not (or, at least, not wholly) a consequence of despair over the possibility of success. Rather, it was seen as an appropriate scholarly outcome. In the tradition of the best scholarship, the contents of this volume are presented not so much as conclusions as they are invitations to further debate. Thus this, while the epilogue to the efforts of the GTOL group, is merely intended as the prologue for a continuing discourse concerning the integration of the varied understandings of leadership.

The challenges persist; the quest for a grand theory of leadership continues.

As the initial chapter of this collection, this piece has attempted to provide the reader with a glimpse into the dynamics of a fascinating experiment into multidisciplinary discussion and collaboration in the emerging field of leadership studies. As suggested in the introductory paragraphs, this process may prove as interesting to our fellow scholars in the field as our ultimate substantive conclusions. The remaining chapters, beginning with one by Michael Harvey addressing the nature of the human condition, provide more of the substance of the deliberations over the creation of a General Theory of Leadership.

NOTES

1.   Georgia Sorenson, from J. Thomas Wren's informal notes of Mount Hope meeting, June 22, 2002. Note that the bulk of the citations in this paper will be to unpublished papers circulated among group members in several rounds of exchanges. On occasion, reference will be made to informal notes of group meetings, which will be identified as such. In the interests of a coherent narrative, some chronological liberties have been taken with respect to the timing of when points were made in the discussions.

2. Joanne B. Ciulla, ibid.
3. Joanne B. Ciulla, 'Some Thoughts on the Mount Hope Meeting,' (unpub. ms., ca. May, 2002), p. 5.
4. Founding members were: James MacGregor Burns, Jepson School of Leadership Studies, University of Richmond; Georgia Sorenson, Jepson School and the University of Maryland; George Goethals, Williams College; Joanne Ciulla, Jepson School; Richard Couto, Jepson School; Elizabeth Faier, Jepson School; Zachary Green, Alexander Institute; Gill Robinson Hickman, Jepson School; Douglas A. Hicks, Jepson School; Frederic Jablin, Jepson School; Terry L. Price, Jepson School; and J. Thomas Wren, Jepson School. The current roster also includes: Bruce Avolio, University of Nebraska; Michael Harvey, Washington College; Ed Hollander, Baruch Center; Robert E. Kelley, Carnegie-Mellon; Jean Lipman-Blumen, Claremont; Deborah Meehan, Leadership Learning Community; Sonia Ospina, Wagner School, New York University; Ron Riggio, Claremont McKenna; Mark Clarence Walker, American University; Ron Walters, University of Maryland; and John L. Johnson, University of the District of Columbia.
5. Katherine Managan, 'Leading the Way in Leadership: The Unending Quest of the Discipline's Founding Father, James MacGregor Burns,' *Chronicle of Higher Education*, May 31, 2002, p. 1.
6. Ibid.
7. Georgia Sorenson, 'Preliminary Ideas about a General Theory of Leadership,' (unpub. ms., ca. Dec., 2001), p. 1, citing James Hunt and Lars Larsen, eds., *Leadership, the Cutting Edge* (Carbondale: Southern Illinois University Press, 1977), and Ralph Stogdill, *Handbook of Leadership* (New York: Free Press, 1974), p. vii.
8. Sorenson, 'Preliminary Ideas about a General Theory of Leadership,' p. 1.
9. Ibid., p. 3.
10. Georgia Sorenson, quoted in Managan, 'Leading the Way in Leadership,' p. 1.
11. Joanne B. Ciulla, 'Some Thoughts on the General Theory of Leadership Project,' (unpub. ms., ca. Feb., 2002), p. 1.
12. Douglas A. Hicks, '"But Is It Leadership?": On Disciplinary Identity and a General Theory of Leadership' (unpub. ms., ca. Feb. 2002), pp. 1–4.
13. Ciulla, 'Some Thoughts on the General Theory of Leadership Project,' p. 3.
14. Ibid.
15. James MacGregor Burns, quoted in Managan, 'Leading the Way in Leadership,' p. 1.
16. Richard A. Couto, 'Towards A General Theory of Leadership,' (unpub. ms., ca. March, 2002), p. 11. *See also* J. Thomas Wren, 'Toward a General Theory of Leadership,' (unpub. ms., ca. Feb., 2002), p. 1.
17. James MacGregor Burns, 'Toward a General Theory of Leadership?' (unpub. ms., ca. Mar., 2002), p. 1.
18. Elizabeth A. Faier, comments made in meeting, Richmond, Virginia, March, 2002, from J. Thomas Wren's informal discussion notes.
19. Terry L. Price, 'Reflections toward the Mt. Hope Meeting,' (unpub. ms., ca. June, 2002), p. 1
20. Ibid., pp. 1, 3.
21. Douglas A. Hicks, comment made in meeting, Richmond, Virginia, March, 2002, from J. Thomas Wren's informal discussion notes.
22. Sorenson, 'Preliminary Ideas about a General Theory of Leadership,' p. 2.
23. Burns, 'Toward a General Theory of Leadership?' pp. 2, 3.
24. Terry Price, comment made in group discussion, Richmond, Virginia, March, 2002, from J. Thomas Wren's discussion notes.
25. Richard Couto, 'Toward a General Theory of Leadership,' (unpub. ms., ca. Feb., 2002), p. 1.
26. Ibid.
27. Frederic Jablin, 'Thoughts on Richmond and Mt. Hope,' (unpub. ms., ca. June, 2002), p. 2.
28. Jablin, from Carmen Foster's discussion notes of meeting at Richmond, Virginia, March 23, 2002, p. 8.
29. Ciulla, 'Some Thoughts on the General Theory of Leadership Project,' pp. 3, 1.

30. Commentator not identified. From Carmen Foster's discussion notes of meeting at Richmond, Virginia, March 23, 2002.
31. Jablin, 'Thoughts on Richmond and Mt. Hope,' p. 2.
32. Joanne Ciulla, from informal discussion notes of J. Thomas Wren, Richmond, Virginia, March 23, 2002.
33. Frederic Jablin, from informal discussion notes of J. Thomas Wren, Richmond, Virginia, March 24, 2002.
34. James MacGregor Burns, from informal discussion notes of J. Thomas Wren, Richmond, Virginia, March 23, 2002.
35. Elizabeth A. Faier, 'What Anthropology Contributes to Leadership Studies,' (unpub. ms., ca. Feb., 2002), pp. 3–4.
36. Couto, 'Toward a General Theory of Leadership,' p. 1.
37. Ibid., pp. 2, 5, 7.
38. Terry L. Price, 'Preliminary Ideas on a General Theory of Leadership,' (unpub. ms., ca. Feb., 2002), pp. 2–3.
39. Jablin, 'Thoughts on Richmond and Mt. Hope,' p. 2.
40. See Managan, 'Leading the Way in Leadership,' p. 2.
41. Faier, 'What Anthropology Contributes to Leadership Studies,' p. 4.
42. Price, 'Preliminary Ideas on a General Theory of Leadership,' p. 2.
43. Zachary Gabriel Green, 'Preliminary Ideas about a General Theory of Leadership,' (unpub. ms., ca. Feb., 2002), p. 1.
44. George R. Goethals, 'Preliminary Ideas about a General Theory of Leadership,' (unpub. ms., ca. Feb., 2002), p. 1.
45. Faier, 'What Anthropology Contributes to Leadership Studies,' pp. 1, 3.
46. Hicks, '"But Is It Leadership?": On Disciplinary Identity and a General Theory of Leadership,' p. 3.
47. Couto, 'Toward a General Theory of Leadership,' p. 2.
48. Ciulla, 'Some Thoughts on the General Theory of Leadership Project,' p. 2.
49. Ibid., pp. 1–2.
50. Wren, 'Toward a General Theory of Leadership,' p. 1.
51. Gill Robinson Hickman, 'General Theory of Leadership,' (unpub. ms., ca. Feb., 2002), p. 1.
52. Couto, 'Towards a General Theory of Leadership,' p. 1.
53. Burns, 'Toward a General Theory of Leadership,' pp. 1, 3, 6.
54. Sorenson, 'Preliminary Ideas about a General Theory of Leadership,' p. 1.
55. Price, 'Reflections toward the Mt. Hope Meeting,' p. 2.
56. James MacGregor Burns, informal discussion notes of J. Thomas Wren from meeting at Richmond, Virginia, March 23, 2002.
57. George Goethals, from informal discussion notes of J. Thomas Wren, Richmond, Virginia, March 22, 2002.
58. Burns, in ibid.
59. From J. Thomas Wren's informal notes of general discussion, Richmond, Virginia, March 23, 2002.
60. Hickman, from J. Thomas Wren's informal notes of general discussion, Richmond, Virginia, March 23, 2002. See also Carmen Foster, 'Flip Chart Notes from General Theory of Leadership Session, March 23, 2002,' p. 4.
61. Hicks, from Wren's informal notes of general discussion, Richmond, Virginia, March 23, 2002.
62. From Wren's general discussion notes, March 23, 2002; Foster 'Flip Chart Notes,' pp. 6–7.
63. General discussion notes by J. Thomas Wren, Richmond, Virginia, March 23, 2002.
64. Ibid.
65. Ibid., March 24, 2002.
66. Price, 'Reflections toward the Mt. Hope Meeting,' p. 1.
67. J. Thomas Wren, 'The Mount Hope Accords,' (unpub. ms., ca. June, 2002), p 1.

68. James MacGregor Burns to GTOL group, 'Supplement to Earlier Statement,' ca. June, 2002, p. 1.
69. George Goethals to GTOL group, 'Planning Suggestion,' June 6, 2002, p. 1.
70. James MacGregor Burns to GTOL group, 'Pre-Mt. Hope Conference Notes,' ca. June, 2002, p. 1; Burns, 'Supplement to Earlier Statement,' p. 1.
71. Elizabeth Faier, 'Is Leadership Greater than the Sum of Its Parts?' (unpub. ms., ca. June, 2002), p. 1.
72. Ciulla, 'Some Thoughts on the Mt. Hope Meeting,' pp. 4–5.
73. Faier, 'Is Leadership Greater than the Sum of Its Parts?', p. 4.
74. Ciulla, 'Some Thoughts on the Mt. Hope Meeting,' pp. 4–5.
75. Wren, 'The Mt. Hope Accords,' p. 3.
76. Price, 'Reflections toward the Mt. Hope Meeting,', p. 1
77. Ibid., pp. 1–2.
78. Red Team members were Georgia Sorenson, Joanne Ciulla, Fred Jablin, and Michael Harvey, a new addition to the GTOL process; Purple Team members were Carmen Foster, George Goethals, Terry Price, and J. Thomas Wren; Gold Team members were Richard Couto, Elizabeth Faier, Gill Hickman, and Douglas Hicks.
79. Michael Harvey, 'Leadership and the Human Condition,' (unpub. ms., Jan., 2004).
80. Sorenson, Ciulla, Jablin, and Harvey, 'The Leadership Creation Parable' (Red Team report, June 22, 2002).
81. Foster, Goethals, Price, and Wren, 'What Makes Leadership Necessary? What Makes Leadership Possible?' (Purple Team report, June 22, 2002).
82. Couto, Faier, Hickman, Hicks, 'The Integrated Leadership Report,' (Gold Team report, June 22, 2002).
83. Burns, 'Supplement to Earlier Statement,' p. 1.
84. Price, 'Reflections toward the Mt. Hope Meeting,' p. 3.
85. Burns, 'Pre-Mt. Hope Conference Notes,' p. 1; Burns, 'Supplement to Earlier Statement,' p. 1.
86. Price, 'Reflections toward the Mt. Hope Meeting,' p. 3.
87. Faier, informal discussion notes by J. Thomas Wren, Williamstown, Massachusetts, June 22, 2002.
88. J. Thomas Wren, 'The Mt. Hope Disaccords: Reflections on Varying Assumptions,' (unpub. ms., ca. Sept., 2002), p. 1.
89. Ibid., pp. 1–2.
90. Ibid., pp. 2–3.
91. Ibid., pp. 3–4.
92. Ibid., p. 4.
93. Ibid., pp. 4–5.
94. Ibid., pp. 5–6.
95. James MacGregor Burns, 'Mount Hope and Seattle Follow-up,' (unpub. ms., Nov., 2002), p. 1.
96. Ibid.
97. Ibid., p. 2.
98. Ibid., pp. 2–3.
99. Ibid., p. 6.
100. Mark Clarence Walker and J. Thomas Wren to GTOL group, 'General Theory of Leadership Group May–September 2003 Work Plan,' (unpub. ms., ca. May, 2003), p. 1.
101. Ibid.
102. Ibid., pp. 1–3.
103. Ibid., pp. 2–4.
104. Ibid., pp. 4–5.
105. Mark Clarence Walker, 'Schools of Thought in the Study of Leadership,' from Walker, 'Reconciling Morality and Strategy in the Study of Leadership,' (unpub. ms., 2003).
106. J. Thomas Wren, 'Theoretical Matrix' (September, 2003).
107. Gill Robinson Hickman, 'Leadership Perspectives' (November, 2003).
108. Terry L. Price, untitled matrix (November, 2003).

109. Gill Robinson Hickman, 'Concepts in Leadership Studies' (November, 2003).
110. Joanne Ciulla, from informal discussion notes of J. Thomas Wren, November, 2003.
111. Georgia Sorenson to GTOL group, November 23, 2003.

2.   Leadership and the human condition

Michael Harvey

I'd shape one impulse through the contraries
Of vain ambitious men, selfish and callous ... .
    ... All that's low I'll charm;
Barbaric love sweeten to tenderness.
Cunning run into wisdom, craft turn to skill.
                    Isaac Rosenberg, *Moses*

In June 2002 a dozen scholars met at Williams College's auspiciously named Mount Hope retreat to think and talk about leadership. Amid the wild profusion of leadership theories and topics, and notwithstanding the epistemological diversity of modern academics, we hoped to find common ground in our thinking about leadership. We began with two simple but in our opinion fundamental questions: 'In the human condition, what makes leadership necessary? And what makes leadership possible?' We broke into three groups, and each group wrote a short essay seeking to answer these questions. These papers displayed all the richness of thinking that typifies modern interdisciplinary approaches to leadership – signs of psychology, anthropology, history, political science, sociology, ethics, philosophy, religious studies, and cultural and literary studies. But some thoughts or suppositions about leadership could be traced throughout the essays. What follows is a loose synthesis or free translation of these three short essays – a meditation on the place of leadership in the human condition.

*   *   *

Leadership is part and parcel of the human condition. A mystery as modern as the nation-state and as ancient as the tribe, it brings together the best and worst in human nature: love and hate, hope and fear, trust and deceit, service and selfishness. Leadership draws on who we are, but it also shapes what we might be – a kind of alchemy of souls that can produce both Lincoln's 'better angels of our nature' and Hitler's willing executioners. In its constituent parts leadership includes three basic social organizing patterns – kinship, reciprocity, and command. From kinship it draws a sense of connection (if often exploited) between leaders and followers. From reciprocity it draws a sense of mutual

39

exchange and benefit (if often betrayed). But from command it takes its most visible aspect, for leadership is above all a social relation of dominance and consent (if often constrained), yoked uneasily together. At the heart of leadership is a tension precipitated by our double nature – social animals with self-reflective and often selfish minds. What is it about the human condition that makes leadership necessary – and that makes it possible? What problems does leadership solve? And what problems does it cause?

Leadership presupposes the group (the leader–follower subunit, the dyad, is essentially an analytic artifact). From an evolutionary perspective, groups exist because, for certain kinds of tasks and certain kinds of creatures, groups can outcompete individuals. Wolves, for instance, hunt and live in packs. Within the animal group, leadership originates in inequality. In a wolf-pack the alpha male and alpha female claim their position through strength or spiritedness, dominating other members of the pack and defeating or driving out rivals. Among social predators like wolves, and among our closest group of relatives, the two hundred or so species of primates, the social group is structured by a well-defined hierarchy, by ritualized behaviors that economize the costs of violence, and by constant attention to membership and ranking. Dominant animals gain privileged access to food and reproduction (in a wolf-pack, for instance, typically only the alpha male and female mate). The group gains security or access to desirable resources. In such groups youth is a time of learning and testing. Through play the young practice behavioral displays and sign-stimuli, try their strength against each other, and assume their place in the social hierarchy. They learn lessons, in other words, in how to follow and how to lead. Some of these lessons are astonishingly powerful and redolent of human values: young adult African wild dogs, for instance, will masticate and regurgitate meat for their toothless elders rather than let them starve.

Analogies with other species, especially social predators and our fellow primates, are a tempting place to begin when thinking about leadership and the human condition. We share 98 percent of our DNA with our closest cousins, chimpanzees. We know that our hominin ancestors, in a line that stretches back five to seven million years, lived, scavenged, and hunted in small groups, and must have faced the same pressures and difficulties that other groups of social predators face. And we find pronounced hierarchies in every human community anthropologists have ever observed. Nevertheless, such analogies may lead us to false conclusions. For human beings, the relationship between leadership and inequality is much more complex than it is for other animals. Because of *Homo sapiens sapiens'* radically greater cognitive abilities, human strength encompasses more than force and spiritedness. Complex activities like hunting and gathering, tool-making and butchering (at least 2.6 million years old in the ancestral record), exploration and invention, or conquest and defense require coordination and communication. In human communities we find inequalities along many salient dimensions: not only physical strength and boldness but also cleverness, empathy, memory, imagination, vision, humor, and artistry. 'Inequality' tends to reduce these many differences into a single false scale, as the manifold ideologies and fantasies of patriarchy and racism amply show. Thus while we may begin with animal models to shape our original insight – that leadership originates with inequality – we come quickly to the realization that inequality in itself is too limiting a term to generate much useful thinking about the nature of leadership. A first conclusion, then: when we speak of the *human* condition, we may say that leadership originates in differences deployed in particular situations. We may expect to find not one ideal instance or type of leader, but leadership in many guises, in different situations and for different problems.

The first problem of the human condition is simply to survive. The material circumstances of life on earth are rich but precarious. The world of our earliest dreams is a mythic landscape charged with energy. Earth and sky, fire and water bring both life and death. The days, the seasons, the years beat out a rhythm we feel in our blood. But accident and chance, storm and earthquake, also play their part. Stars fall from the heavens, order collapses into disorder, growth into decay, birth into death – but then chaos is recognized as a new rhythm: change and continuity in an endless cycle. To live in this world means to learn, to remember, to overcome scarcity, to defend against insecurity, to solve problems, to make mistakes. Just as walking is a constant (and painfully learned) almost-falling-down, physical survival is a constant almost-failing. The more successful that people are at solving the problems of life – surmounting scarcities of food and water, accumulating surpluses, safeguarding the young, harnessing new ideas, devising new comforts and pleasures – the more jealous attention they attract. Success carries the seed of ruin. To seize and waste will always be simpler than to build and preserve – thus the ancient enmity of city and steppe.

The challenges of physical survival – hunger, disease, predation – may afflict individuals but they are countered for the most part by common effort. (This simple truth is sometimes obscured in the West by the remarkable success of markets and technology in atomizing social relations. But markets and machines are the end-products of intricate and long-standing collective endeavors: a market is in fact the most complex community ever devised.) The human condition is one of interdependent but self-regarding individuals capable of both cooperation and betrayal. For the past 30,000 years, at least, human communities have hummed with all the dynamics of modern social life – emotion, art, intrigue, politics, the yearnings and strivings of men and women. People interact both for instrumental reasons – to survive and live as well as possible – and for intrinsic reasons – the pleasure of human contact, wired into our makeup. Within this swirl of collective life, people take on different roles, including those of leaders and followers. (Adam Smith would emphasize the efficiency gains of such division of labor.) Many roles include leadership 'pieces' – where collective work requires some measure of coordination, of dominance and consent. And individuals will have multiple roles, so that an individual may be primarily a leader in one setting, primarily a follower in another. Roles are distributed based on difference or negotiation or contestation (with no assurance that any given distribution of roles – absent a Rawlsian veil of ignorance – will be sensible or 'fair' or satisfactory to all concerned). If a group endures, over time a set of folkways, a culture, emerges as a known way to survive in the world. Roles quickly adopted and contingently devised harden into identities – what it means to be a man or a woman, warrior or shaman, lord or peasant, white-collar or blue-collar. The roles are never really fixed, but always subject to the impact of new (or newly salient) differences, negotiation, contestation, or external shock.

After survival, the second problem of the human condition is to make sense of the world. To be human means to have imagination and creative capacity, to be self-reflective, to use language to create and communicate meaning with each other. We want to understand the world, and we want to share and affirm our understanding with others. Modern Western thought has tended to make a hero of the lone thinker – *cogito ergo sum* – but (as the older, wiser Greeks knew) we are really social animals who make sense of the world together. No man is really an island of thought. 'Social reality,' a shared definition of what is true, what is valuable, and how people should behave, is lodged within the group. It is within this framework that individuals imagine and invent, and it is from the repository of the group's memory and experiences, stored in images, symbols, and in language itself, that individuals express their thoughts and dreams, even if only to themselves.

One way by which humans construct their reality is through storytelling. Narratives fulfill many purposes: to motivate, to reassure, to challenge, to provoke, to define identities, to unite, to divide, to scapegoat, to set goals or limits, to teach lessons, to inspire wonder, and to establish particular uses of power as legitimate or illegitimate. Stories connect reason, emotion, intuition, and the subconscious; they help us 'see feelingly,' in Shakespeare's words. A story offers an account of reality that seeks either to affirm or contest an existing terrain of meaning. Because of the power of human imagination – the never-distant thought that things might be different – social reality is always in play. Leaders frame stories and events to help the group understand the world, themselves, and other groups, as well as to identify or solve problems. Often leaders are the authors and tellers of stories; but they may also merely authorize particular stories or interpretations. Often narratives concern the proper roles for group members and proper degrees of agency and dependency. But followers are active in this process, contributing elements in an evolving, negotiated narrative about group roles, group identity, group history, and the world. In addition, while leadership fashions an 'official story,' there are always counter-stories, subversive and challenging authority to one degree or another. Thus social reality is a contested terrain. Complicating all this is that we are deeply ambivalent about mystery and explanation, about what narrative is supposed to do. We seek to plumb the mysteries of our existence, for there is comfort in understanding. But at the same time we crave a further experience of mystery, as if the experience of wonder is one of our innate desires. Through framing and narrative, leadership plays with this tension of mystification and demystification.

The third enduring problem of the human condition, after survival and sensemaking is to manage power – finding a path between the way of the group and the way of the individual that respects the needs of both (I define 'power' as the capacity of an individual to influence the actions and thoughts of another). Ants and bees have no leadership, because in their life 'the individual' has no meaning. The need for – and the possibility of – leadership only emerge in a collective made up of self-reflective, self-regarding individuals, among whom trust and cooperation are fragile and easily betrayed. Hobbes noted that in the state of nature even the strongest individual is insecure; no one can survive without some measure of consent from at least some key constituency. Again, our divided double nature – both social and self-regarding – exacerbates the problem of the divide between group and individual. We want to gain autonomy and independence – but at the same time we want to share our lives with others, and rely on them. And it is more than a desire; it is a fact of existence that we depend on others to live. Solving – or at least coping with – this riddle and balancing dominance and consent is the highest achievement of leadership.

The management of power takes place over time; so the time frame for thinking about leadership must be broader than singular or specific moments of leadership. Dominance and consent exist almost as currencies within the group, closely tracked by individuals (visible in such statements as 'she owes me one' and 'I'm calling in my chits on this one'). And like other kinds of currency, dominance and consent can change in value; thus those with power tend to husband it, and those whose consent is sought are always looking back, to past actions and outcomes, and to the future, to their expectations, in order to gauge their degree of consent. Leaders derive benefits (material and psychic) from effectiveness; how to be effective varies over time, and requires judgment and flexibility. Followers accept their place in the bargain as long as they perceive they are benefiting from the relationship. When followers no longer perceive these benefits, they are less likely to comply or follow. Leadership in such situations may turn increasingly into coercion, and lose legitimacy.

The workings of power are subtle, and much occurs in shadows. The constant re-metering of dominance and consent can play out almost invisibly, the participants seemingly unaware of their immersion in the group's roiling social calculus. In a similar way, many instances and acts of leadership within the group will be in a sense invisible – unseen and unacknowledged within the public space, often performed by those not recognized as leaders. (It is a mistake to think that 'leadership' is owned by the most easily seen leaders – leadership is a function of the group, a play of social relations, rather than a quality of individuals.) Complicating the effort to see power in action, what does *not* happen is often as significant as what does. The willingness of followers to refrain from exercising certain forms of power is indispensable to stable leadership. Followers typically have far more power than they employ, and more than leaders themselves – when this potential energy becomes actual, as for instance in the rise of the Solidarnosc movement in Poland the 1980s, a moment of crisis is reached, and suddenly a long-standing leadership pattern can collapse.

We have looked at three basic problems of the human condition, problems that make leadership necessary but also make it possible. The thee problems – how to survive in the world, how to make sense of the world, and how to wield power – are linked. The large and costly human brain – 2 percent of the body's weight, but consuming 20 percent of the body's caloric intake – virtually compels human beings to take an aggressive orientation to life itself. Humans are not designed to graze and stroll, but to strive and contend and invent and imagine.

To imagine that the basic hominin tool kit of flaked stone hand tools was devised millions of years ago is an extraordinary sign of their – our – imagination. But that this tool kit did not change again for a million years is no less extraordinary, and reveals how much greater is the capacity of our young species (at most 200,000 years old) to imagine. It is only when we became able to imagine what was not there that truly human leadership became necessary, and possible. Human imagination takes place within free spaces that allow individuals to glimpse alternative terrains, 'might-be' worlds. Totalitarianism and other systems of oppression ultimately try to stamp out this capacity to imagine other realities (think of the claustrophobic joylessness in Kafka, Koestler, Orwell, or Primo Levi). Leadership may enlarge or it may constrict the space for human freedom and imagination. Enabling the conditions for survival, while enlarging the space for freedom and imagination – these are the true and highest ends of leadership, its lasting contribution to the human condition. If we consider the words of Moses as imagined by the poet at the beginning of this chapter, leadership may seem to be an enchantment of the simple by the sharp. But that is the Machaivellian romance that leaders – and even their critics – like to tell. More deeply and enduringly, leadership is a relation of the many, a dynamic of the group, that promises – and sometimes attains – a unity out of the diversity of individual experience, faculties, and imagination.

FURTHER READING

Tattersall, Ian. 1998. *Becoming Human: Evolution and Human Uniqueness.* San Diego: Harvest.

3. The theory and metatheory of leadership: the important but contested nature of theory

Mark C. Walker

INTRODUCTION

> In our description of nature the purpose is not to disclose the real essence of the phenomena but only to track down, so far as it is possible, relations between the manifold aspects of our existence.
>
> Niels Bohr, 1885–1962, *Atomic Theory and the Description of Nature* (1934)

Before Sir Isaac Newton, no one thought to link the reason why an apple falls to the ground with the rotation of the moon around the earth. It had simply never occurred to anyone to ask the question. It was Newton's insight, his vision, that offered a hypothesis about a more general, theoretical force called gravity; no amount of empirical observation alone suggests such a relationship. It was theoretical not because it was as of yet unproven or unproveable, but because the terms it uses to describe phenomena cannot be measured in any direct way (Carnap 1988, pp. 162–4). Newton's genius was that he suggested the existence of a general force that could describe similar but distinct phenomena.

Scholars of leadership have presented themselves, as illustrated in Tom Wren's introductory chapter, with a similar and no less admirable, no less attainable task: what are the general, theoretical laws that govern the leadership phenomena in all of its variety? Chapter 1 describes in detail the quest that a group of scholars set out to fulfill with no less integrity and diligence than similar quests in the natural sciences. In doing so, the introductory chapter also illustrates several challenges that have arisen in the attempt to build a general theory of leadership. First, we need a better understanding of the nature of theory in leadership. What role does theory play? Where should it come from? The second challenge concerns making generalizations about leadership (Couto, unpublished manuscript). Given the numerous and differing fields of study and practice that pay attention to the leadership phenomenon, what does a general theory actually generalize about?

Scholars, educators, and practioners – both in business and the non-profit world – see the need for theory – its importance, in other words – differently. The importance of theory even varies among the scholarly disciplines. In general, the social sciences hold steadfast to the belief that theory, like theory in the natural sciences, not only explains phenomena but also should enable social scientists to predict future events. Phenomena such as economic cycles, dysfunctional behavior within groups, and the causes of war have all been targets of scientific inquiry. Other social scientists resist the effort to make a direct application of the scientific method and other theory-making tools from the natural sciences – which study physical matters – to explanations of human behavior.

Similarly, many philosophers, humanists, and postmodern social scientists find the effort to discover a general theory of leadership akin to a quixotic Enlightenment-era quest promoted by an outdated Newtonian view of a mechanical universe (Ciulla, unpublished manuscript). Others suggest that if a general theory of leadership is to be found, it will spring from systems or probability theory; even chaos theory. In sum, it seems that leadership scholars can be divided into two groups along the lines of whether or not they believe general theories of leadership are even possible (Couto, unpublished manuscript).

Being able to make generalizations about leadership is directly related to the above concerns. How do we synthesize what we know about leadership in order to construct a common language? How do we incorporate the vast range of approaches? The effort taking place in leadership studies, though new to us, is nothing new in the history of science and social science. Scholars have been attempting to understand the intellectual nature of what they do, how they do it, and how to do what they do better for centuries if not millennia; a recent example of this type of intradisciplinary struggle – often described as 'war' between scholars – can be found in the study of linguistics in the 20th century (Harris 1995). Thomas Kuhn and his study of paradigms, Larry Laudan and his studies within the philosophy of science, Karl Popper's plea for empirical science, and a regiment of constructivists have offered scholars general ways to order our thinking about how we 'think' about the world. This chapter is an attempt to help order our own reflections as we proceed.

The development of leadership theory is one of the few ways we have to determine if we are making any progress in understanding the leadership phenomenon. As noted by Georgia Sorenson (unpublished manuscript), the call to this task has been broad and long coming. Ralph Stogdill (1974) in the *Handbook of Leadership* wrote, 'the endless accumulation of empirical data has not produced an integrated understanding of leadership.' In 1977, James Hunt – a noted leadership scholar and future editor of *Leadership Quarterly* – stated 'What is missing, in addition to quantity of theoretical formulations or models is a "grand" or generalized theory of leader-subordinate relationships – if indeed, such a theoretical development is possible' (Hunt and Larsen 1977). James

MacGregor Burns helped to put out this most recent call for a 'general theory of leadership' in part to 'legitimize a field that some skeptics still dismiss as lightweight and ill-defined ... We are intent on making [leadership studies] an intellectually responsible discipline' (Managan 2002, p. 1).

This chapter has been organized to provide some illumination on all of these issues. The first section discusses what theory is and is not, and how it has been used and developed in other disciplines like international relations and physics. In physics we find a very effective use of theory with respect to the scientific method. In international relations the use of theory has been agreed upon less by scholars; nevertheless, significant progress in the discipline has been made. These comparisons both give us pointers as to what we can do and solace in that other disciplines have faced similar challenges. The second section shows how a set of leadership scholars conceptualize the theoretical landscape of our discipline with attention given to both what they agree upon and how they differ. The third section attempts to explain why leadership scholars differ on the theoretical landscape of the discipline and in their general approaches through an understanding of metaphor and metaphysics. The final section, in conclusion, discusses how we will know if progress has been made in our understanding of the leadership phenomenon.

A CALL TO WHAT? GENERAL, GRAND, UNIFIED, OR (JUST) THEORY?

James MacGregor Burns has said that we seek a general theory of leadership in order to 'provide people studying and practicing leadership with a general guide or orientation – a set of principles that are universal which can be then adapted to different situations' (Managan 2002, p. 1). But because all theory generalizes, what do we mean by a 'general theory' of leadership? Is it distinct from a 'grand,' 'unified,' 'integrated' or just 'plain' or 'average' theory?

Albert Einstein's success not only as a scientific genius but also his elevation to a cultural hero first introduced the non-physicist world to 'general' theory. The notion of general theory has its popular origins in Einstein's successful attempts to explain the relationship between space, time, moving bodies, and gravitation. Einstein (1905) first argued in a paper that the speed of light is the same for all observers regardless of their motion relative to the light source and that observers moving at the same constant speed will observe the same physical laws. For this to be true, space and time must be relative to one another: in other words, depending upon how fast one is moving with respect to the speed of light, time intervals may be longer or shorter relative to another observer moving at a different speed. This profound insight, later supported through empirical tests, essentially gave birth to an equally important but more famous corollary:

that matter and energy are interchangeable where E (energy) = m (mass) $\times c^2$ (speed of light, a constant, squared). Einstein only later referred to this as the special theory of relativity because it did not encompass the effects of gravity. In other words, 'special' denoted a narrow treatment of the subject. Einstein (1916) published a paper 11 years later in which he argued for his general theory of relativity; now more 'general' because it encompassed what happens to moving bodies and light in the presence of a gravitational field.

The notion of unified theory probably had its popular origins in part also due to Einstein. Einstein's original papers published in 1905 were an attempt to resolve inconsistencies in James Clerk Maxwell's equations that governed electromagnetic theory. Maxwell, one of the greatest theoretical physicists of the 19th century, developed equations that illustrate a 'unified' field theory that show the basic interrelationship between two concepts: electricity and magnetism. Einstein's paper that established what would later be known as special relativity was actually entitled 'The Electrodynamics of Moving Bodies' (Einstein 1905).

'Grand' theory also probably has its popular origins due to the diligence of physicists to explain the world. Beginning in the middle of the 20th century to the present-day, the 'Holy Grail' that all physicists have lusted after is the discovery of the Grand Unified Theory, or GUT, that unifies electromagnetic forces with the 'strong' and 'weak' forces found inside of atoms. To date there are various GUT theories, and they have had some success, for example, in being able to explain the absence of antimatter in the universe, but none have been empirically substantiated and some scientists still challenge their ability to accurately describe physical phenomena. At extremely high levels of energy, it has been shown experimentally that the electromagnetic and weak force are the same force, but no particle accelerator has been built with enough power in order to provide an empirical test to go beyond that. Physicists have specified their world so thoroughly that these grand theories are an attempt to explain phenomena that existed in nature only in the first few seconds of existence.

What Does Theory Do: Description, Explanation, or Prediction?

The contested nature of the concept of theory itself illustrates the difficulty of creating a general theory of leadership: we can barely agree on what a 'theory' is in the first place. Even in the hard sciences, the definition of a theory can either be broad or strict even though it describes the same essential idea. In short, different disciplines have evoked that part of the construct known as theory that best illustrates what happens within that discipline. Thus, theory could 'describe' historical events, 'explain' the origin of disease, or 'predict' that light, in the presence of a substantially strong gravitational field, would actually bend.

Even so, one would be hard-pressed to argue that theory is not explanation. The distinction between description and explanation, though the subject of great debate at times, is often moot because each is a part of the same scientific process. Those who 'explain' may expect that there should be some empirical verification to the process, for example, while those who 'describe' may say that empirical confirmation is not necessary. But there is no real opposition between description and explanation (Carnap 1988, p. 175). Even though most physicists would say that explanation is only of minor value and that 'the supreme power of a theory is its power to predict new empirical laws,' explanation nevertheless is a valid and not insubstantial part of the scientific process that they adhere to (Carnap 1988, p. 166).

Something should be said here about 'empirics.' The term empirical verification, as used in the paragraph above, refers to the step in the scientific process in which an hypothesis is tested by new information; note that an hypothesis could either have been deduced from a theory (deductive reasoning) or derived inductively from an earlier set of facts (inductive reasoning). Facts, by themselves, tell scientists very, very little. It is only the marshalling of facts at different stages of the scientific process that helps scientists verify hypotheses and/or theory that makes 'facts' or 'empirics' useful. As noted by Louis Goodman several decades ago, 'A fact, in fact, is quite abstract.' This is also, in part, a reason why generalizing about leadership is so difficult: people argue about the meaning of and the conclusions that should be derived from the same set of facts.

Making Generalizations about Leadership

What is the question?

Unfortunately, there are far more pernicious challenges – two to be exact – which must be dealt with in order to explain leadership phenomena. First, there has been an attempt to provide an answer – in the form of a general theory – without first deciding upon the question; in some sense this is a metaphysical issue but in a concrete way it is not. Second, there is no empirical test or validation that can help us answer prescriptive questions or questions that ask, 'What should leaders do?' The best way to show how to overcome the first challenge requires an examination of how other disciplines have achieved focus.

Theory usually develops in response to a particular problem. Einstein illustrates this with his attempt to answer particular inconsistencies in Maxwell's equations with the special theory of relativity and his later attempt to integrate gravitational forces into his theory with the general theory of relativity. In international relations, a sub-discipline of political science that has well-established theories and a successful history of theory-making, the problem has always been the cause of war between states, or, in the form of a question, what is the cause of war (Waltz 1959)? This clearly stated query has allowed international relations scholars to develop a set of well designed theories that at a minimum has disallowed different camps of scholars to speak past one another and at best has shown some accumulation of knowledge over time.

Example: Schools of thought in international relations
The delineation of different schools of thought in international relations theory has arguably shown some accumulation of knowledge by identifying elements that are common among several different, but progressively advanced schools (see Table 3.1). Neoliberalism, the newer study, acknowledges the parts of the well-established school of realism that it finds convincing: the selfishness of human nature, the tenet that states are the most important actors, and the initial description of the international system as anarchy. Neoliberalism as a school of thought builds upon these elements of realism in order to create a perspective that effectively explains more by showing that there are examples of cooperation in the world based upon mutual self-interest. Feminist, postmodernist, and constructivist schools of thought do not explicitly build upon earlier schools of thought but they do offer important critiques that have been effective at helping scholars analyze not only the practice of international affairs but also issues within its study. Most of these schools are still actively involved in theory creation by remaking and reforming themselves as the world changes; most notably realism has spawned an updated, more sophisticated version of itself in neorealism beginning with Kenneth Waltz's publishing of the *Theory of International Politics* in 1979.

In fact, these different schools of thought in international relations have been so successful that there has actually been little change in them over the last 15 years or so. This has frustrated some but to others this has done nothing but justify the faith put into these schools of thought in the first place. Although new theories are presented every year, they must show themselves not only to be distinct from what has come before but also able to explain more in order to receive much praise.

For example, although some observers may see the Bush administration's handling of foreign policy in a new light beginning in the spring of 2005, international relations scholars see three clear 'eras' in Bush administration policy that fall within three distinct and well-known schools. Realism describes foreign policy in the White House from the first inauguration to 9/11. Wilsonian idealism explains it from 9/11 through the Iraq war until about the time of the first election held in Iraq in January 2005. Currently, many scholars believe that neorealism explains the current shift in US policies as the checks and balances of the international system and the fact that unilateralism has become too expensive for the USA. In late 2005 the USA began to reinvigorate its alliances and be more in unison with other countries, e.g. now openly discussing 'incentives' in

Table 3.1 Schools of thought in international relations

Issue \ School	Realism	Idealism/ Liberalism	Neo-liberalism	Feminism	Post-modernism	Constructivism
Human Nature	Selfism	Altruistic	Selfism	Gendered	Diverse	Diverse
Most Important Actors	States	States and others including individuals	States	Individuals	Everything and everyone	People and society
Causes of State Behavior	Rational pursuit of self-interest over short term	Psychological motives of decision makers	Rational pursuit of mutual gain over long term	Masculinity	Multiple	Language, rules, and norms
Nature of International System	Anarchy	Community	Anarchy tempered by institutional norms and regimes	Masculine	None; the international system is non-existent	Constructed (by language, norms, rules, and/or culture)

its policy toward Iran and its nuclear program as opposed to rhetoric that places Iran within an 'Axis of Evil.'

The persistence of prescription and Laplace's demon

Similar progress may be shown within schools of thought in leadership but the issue of prescription must be discussed first. International relations is a relatively coherent field with scholars being trained in similar – if not identical – perspectives. In contrast, leadership studies varies significantly because of its interdisciplinary nature. The distinctions made between humanists, social scientists, and others are substantial and they express themselves in both subject matter and methodological approach.

For example, the different scholarly disciplines that study leadership have put different emphases upon the role of prescription. Social science often avoids 'should' questions while the humanities often embrace them, and thus, one of the most significant obstacles to the creation of general theory is the divide over prescription (Price, unpublished manuscript).

Within the philosophy of science, some believe that empirical tests and observations cannot ever provide a moral answer. For example, what if there was a being that could instantaneously understand and predict all cause and effect in the universe? Marquis Pierre Simon de Laplace (1951) [1918] illustrates this in the following passage:

> We may regard the present state of the universe as the effect of its past and the cause of its future. An intellect which at any given moment knew all of the forces that animate nature and the mutual positions of the beings that compose it, if this intellect were vast enough to submit the data to analysis, could condense into a single formula the movement of the greatest bodies of the universe and that of the lightest atom; for such an intellect nothing could be uncertain and the future just like the past would be present before its eyes.

Laplace used the above passage to illustrate his belief in causal determinism, but others have used it to pose a question about morality. What if we hired the being above – described by others as a demon given that Laplace was an atheist – to help us choose one of several actions to take. We want to know what we ought to do. The demon could tell us 'for any contemplated choice, what its consequences would be for the future course of the universe, down to the most minute detail, however remote in space and time. But, having done this for each of the alternative courses of action under consideration, the demon would have completed his task: he would have given us all the information that an ideal science might provide under the circumstances' (Hempel 1988, pp. 340–341).

The demon could not resolve our problem because it requires a decision made by us as to which alternate action is best. We must still make an unconditional value judgment between alternative sets of consequences (Hempel 1988, pp. 341). Fields that utilize mathematical decision-making recognize this limitation by having the researcher assign preference orderings or values over potential outcomes. Instead of being sidelined by this challenge, formal theory – whether it be rational choice, game theory, or strategic choice – recognizes this limitation and allows the researcher to make the value judgment – often itself based upon empirical observations – and move on (Walker 2004). As we shall see in the next section, it is not always obvious how prescriptive questions should be handled in leadership studies.

FUNDAMENTAL ISSUES AND PERSPECTIVES IN LEADERSHIP THEORY

> Your theory is crazy, but it's not crazy enough to be true.
>
> Niels Bohr, to a young physicist

Even given an understanding of the above caveats that may challenge our general thinking about leadership, scholars still differ on the way in which they conceptualize the field of leadership studies. These differences often reflect how scholars are trained in different disciplines and their own individual biases and perspectives. These different perspectives on theories of leadership, however, do not preclude the idea of an accumulation of knowledge within the study of leadership. In fact, our ability to conceptualize the field to any degree shows that there is a substance to our work that can be manipulated, discussed, and disagreed with but not easily dismissed. These foundational differences based upon our diverse disciplinary perspectives do not simply provide limitations but also possibilities for the future of leadership studies.

The next sub-sections provide some illustrations of these different perspectives in the form of matrices prepared by a diverse set of scholars. These matrices are an attempt to describe the different schools of thought within the interdisciplinary study of leadership and the basic or fundamental issues along which they can be distinguished. The categories that describe these fundamental issues or elements are just as important themselves as the distinctions that exist between schools of thought. At a minimum, by delineating both the schools and the fundamental issues that divide them, these matrices are an attempt to disallow scholars of leadership from talking past one another and serve as a basis for constructive debate. At best, these matrices may show us some accumulation of knowledge.

Mark Walker's Matrix and Perspective[1]

From this scholar's perspective, the study of leadership has gone through several stages of development, some of which have paralleled broader movements in the social sciences (see Table 3.2). Although leadership studies has not seen the type of paradigm shift described by Thomas Kuhn (1996) [1962], it has seen a change in thinking by scholars that has exhibited more progress than one might at first realize. This matrix identifies six schools of thought starting with the 'Great man' or trait theories of leadership. These theories were once popular among ordinary citizens and scholars, of whom Thomas Carlyle (1902) was the most famous proponent, but they have been widely discredited by both empirical evidence and sound theoretical arguments. Some still believe, however, that the best leaders are determined by possessing certain characteristics, whether it is a certain race, gender, height, intelligence, or just general good looks. Even more people can easily be caught admitting that some people are *born* leaders while others clearly are not.

One of the tenets of modern leadership theory is that leadership can be learned. This does not mean, however, that having certain characteristics cannot help to improve one's skill set with respect to certain leadership tasks. Before the age of radio and television, leaders often depended upon how far their voice could carry in front of a crowd in order to communicate with them. Correspondingly in today's world, individuals who are accomplished in front of a television camera have an advantage.

Behavioral theories paralleled movements in other parts of the social sciences, but in leadership studies it primarily provided the idea that leadership style is very important. One popular analytical distinction that was made was between *task*-oriented persons vs. *people*-oriented persons (Stogdill and Coons 1957; Kahn and Katz 1953; Bales and Slater 1945). This distinction basically said that *people*-oriented workers were more proficient when their primary job depended upon interaction with persons while *task*-oriented people were more efficient when given particular goals to satisfy where they were not dependent upon their interaction with others. The related school of contingency theory improved upon behavioral theory by suggesting that leadership style must be considered in the particular situational context in which it was found (Fiedler 1972; Vroom and Yetton 1973).

Leadership theories based upon internal processes of individuals include both cognitive and moral theories. Cognitive theories of leadership perceive behavior as being due to internal factors of individuals, and both leaders and followers are perceived through the lens of individuals that may be affected by learning, culture, past history, psychology, emotion, and anything that alters their conscious state such as drugs, hunger, or perceived threats (Green and Mitchell 1979; Calder 1977; Ayman and Chemers 1983). Moral theories are also based

Table 3.2 Mark Walker's matrix: schools of thought in the study of leadership

School of Thought / Element	'Great man' or trait-based leadership theory	Behavioral leadership theory	Contingency leadership theory	Cognitive leadership theory	Moral leadership theory	Strategic/ transactional leadership theory
Key component	Traits of the individual leader are the determinant of effectiveness	Leadership style is the determinant of effectiveness	Leadership style in a particular situational context is the determinant of effectiveness	Behavior perceived as being due to internal factors of individuals observed	Attention to or elevation of morality as the most desirable goal	Individual decision-making that leads to goal fulfillment
Relative role of leaders and followers	Leader-centered	Leader-centered	Leader-centered	Individual perception of leaders and followers	Leader–follower relationship	Leader–follower relationship
Related theories and concepts	Heroic leadership	'Task'- vs. 'people'-oriented leaders	Situational leadership	Culture-based or -sensitive theories	Servant leadership; citizen leadership; transforming leadership	Exchange & transactional theories; formal & game theory; LMX, strategic theory in management; military theories.
Theorists	Carlyle	Lewin; Stogdill and Coons; Kahn and Katz; Bales and Slater	Fiedler; Vroom and Yetton	Green and Mitchell; Calder; Ayman and Chemers (cross-cultural theories)	Greenleaf (servant leaders); Burns (transforming leaders)	Frohlich, Oppenheimer, and Young; Riker; Burns (transactional leaders); Lake and Powell; Hunt

upon an internal, individual process; however, leadership is now seen as a relationship between leaders and followers where they all strive to attain mutual goals (Burns 1978). Morality becomes the central component in these theories and is often elevated to the most desirable goal. Various prominent theories fit into this category, including servant leadership (Greenleaf 1977), citizen leadership (Couto 1992), and transformational or transforming leadership (Burns 1978, 2003). But morality is not a strategy; it is a goal (Zakaria 2003). Sometimes these works have emphasized morality as a goal without reflection on the strategic consequences of a leader's decisions; other times moral action is emphasized as a tactic but still without reflection on the leader's ability to succeed at bringing into existence a particular outcome – hence part of the dilemma of leadership studies from this scholar's perspective.

Walker believes that various strategic and transactional theories capture much of what is effective in the application of leadership theory in practice (Walker 2004); this set of approaches encompasses strategic choice in political science (Lake and Powell 1999), for example, and the strategic leadership theory found in management and organizational studies (Boal and Hooijberg 2001; Phillips and Hunt 1992). Helpful leader characteristics feed into a leader's skill set and his/her competence in taking certain actions, such as giving a speech. Style can be captured by an individual's preferences over actions, and modeling the environment captures the situational context in which an individual may find him or herself. Both cognitive and moral theories are related to a strategic approach because they depend upon internal individual preferences and beliefs that have an effect upon the environment and the strategic interaction of actors.

Tom Wren's Matrix and Perspective

Tom Wren explicitly labeled his approach a 'theoretical' matrix in which he categorized the type of scholars involved in the study of leadership and then showed how they might respond to five key questions (see Table 3.3). His scholarly categories included (1) social scientists or 'positivists,' (2) humanists or 'interpretativists,' and (3) postmodernists or 'constructivists.' He showed distinctions between these scholars through the following sets of questions: How is the problem defined? What type of information/data is used in seeking an answer? What method is used? How does one judge the validity of the outcome? How should the outcome be applied?

Wren illustrated in his matrix some of the differences in premise that have hampered the efforts of scholars to come to some integrated result. These differences can be pithily summarized in the degree to which the 'scientific' method is applied to leadership studies. Social scientists have been described as strict positivists in approach through the application of empirical tests, col-

Table 3.3   J. Thomas Wren's theoretical matrix

Central Questions	Social Scientists (Positivists)	Humanists (Interpretavists)	Postmodernists (Constructivists)
How is the problem defined?	There are extant causal patterns that can be discovered, articulated, and tested	Ask a (general) question about the topic under study, often shaped by discipline (e.g. history: what were long-term causative elements; ethics: was a certain action justified?)	There are no fixed and immutable institutions, processes, or relationships. Individuals, societies or institutions negotiate their own reality. The task is to understand the sources, process, and product of this process of construction
What type of information/data is used in seeking an answer?	Look to data that can be measured (directly or indirectly)	Explore a wealth of quantitative and qualitative information that is not replicable (historians); draw upon understanding of moral reason (ethicists)	Look to wide range of physical, historical, psychological, and anthropological evidence (non-replicable)
What method is used?	Emulates scientific method to extent possible: is empirical, subject to empirical verification, is explicit and replicable	Method is to draw logical conclusions either by looking to unique non-replicable sources (historians) or through the logical application of moral reason (ethics)	Go beyond description, and seek to deconstruct the values and processes that created the perceived reality
How does one judge validity of outcome?	Is it predictive?	Does the logic or argument have cogency and consistency? Does it bring increased understanding?	Is it explanatory?
How should the outcome be applied?	It is perceived to be non-normative (other than the occasional reference to 'effectiveness'). Goal is to understand and predict	Can be either normative or non-normative. Goal is to understand and to reflect critically upon the topic	Goal is to understand. Some postmodernists have social agendas, others do not. While some seek enhanced clarity regarding societal processes and institutions, others take a more critical stance concerning power and inequality

lection of measurable data, and the use of a non-normative frame of reference. Theory that can predict is the ultimate goal, much like the perspective of physicists.

Humanists, according to Wren, have a much broader mandate. Humanists ask more general questions, unlike social scientists who search for causal patterns that can be articulated and tested. This does not mean that humanists are not concerned with causality, e.g. history often looks for long-term causative factors. The data that humanists collect span a range from quantitative to qualitative that is, unlike in the physical sciences, not replicable in the case of historians or based upon moral reason in the case of ethicists. Instead of having prediction as a goal, the validity of an outcome is judged by the cogency and consistency of an argument, and if it brings about increased understanding.

The main task of postmodernists and constructivists is to understand and explain the world around them. Their methodology, though more complex than this, is to go beyond description and deconstruct the values and ideas that make up one's perception of reality. The evidence of postmodernists is also usually nonreplicable, but with explanation as the goal of the theory-making process, postmodernists are not as dissimilar from other groups of scholars as one might initially guess. One of the key tenets of postmodernism is that reality is 'constructed' and thus not based upon any immutable criteria.

Gill Hickman's Matrix and Perspective

Gill Hickman's matrix has components of both Walker and Wren, but it also goes farther than either of the above attempts in the number of categories of scholars presented and the issues upon which they are contrasted (see Table 3.4). These scholars are broken down into six different camps: humanists, essentialists (positivists), social constructivists, environmentalists, feminists, and pluralists. Most importantly, Hickman's matrix illustrates some significant consistencies between the different groups of scholars.

While most of these camps differ on issues such as human nature and the purposes of leadership (see Table 3.4), Hickman identifies four out of six as viewing ethics as being 'essential' to their task. Moreover, in the category of context, all of the groups are posited with some type of system whether it is social, socially constructed, natural, human, or an ecosystem. Although this may be a semantic tick, the use of 'system' as a metaphor suggests something quite specific about how context in a leadership environment is viewed across the board. All of the groups have participants serve as initiators, partners, challengers, and passives. The level of analysis between the different scholarly perspectives also has some interesting continuities given that the 'groups and collectives' exist in every perspective whereas individuals do not. It could be argued, however, that the individual level is important to constructivists along

Table 3.4 Gill Hickman's matrix

Differing Perspectives / Issues	Humanism	Essentialism (Positivism)	Social Constructivism	Environmentalism	Feminism	Pluralism
Human Nature	• Self-determining • Problem-solving • Capable of choice • Rational	• Observable & Discernible • Verifiable • Questioning • Analytical	• Meaning-making • Categorizing • Relational – Alliance building • Generative Reorganizing	• Interdependent • Sustainable	• Gendered	• Diverse – Multiple
Mobilizing Forces ■ **Purpose of Leadership**	• Create, change or sustain human course of action • Solve human problems	Influence human and environmental functioning or actions using factual information	• Legitimate human needs and wants • Create or change common meanings • Imagine & communicate alternative social realities or arrangements • Create, sustain or change constructed realities or arrangements	• Sustain and balance human and environmental needs	Create human systems of gender equality, freedom and opportunity	Expand tolerance of multiple human differences, identities and beliefs among interdependent groups

60

	Essential	Differing or Nonessential	Essential	Essential	Essential	Differing
Ethics						
Context	Human Systems (Humanity)	Social and Natural Systems	Socially Constructed Systems (Terrains of meaning – e.g. economic, political, social cultural, religious, ecological, and so on)	Ecosystems	Social Systems	Social Systems
Participants	• Initiators and partners • Challengers and passives	• Initiators and partners • Challengers and passives	• Initiators and partners • Challengers and passives	• Initiators and partners • Challengers and passives	• Initiators and partners • Challengers and passives	• Initiators and partners • Challengers and passives
Power	Function of human self-determination & problem-solving	Function of human interaction	Function of social relationships (within and between terrains of meaning)	Function of human interaction & natural forces	Function of male systems	Function of dominant systems
Level of Action & Analysis	Individuals, Groups, Collectives	Individuals, Dyads, Groups & Collectives	Groups & Collectives	Groups & Collectives	Individuals, Dyads, Groups & Collectives	Groups & Collectives

61

with humanists, essentialists, and feminists but less of an argument may be made for environmentalists and pluralists.

Terry Price's Matrix and Perspective

Terry Price goes even farther than Hickman in showing some of the similarities among schools of thought (see Table 3.5). In fact, he essentially sees only two categories of scholars separated on a descriptive/explanatory vs. prescriptive/ justificatory divide. Harkening back to the earlier discussion of prescription and Laplace's demon, Price believes that this challenge to leadership scholars so dominates the discussion that, indeed, there is no basic distinction between description and explanation, as also per an earlier discussion. Only Burns's theory of transforming leadership and Rousseau's social contract bridge this divide within the issue of transformation. Otherwise, descriptive/explanatory and prescriptive/justificatory disciplines have a different basis for personal characteristics, situational response, and transaction in leadership – the issues Price identifies as important in the study of leadership.

Toward an Integrative Theory of Leadership?

The similarities and continuities illustrated above not only show some possible accumulation of knowledge but also point toward a possible integrated theory of leadership. But for an integrated, or 'unified,' theory to have validity, scholars must agree upon the essential or basic elements that are being integrated. For example, physics demonstrates this through a common understanding among its scholars of not only electricity and magnetism but also such abstract concepts as 'strong' and 'weak' forces. Without this basic, scholarly agreement as a pre-requisite, we in the study of leadership would be providing integration without substance, or a map without landmarks.

Mapping the territory: a metaphor offered by Joanne Ciulla
Joanne Ciulla contributed what many consider to be a very helpful metaphor in the task of constructing an integrated theory of leadership: a map. This map would include the fundamental elements of leadership and how they fit together within the context of features with which we are all familiar: terrain, roads, hills, oceans, etc. The above exercise of developing a matrix appeals to those who do not mind making 'classic' distinctions between concepts. Ciulla's contribution suggests that the study of leadership may be more fruitfully theorized based upon metaphor and a universal typology of concepts. This is opposed to a clas-sical view of the accumulation of knowledge, where a scholarly consensus comes about unconsciously through discoveries – paradigm creations and shifts – in some kind of evolutionary process. Natural scientists have done a better

Table 3.5 *Terry Price's matrix*

	Leadership As			
Descriptive/Explanatory Fields/Disciplines	Personal Characteristics	Situational Response	Transaction	Transformation
Organizational Leadership	Trait Theories	Contingency Theories (e.g., Path – Goal)	Social Exchange Theories (e.g., LMX)	Bass's *Transformational Leadership* (1985)
Other Fields/Disciplines?				Burns's *Transforming Leadership* (2003)
Prescriptive/Justificatory Fields/Disciplines				
Social and Political Philosophy	Plato in the *Republic*	Machiavelli in *The Prince* and *Discourses*	Social Contract Theory (e.g., Hobbes, Locke)	Rousseau on the *Social Contract*

job than social scientists in creating consensus among themselves; is there a reason for this based upon some correspondence between the nature of physical and social phenomena?

The linguistic theories of George Lakoff (1987, 1992; and Johnson 1980) for example, provide an alternate approach for how scholars categorize things and the consequences for the way in which humans think, reason, and carry out scientific investigations. These alternative classifications, based upon sound empirical evidence in linguistics, cognitive science, psychology, anthropology, and biology, may challenge the scope and explanatory ability of classical theories, which suggest a Kuhnian paradigm shift in all modes of scientific discourse.

Lakoff argues that metaphor is not only a valid way of thinking about concepts, but that it and other imaginative ways are essential. Simply put, the classical, or 'objectivist,' view holds that categories are defined in terms of common properties of their members. But evidence has supported a view referred to as experiential realism or experientialism that is explained by the theories of prototypes and basic-level categories (see Table 3.6). The objectivist view holds that thought is the mechanical manipulation of abstract symbols. The experientialist view holds, for example, that the structures used in thought come directly from our bodily experience. Table 3.6 organizes and contrasts the two positions.

Metaphorical systems impose a tremendous number of constraints on a conceptual system. This is because metaphor goes beyond language; metaphorical systems are general mappings across conceptual domains. 'In short, the locus of metaphor is not in language at all, but in the way we conceptualize one mental domain in terms of another. The general theory of metaphor is given by characterizing such cross-domain mappings. And in the process, everyday abstract concepts like time, states, change, causation, and purpose also turn out to be metaphorical' (Lakoff 1992). The most important point drawn from above is that those concepts that are not drawn directly from experience; we must employ imagination to link them to experience.

A holistic, social constructive model of leadership by Gill Hickman

As a precursor to an integrated theory of leadership, Hickman offered a holistic, socially constructed model of leadership that succeeded in including most of the elements and issues that had occupied the GTOL group (see Figure 3.1). Though drawn in two dimensions on a page, in reality it would be best represented by a three-dimensional model that, unbeknownst to her, resembles the core instrumental device of an atomic bomb. At its center is the perfectly round sphere of uranium, here denoting 'leadership purpose,' that serves as the source of energy. A spherical shell surrounds this core representing different levels of analysis through individuals, dyads, collectives, and groups. This core and spherical shell sits in a device that provides explanatory power in the form of

Table 3.6   The objectivist vs. experientialist view

The Objectivist View	The Experientialist View
• Thought is the mechanical manipulation of abstract symbols	• Thought is *embodied*; that is, the structures used to put together our conceptual systems grow out of our bodily experience and make sense in terms of it; moreover, the core of our conceptual systems is directly grounded in perception, body movement, and experience of a physical and social character
• The mind is an abstract machine, manipulating symbols essentially in the way a computer does, that is, by algorithmic computation	
• Symbols (e.g., words and mental representations) get their meanings via correspondences to things in the external world. All meaning is of this character	
• Symbols that correspond to the external world are *internal representations of external reality*	• Thought is *imaginative*, in that those concepts which are not directly grounded in experience employ metaphor, metonymy, and mental imagery – all of which go beyond the literal mirroring, or *representation*, of external reality. It is this imaginative capacity that allows for 'abstract' thought and takes the mind beyond what we can see and feel. The imaginative capacity is also embodied – indirectly – since the metaphors, metonymies, and images are based on experience, often bodily experience. Thought is also imaginative in a less obvious way: every time we categorize something in a way that does not mirror nature, we are using general human imaginative capacities (Lakoff, 1987, pp. xii–xv)
• Abstract symbols may stand in correspondence to things in the world independent of the peculiar properties of any organisms	
• Since the human mind makes use of internal representation of external reality, the mind is a *mirror of nature*, and correct reason mirrors the logic of the external world	
• It is thus incidental to the nature of meaningful concepts and reason that human beings have the bodies they have and function in their environment in the way they do. Human bodies may play a role in *choosing* which concepts and which modes of transcendental reason human beings actually employ, but they play no essential roles in *characterizing* what constitutes a concept and what constitutes reason	
• Thought is *abstract* and *disembodied*, since it is independent of any limitations of the human body, the human perceptual system, and the human nervous system	

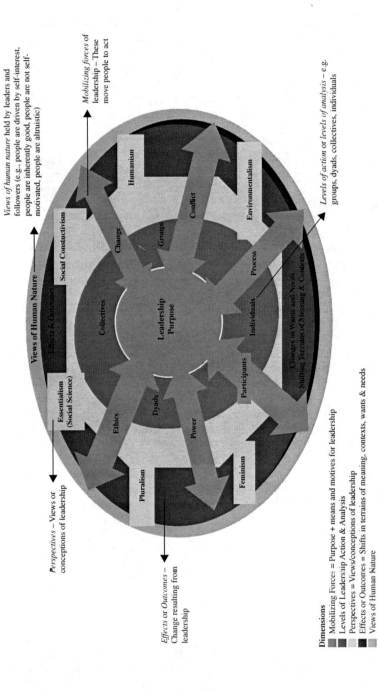

Views of human nature held by leaders and followers (e.g., people are driven by self-interest, people are inherently good, people are not self-motivated, people are altruistic)

Mobilizing forces of leadership – These move people to act

Views of Human Nature

Social Constuctivism

Humanism

Effects & Outcome

Change

Groups

Conflict

Environmentalism

Collectives

Leadership Purpose

Process

Individuals

Essentialism (Social Science)

Dyads

Participants

Changes in Wants and Needs Shifting Terrains of Meaning & Contexts

Ethics

Power

Pluralism

Feminism

Perspectives – Views or conceptions of leadership

Levels of action or levels of analysis – e.g. groups, dyads, collectives, individuals

Effects or Outcomes – Change resulting from leadership

Dimensions
Mobilizing Forces = Purpose + means and motives for leadership
Levels of Leadership Action & Analysis
Perspectives = Views/conceptions of leadership
Effects or Outcomes = Shifts in terrains of meaning, contexts, wants & needs
Views of Human Nature

Figure 3.1   Gill Hickman's holistic, social constructive model

different perspectives such as essentialism, social constructivism, humanism, environmentalism, feminism, and pluralism. This entire mechanism is posited within an environment of effects and outcomes based upon the shifting terrain of meaning, contexts, wants, and needs of people.

The dynamic nature of this model of leadership is captured by forces, represented by arrows that travel between the core of leadership purpose through the shell and device into the environment. These forces include change, conflict, process, participants, power, and ethics. These forces operate in both directions and through the different levels of analysis of the shell and the perspectives of the device. These forces operate with leadership purpose to create an overall mobilizing force that captures, then, the leadership phenomenon.

METATHEORETICAL CONCERNS OF LEADERSHIP THEORY

> The engineer is the key figure in the material progress of the world. It is his engineering that makes a reality of the potential value of science by translating scientific knowledge into tools, resources, energy and labor to bring them into the service of man ... To make contributions of this kind the engineer requires the imagination to visualize the needs of society and to appreciate what is possible as well as the technological and broad social age understanding to bring his vision to reality.
>
> Sir Eric Ashby

Why is it important to understand the metatheory of leadership studies? Throughout our attempts to develop a general theory of leadership, certain metaphors and perspectives keep resurfacing without sufficient explanation. Why does or should morality play a central role? Why are the wants and needs of society a factor in leadership studies? Why do some emphasize the transformation of leaders and followers and neglect the more mundane transactional relationships? Why do a significant number of leadership programs and practitioners emphasize ethics and service?

We need to understand what concepts and ideas keep resurfacing and why; this is crucial to our goal of furthering the scholarly 'progress' of leadership studies. Moreover, we need to be self-conscious about the process we use to think about leadership in order to change how practitioners actually practice leadership. For example, even the engineer quoted above perceives that he plays a role in society; similarly, 'service' is one of the most durable metaphors to be found in the study of leadership.

Metatheories are 'theories of theories,' or the explanations for the explanations we use to describe, explain, predict, and prescribe the world. At its root, the simplest way to think of it is as metaphor, literally. For example, in international relations theory, we can group different theories by the metaphor that best describes how they operate. There are 'mechanical' theories that are based upon mechanics in physics. Examples of these have to do with theories of the 'balance' and 'distribution' of power, the 'structure' of the international system, and so on. There are biological theories that talk about the international relations 'system' and how everything is connected much like organs and tissue are connected in the human body. The global perspective or level of analysis would fit into a 'biological' metaphor. There are economic or market metaphors; this is where politics is literally seen taking place like the transactions in a market place and not necessarily as politics being influenced by economics per se.

One challenge would be to attempt to find the metaphors that help to explain various leadership theories. As noted above, one possible metaphor might be of 'service.' There are many theories that belong in this metatheoretical category, including most if not all of the theories explicitly based upon a morality, and all those including servant leadership, citizen leadership, and transforming leadership. Another possible metaphor would be that of the 'market' with transactional leadership being an example. Behavioral, contingency, and 'Great man' theories all could fall into a 'paternal' metaphor of leadership because at its core each of these is focused solely upon the leader and not upon a relationship between leaders and followers. Cognitive leadership theory, along with theories based upon culture, might be based upon a metaphor of 'perception, equality, or diversity' because at their heart these theories all trumpet how different viewpoints, whether individually or group-based, are all valid.

The philosophy of science and social science gives us a rubric or shorthand for describing various theories of leadership (see Table 3.7). In this literature there are four essential ways that people look at the world and they are all intimately tied to one's conception of truth. Table 3.7 presents a theory of how theories and theorists differ from one another. By applying this metatheory to our study of leadership, we have the opportunity to end the practice of talking past one another and perhaps understanding from where we derive our beliefs and perspectives.

In the philosophy of science, how individuals – including scholars – conceptualize the truth goes a long way in helping us explain how we can observe the same person, place, thing, or event and assign to it different value or even meaning. Essentially, there are four different categories of individuals: positivists, realists, pragmatists, and relativists. Positivists believe that there is one and only one correct answer to a question; they also believe that the answer can be learned or discovered. Realists believe that there are many answers to a question but that there is one best answer. Pragmatists believe that there are many different potential answers to a question but that the best answer depends upon the situation and what is needed. The relativist believes that there is no such thing as a best answer; in fact, all answers are equally valid. Because questions have no true answers, many relativists believe there is no such thing as the truth (Laudan 1990).

Table 3.7   Four perspectives on the nature of truth in the philosophy of science

Positivist	Realist	Pragmatist	Relativist
'There is one and only one correct answer to a question, and it can be learned and/or discovered.'	'There are many answers to a question, but there is one best answer.'	'There are many different answers to a question, and the best answer depends upon the situation and what is needed.'	'There is no best answer to a question: all answers are equally valid. Questions have no true answer; thus there is no such thing as the truth.'

Given the above framework, it is clear that leadership scholars come to the table with significant metatheoretical differences. Postmodernists and constructivists are relativists. Some social scientists come very close to being positivist. Humanists and social scientists in general often range somewhere in between being realist, pragmatist, or moderately relativist. Individuals run a significant risk of talking past one another – listening without hearing and speaking without understanding – unless they recognize the metatheoretical perspective not only of those they are in dialogue with but also themselves.

There are other consequences of these underlying metaphorical attributes. Positivistic and realist thinking can usually be described as linear while the thinking of pragmatists and especially relativists is not. Linearity means that one can achieve an accumulation of knowledge over time because things, in general, improve with time; therefore, progress is a viable concept if one subscribes to linear thinking. Non-linear thinking may not completely disallow progress, but it comes about with greater difficulty and is certainly not assumed. For example, if one believes strongly that history repeats itself and that human beings are essentially the same now as they have always been – no more moral or effective in their relations with one another and their environment – then one believes very little in the notion of progress. On the other hand, if one teaches leadership in a high school or undergraduate program, there is an implicit belief in progress because one believes that students will become better leaders if not also better people by the end of the program. Leadership scholars, therefore, are confronted not only with differing theoretical and metatheoretical perspectives, but also with different ideas of progress in the study of leadership.

DISCERNING WHAT CONSTITUTES PROGRESS IN LEADERSHIP THEORY

Honest differences are often a healthy sign of progress.
                                        Mahatma Gandhi, 1869–1948

When will we know when we have begun to make progress in the study of leadership? What constitutes an accumulation of knowledge? Can this determination be made empirically, or does it necessarily involve a value judgment? Indeed, the answer to this basic question has eluded the GTOL group during its entire tenure. Is it good enough to show that there are different and significant schools of thought in leadership; is that progress? Or is there a need for an integrated theory that brings some, most, or all theories under the same framework? Although a general theory of leadership, if developed, would certainly denote progress, are there steps that can be taken short of a general theory that would also signal progress? Can any of this be achieved without agreement on the basic elements of leadership?

It should be recognized that there are different kinds of progress noted within science. Economic progress denotes an increase in funding for research. Professional progress means a rising status of the scientists and the institutions they belong to. Educational progress means an increase in the skills and expert knowledge of scientists. Methodological progress means the development of new methods of research or the refinement of instruments. Cognitive progress denotes the increase or advancement of scientific knowledge. Technical progress means an increase in the effectiveness of tools and techniques. Social progress means an improvement in economic prosperity, quality of life, and justice in a society (Niiniluoto 2002).

Moreover, it has been argued that the term 'progress' is value-laden or normative itself as opposed to more neutral terminology such as 'change' (Niiniluoto 1995). However, this aspect allows it to be a goal-oriented term that allows for the use of backward-looking or forward-looking criteria. Should success in leadership theory be judged by how far it has come over the last few decades, or should it be judged by some ideal measure, such as the power and elegance of general or unified theory in physics? Specifically, should 'unification,' 'simplicity,' or explanatory power be the criteria used to judge progress in leadership theory?

This chapter will provide no answer to this debate as it is much larger than a discussion of theory and metatheory. However, it should be noted that there seem to be several different kinds of progress being sought after and not just one; both cognitive (Stogdill 1974; Hunt and Larsen 1977) and professional progress (Managan 2002) seem to be goals of many scholars of leadership. Moreover, social progress seems to be a crucial element for others, including those who see the needs and wants of a people as a central component (e.g. Burns 2003). These distinct, possibly conflicting, but clearly enormous single goals only serve to make the task of constructing a 'general' theory that much more difficult given the collective criteria – cognitive, professional, and possibly social – implied for its success.

NOTE

1. This summary description is drawn in part from Martin Chemer's chapter 'Contemporary Leadership Theory', in J. Thomas Wren's (1995) edited volume *The Leader's Companion*.

REFERENCES

Ayman, Rova and Martin M. Chemers (1983), 'The Relationship of Leader Behavior to Managerial Effectiveness and Satisfaction in Iran', *Journal of Applied Psychology*, **68**, 338–41.

Bales, Robert F. and Paul E. Slater (1945), 'Role Differentiation in Small Decision Making Groups', in Talcott Parsons and Robert F. Bales (eds), *Family, Localization, and Interaction Processes*, New York: Free Press.

Bass, B.M. (1985), *Leadership and Performance Beyond Expectation*, New York: Free Press.

Boal, Kimberly B. and Robert Hooijberg (2001), 'Strategic Leadership Research: Moving On', *Leadership Quarterly*, **11** (4), 515–49.

Burns, James MacGregor (1978), *Leadership*, New York: Harper & Row.

Burns, James MacGregor (2003), *Transforming Leadership: A New Pursuit of Happiness*, New York: Atlantic Monthly Press.

Calder, Billy J. (1977), 'An Attribution Theory of Leadership', in Barry M. Straw and Gerald R. Slancik (eds), *New Directions in Organizational Behavior*, Chicago: St Clair.

Carlyle, Thomas (1902), *On Heroes, Hero Worship, and the Heroic in History*, New York: Ginn & Co.

Carnap, Rudolf (1988), 'The nature of theories', in E.D. Klemke, Robert Hollinger, and A. David Kline (eds), *Introductory Readings in the Philosophy of Science*, rev. edn, Buffalo, NY: Prometheus Books.

Chemers, Martin M. (1984), 'The Social, Organizational, and Cultural Context of Effective Leadership', in Barbara Kellerman (ed.), *Leadership: Multidisciplinary Perspectives*, Englewood Cliffs, NJ: Prentice Hall.

Chemers, Martin M. (1995), 'Contemporary Leadership Theory', in J. Thomas Wren (ed.), *The Leader's Companion*, New York: Free Press.

Ciulla, Joanne, 'Some Thoughts on the General Theory of Leadership Project', unpublished manuscript.

Couto, Richard A. (1992), *Public Leadership Education: The Role of the Citizen Leader*, Dayton, OH: The Kettering Foundation.

Couto, Richard A., 'Toward a General Theory of Leadership', unpublished manuscript.

Einstein, Albert (1905), 'Zur Elektrodynamik bewegter Körper', *Annalen der Physik*, **17**, 891–921.

Einstein, Albert (1916), 'Die Grundlage der allgemeinen Relativitatstheorie', *Annalen der Physik*, **49**, 769–822.

Fiedler, Fred E. (1972), 'The Effects of Leadership Training and Experience: A Contingency Model Interpretation', *Administrative Science Quarterly*, **17**, 453–70.

Frohlich, Norman, Joe A. Oppenheimer, and Oran R. Young (1971), *Political Leadership and Collective Goods*, Princeton: Princeton University Press.

Green, Stephen G. and Terrence R. Mitchell (1979), 'Attributional Processes of Leaders in Leader–Member Interactions', *Organizational Behavior and Human Performance*, **23**, 429–58.

Greenleaf, Robert K. (1977), *Servant Leadership: A Journey into the Nature of Legitimate Power and Greatness*, New York: Paulist Press.

Harris, Randy Allen (1995), *The Linguistics Wars*, Oxford: Oxford University Press.

Hempel, Carl G. (1988), 'Provisos: A Problem Concerning the Inferential Function of Scientific Theories', in Wesley C. Salmon and Adolf Grünbaum (eds), *The Limitations of Deductivism*, Berkely: University of California Press.

Hunt, James G. and Lars Larsen (eds) (1977), *Leadership, The Cutting Edge*, Carbondale, IL: Southern Illinois University Press.

Kahn, Robert L. and Daniel Katz (1953), 'Leadership Practices in Relation to Productivity and Morale', in Dorwin Cartwright and Alvin Zander (eds), *Group Dynamics*, New York: Harper & Row.

Klemke, E.D., Robert Hollinger, and A. David Kline (eds) (1988), *Introductory Readings in the Philosophy of Science, rev. edn*, Buffalo, NY: Prometheus Books.

Kuhn, Thomas S. (1996) [1962], *The Structure of Scientific Revolutions: 3rd edn*, Chicago: University of Chicago Press.

Lake, David A. and Robert Powell (eds) (1999), *Strategic Choice and International Relations,* Princeton: Princeton University Press.

Lakoff, George (1987), *Women, Fire, and Dangerous Things,* Chicago: University of Chicago Press.

Lakoff, George (1992), 'What is Metaphor?', in K.J. Holyoak and J.A. Barnden (eds), *Advances in Connectionist and Neural Computational Theory, Vol. 2 Analogical Connections*, Norwood, NJ: Ablex.

Lakoff, George and Mark Johnson (1980), *Metaphors We Live By*, Chicago: University of Chicago Press.

Laplace, Pierre Simon de (1951) [1918], *Philosophical Essay on Probabilities*, New York: Dover Publications.

Laudan, L. (1990), *Science and Relativism: Some Key Controversies in the Philosophy of Science*, Chicago: University of Chicago Press.

Managan, Katherine (2002), 'Leading the way in leadership: The unending quest of the discipline's founding father, James MacGregor Burns', *Chronicle of Higher Education*, May 31, p. 1.

Niiniluoto, Ilkka (1995), 'Is there progress in science?' in H. Stachowiak (ed.), *Pragmatik, Handbuch pragmatischen Denken, Band V*, Hamburg: Felix Meiner Verlag, 30–58.

Niiniluoto, Ilkka (2002), 'Scientific Progress', *The Stanford Encyclopedia of Philosophy,* Winter 2002 edn, Edward N. Zalta (ed.), available at: http://plato.stanford.edu/archives/win2002/entries/scientific-progress/.

Phillips, R.L. and J.G. Hunt (1992), *Strategic Leadership: A Multiorganizational-level Perspective*, Westport, CT: Quorum Books.

Price, Terry, 'Preliminary Ideas on a General Theory of Leadership', unpublished manuscript.

Riker, William H. (1986), *The Art of Political Manipulation*, New Haven: Yale University Press.

Sorenson, Georgia, 'Preliminary Ideas about a General Theory of Leadership', unpublished manuscript.

Stogdill, Ralph (1974), *Handbook of Leadership*, New York: Free Press.

Stogdill, Ralph M. and Alvin E. Coons (eds) (1957), *Leader Behavior: Its Description and Measurement*, Columbus: Ohio State University, Bureau of Business Research.

Vroom, Victor H. and Paul W. Yetton (1973), *Leadership and Decision-Making*, Pittsburgh: University of Pittsburgh Press.

Walker, Mark Clarence (2004), *Must political leaders choose between morality and effectiveness? Or, alternatively, bringing the leader back into political science.* Manuscript submitted for publication.

Waltz, Kenneth (1959) [1954], *Man, the State and War: A Theoretical Analysis*, New York: Columbia University Press.

Waltz, Kenneth (1979), *Theory of International Politics*, New York: McGraw Hill.

Wren, J. Thomas (1995), *The Leader's Companion: Insights on Leadership Through the Ages*, New York: Free Press.

Zakaria, Fareed (2003), 'Morality is Not a Strategy', *Newsweek*, January 13, US edn.

4. Power

Michael Harvey

We have power in ourselves to do it, but it is a power that we have no power to do.
Third Citizen, *Coriolanus* (2.3.4–5)[1]

Coriolanus, a study of early 17th-century English political anxieties set in an-cient Rome, is Shakespeare's most searching meditation on power and leadership. It's a bitter and ambiguous play, filled with largely unlikeable char-acters jostling for power – one critic, Eric Bentley, called *Coriolanus* 'the struggle of wrong and wrong' (1954, 186). Caius Marcius Coriolanus, the im-perious warrior who as a youth helped drive out the last king of Rome and bears the scars of a lifetime of warfare and command, decides to seek the consulship. The move from military to civil power requires him to learn a new kind of leadership and cultivate a truly reciprocal relationship with the commoners he has always disdained, for they have a crucial (though limited) voice in the elec-tion of a consul. Shakespeare begins the play with images of conflict and power as physical force: mutinous citizens with rude weapons, Menenius' fable of the belly with its literal imagining of the body politic ('the arm our soldier' [1.1.105]), war between Rome and the neighboring Volscians, soldiers armed with swords, and standing above all, the haughty, blood-drenched, heroic Cori-olanus (the word 'hero,' a *Coriolanus* scholar reminds us, derives from the Greek word for 'warrior' [Maus 1997, 2785]).

In the play, it is not the aristocratic Coriolanus but an anonymous commoner – one of the city's vital but uncelebrated 'apron-men' (4.6.100) – who gives voice to one of the mysteries of power: how its matter-of-fact corporeal simplic-ity – 'we have power in ourselves' – coils itself into complexities and contradictions: 'a power that we have no power to do.' The Third Citizen puzzles over how moral obligation is itself a kind of power, or curb on power. Picking up his cue, the mob of mutinous citizens in *Coriolanus* soon show themselves to be thoughtful students of power and of the making, meaning, and preservation of community. The citizens' quandary is whether to trust the man who would be their leader – and beyond him, how to understand, use, and safeguard their power. What allegiance do they owe a hero for his past service to the city? Does his valor suit him to peaceful rule? What of his evident contempt for them? If they defy him, what damage will they do to the city's fabric?

'What is the city but the people?' they ask (3.1.198), and this, the central question of the play (ironically first asked by the cynical and demagogic tribunes of the people) leads us to ponder more questions: Where does power come from? From a leader's strength, resolve, or wisdom? From the people's numbers, or bodies, or voices? Or are such metrics of power less important than the power of connections, neighborliness, or mutuality? Power is in one sense whatever we agree or think it is, so that the names we give things (was the 2005 Lebanese uprising against Syria the 'intifada for independence' or the 'Cedar Revolution'?),[2] how we talk (and who talks), what we mean by 'agree,' and how we remember our answers – even how we define this collective 'we' – are themselves vital sources of power. Power, in short, has many faces. That which seems strongest – a general waving a sword at the head of his army – is weak if no one follows him:

MARCIUS. So, now the gates are ope. Now prove good seconds.
　　'Tis for the followers fortune widens them,
　　Not for the fliers. Mark me, and do the like.
　　　　　　　　　　　　　　　　[*He enters the gates*]
FIRST SOLDIER. Fool-hardiness! Not I.
SECOND SOLDIER.　　　　　　　　Nor I.
　　　　　　　　　　　　　　　[*MARCIUS is shut in*]
FIRST SOLDIER. See, they have shut him in.
THIRD SOLDIER.　　　　　　　To th' pot, I warrant him.
　　　　　　　　　　　　　　　[*Alarum continues*]
FIRST SOLDIER.　　… he is himself alone,
　　To answer all the city. (*Coriolanus*, 1.4.43–51)

Following Shakespeare's lead in *Coriolanus* (or Michel Foucault's in *Discipline and Punish*) we'll begin with images of power as strength and violence. Then we'll turn to other ways of explaining power, like charisma, authority, influence tactics, 'soft' power, and how power is embedded in social interactions and culture. The direction of our exploration will be from a view of power as an individual resource, beginning with the physical power of the body, to power as a social relation, a circulation of energy in a human network. For some, like Foucault, this view of power makes it an inescapable, embedded part of the (modern?) human condition. For others, the notion of the 'circulation' of power raises the possibility that power might circulate without any guidance from a 'leader' – and quickens the dream, or the illusion, of 'leading without power' (DuPree 1997).

FORCE

Let us begin where Shakespeare does in *Coriolanus*, with power as physical strength and violence. Force, absolute and stunning, is a kind of primal truth of

power, from the slap in the face to American 'shock and awe' in Iraq. Michel
Foucault calls violence 'the primitive form' of power, 'its permanent secret, and
last resort, that which in the final analysis appears as its real nature when it is
forced to throw aside its mask and to show itself as it really is' (Foucault 2000b
[1982], 340). The God of the Old Testament bludgeons Job into silence with
the crudest of arguments: 'Hast thou an arm like God? or canst thou thunder
with a voice like him?' (Job 40:9).[3] Moses, who learned something about leadership from God, responds to the crisis of the golden calf – when the Israelites
stray from civil order and proper worship of the true God – not by appealing to
the people's better judgment or the newly carved holy commandments (or even
a Clintonian 'I feel your pain'), but by smashing the stone tablets, grinding up
the golden idol, forcing the people to drink the gold dust in water, and com-
manding the deaths of three thousand Israelites (Exodus 32:19–28). *Gilgamesh*,
an even older Near Eastern text, begins with the citizens of Uruk lamenting their
king's unslakeable power, depicted as ravening lust:

> There was no withstanding the aura or power of the Wild
> Ox Gilgamesh. Neither the father's son
> nor the wife of the noble; neither the mother's daughter
> nor the warrior's bride was safe. [4] (*Gilgamesh* 4)

Such 'masculine stories of violence and bloodshed' – the kind that Okwonko,
the brutal village strong man in Chinua Achebe's *Things Fall Apart* (1994), likes
to tell his reluctant son – represent an ancient tradition in thinking about
power.

Is violence perhaps a 'typically' male mode of power? Crime statistics, to
put it bluntly, support such a view. Men commit 80 to 90 percent of crimes in
Europe and North America, according to the United Nations (2003). In the USA
97 percent of inmates in federal prisons for violent crimes (murder, negligent
manslaughter, kidnapping, rape, sexual assault, robbery, and assault) are men
(US Dept. of Justice [DOJ] 1997, Table 4.4). American men are ten times more
likely than women to commit murder, and according to a 1994 DOJ study almost
99 percent of rapists are men. Three decades ago Susan Brownmiller (1975)
argued that rape was a crime of power rather than lust. Certainly the prevalence
of same-sex rape among male inmates in American prisons, and its role in mark-
ing status among inmates (Human Rights Watch 2001), supports the logic of
Brownmiller's argument about power and male identity. (That American criminal justice officials and ordinary citizens tolerate a culture of rape and sexual
slavery in penal institutions suggests a common American view of sexual aggression as part of a kind of useful 'natural' order among men.) East and West,
yesterday and today, rape has long been a 'normal' part of the actions of male
warrior groups. In the Democratic Republic of Congo, for instance, rape and
sexual violence have been routine tactics during the ongoing civil war:

During five years of armed conflict in the Democratic Republic of Congo (DRC, or Congo), tens of thousands of women and girls were raped or otherwise subjected to sexual violence. Victims whose cases HRW [Human Rights Watch] documented were as young as three years old.... . There were several patterns of sexual abuse against civilians. Soldiers and rebel fighters engaged in acts of sexual violence in the context of military confrontations, to scare the civilian population into submission, punish them for allegedly supporting enemy forces or to provide gratification for the fighters, sometimes after a defeat. In Ituri where armed groups of different ethnicity have fought each other for years, combatants often used sexual violence to target persons of ethnic groups seen as the enemy. (Human Rights Watch 2005, 7–8)

Some evolutionary biologists and psychologists seek to explain the 'maleness' of violence as a mode of power by exploring our evolutionary history and the intriguing parallels between human beings and our closest relatives, chimpanzees. The evidence is striking. The most notorious episode from the primatologist Frans de Waal's years-long study of the chimpanzee colony in the Arnhem Burgers Zoo, for example, was the bloody, almost Senecan revenge triangle among the three dominant males, Luit, Yeroen, and Nikkie. One night the alpha male, Luit, was attacked by the other two. His toes and testicles were bitten off and he died from loss of blood (de Waal 1989, 65–68). Such extraordinary violence was rare, to be sure, among the chimps – but physicality, violence, and force were part of the ordinary power 'toolkit' among chimpanzee troops, along with coalition-building, alliances, and betrayals.

As Francis Fukuyama puts it in a summary of research by de Waal and others, 'Only chimps and humans seem to have a proclivity for routinely murdering peers' (Fukuyama 1998, 25). Compared with other species, Fukuyama notes, human and chimpanzee males are unique: 'of the 4,000 mammal and 10 million or more other species, only chimps and humans live in male-bonded, patrilineal communities in which groups of males routinely engage in aggressive, often murderous raiding of their own species' (1998, 25, summarizing Wrangham and Peterson 1996). Some evolutionary biologists conclude from such studies that human males are virtually 'demonic,' to use Wrangham and Peterson's (1996) provocative term. Scholars inclined to this view conclude that evolution has hard-wired men to assert power by committing acts of violence and sexual aggression. Male bonding, it is suggested, centers around such behaviors – thus scholars like Wrangham and Peterson see a clear line from the behaviors of chimpanzee troops and human ancestors to modern male warrior groups, and even to many other manifestations of power by men. But it is important to note that not all evolutionary scholars hold such a view, nor is it unambiguously supported by such data as we have. Women in the armed forces, for instance, played significant roles in the sexual degradation and torture of prisoners at America's prison at Abu Ghraib in Iraq. 'The gendering of war,' concludes one scholar skeptical of the gender explanation for violence, 'results from the combination of culturally constructed gender roles with real

but modest biological differences. Neither alone would solve the puzzle'
(Goldstein 2001, 6).

Whatever we may decide about evolutionary psychology, hard-wired behaviors, and 'demonic males,' we see that when men talk and think about power, the trope of male sexual aggression is likely to arise. Consider what is probably the most famous passage in the Renaissance thinker Niccolò Machiavelli's *Prince*:

> It is better to be impetuous than cautious, because fortune is a woman; and it is necessary, if one wants to hold her down, to beat her and strike her down. And one sees that she lets herself be won more by the impetuous than by those who proceed coldly. And so always, like a woman, she is the friend of the young, because they are less cautious, more ferocious, and command her with more audacity. (Machiavelli 1985, 101)

Machiavelli, as the scholar Harvey Mansfield notes, 'makes the politics of the new prince appear in the image of rape ... ' (Machiavelli 1985, xxiii–iv).

In the Western intellectual tradition, Machiavelli (1469–1527) was the first modern thinker to articulate a worldview based on force and violence. The troubled landscape of 15th- and 16th-century Italy – a patchwork of weak and fractious states relying on timid mercenaries, shaky alliances, and ostentatious pageants, all the while threatened by strong foreign powers like France and the fearsome Muslim 'Turk' – taught Machiavelli a simple lesson: to live, one must be strong. 'Prophets of force,' the historian Felix Gilbert called Machiavelli, Francesco Guicciardini, and the young men of Florence at the beginning of the 16th century, for they no longer believed in the old descriptions or justifications of political power (Gilbert 1984, 129). Guicciardini, Machiavelli's closest friend and 'the first of the Machiavellians' (Ridolfi 1968, 136), distilled this disillusionment into one of his *Ricordi*: 'Considering its origin carefully, all political power is rooted in violence' (Guicciardini 1965, 119). Machiavelli made the study of violence his life's work. He believed that men are predisposed to violence (Machiavelli 1996, 55). Harnessing this power must be the leader's chief task: 'a prince should have no other object, nor any other thought, nor take anything else as his art but the art of war and its orders and discipline; for that is the only art which is of concern to one who commands' (Machiavelli 1985, 58). We live, Machiavelli insisted, in an anarchic world. Human beings must constantly find, make or take the means to live and procreate. Then they must fight to defend what they have gained and constructed. History shows that most settled orders soon fall, because there are always threats on the horizon or dissension within the walls. It is much easier to destroy than to build something that lasts: 'For one can say this generally of men: that they are ungrateful, fickle, pretenders and dissemblers, evaders of danger, eager for gain.' Cooperation is short-lived and usually shallow: 'While you do them good, they are yours,' but when you need them, 'they revolt' (Machiavelli 1985, 66). Force and selfishness tear apart the thin tissue of cooperation in anarchy. For Machiavelli, force is both the great destroyer, and – if properly harnessed – the great hope.

How does Machiavelli propose to harness force? Three points are relevant for our purposes. First, he noted that raw physical strength was not enough. A leader should emulate not only the lion but also the fox, 'because the lion does not defend itself from snares and the fox does not defend itself from wolves. So one needs to be a fox to recognize snares and a lion to frighten the wolves. Those who stay simply with the lion do not understand this' (1985, 69). Second, the foxlike leader must carefully consider the nature of his relationship with his followers. It is vital to avoid hatred, because feelings of hatred will provoke passionate resistance among followers and make leadership impossible. Machiavelli's famous advice on fear and love – 'it is much safer to be feared than loved' (1985, 66) – should be understood in this context. The best leaders use both fear *and* love (religions that combine love of the deity with fear of damnation well understand this linkage); but that is a difficult balance, and if one must choose, choose fear, for it goes deeper. James Hillman, in a recent meditation on the nature of power, makes a similar point: 'Of all the faces of power, fearsomeness seems to serve as a profound stabilizing principle... . Shared fear unifies people' (Hillman 1995, 185–6). When we think of fearsomeness and leadership, we are likely to imagine a leader making himself fearful, but that is only one possible tactic. Skillful leaders often deflect the fear outwards, using fear of an external threat to drive action and win support. Hillman provides a nice example:

> A university administrator explained carefully to me that by predicting financial disasters and scandalous embarrassments he could move his lethargic supervisory boards and academic committees to make decisions. 'I had to make them afraid; it's definitely the best method for overcoming institutional inertia.' (Hillman 1995, 185)

If the leader accurately perceives the external threat, this exercise of power can be considered a kind of virtuous Machiavellianism.

The third point about how Machiavelli proposes to harness power is perhaps the most interesting. For all his attention to the nature of individual power in *The Prince*, Machiavelli preferred republics. Patriotism – shared love for one's country – was for him the surest base on which to build, and the best way to discipline or harness the power of strong individuals.[5] Machiavelli is justifiably seen by scholars as a radical in political thought, the first modern thinker to dare to suggest that people had the power and capacity to govern themselves. (Jean-Jacques Rousseau, for one, held this view, observing in his *Social Contract* that Machiavelli 'professed to teach kings; but it was the people he really taught. His *Prince* is the book of Republicans' [Rousseau 1973, 123].) If a community could solve the problem of trust – a big 'if' – then Machiavelli preferred the power of the many over the power of one. But how to do that was left to an English successor, Thomas Hobbes, to explore.

Hobbes (1588–1679), the first great thinker in the English liberal tradition, recast Machiavelli's poetic insights in the more scientific and mechanical language of the 17th century ('For what is the heart, but a spring; and the nerves, but so many strings; and the joints, but so many wheels, giving motion to the whole body, such as was intended by the Artificer?' (Hobbes 1960, 5). Hobbes applied his self-consciously scientific approach (he was in a sense the first 'social scientist') to the study of human society. His unit of analysis was the individual, and the individual's power. He provides a surprisingly nuanced definition of power, upon which three centuries of scholarship have done little to improve: 'The power of a man, to take it universally, is his present means, to obtain some future apparent good; and is either original or instrumental' (Hobbes 1960, 56). By 'original' power, Hobbes means power that inheres in the self, like strength, intelligence, daring, or eloquence. By 'instrumental' power he means power that inheres in social interactions. Instrumental power – the power to draw on other resources or people – broadens our understanding of power:

> Reputation of power is power ... So is reputation of love of a man's country, called popularity... . what quality soever maketh a man beloved or feared of many, or the reputation of such quality, is power... . Good success is power; because it maketh reputation of wisdom or good fortune, which makes men either fear him or rely on him. Affability of men already in power is increase of power; because it gaineth love. Reputation of prudence in the conduct of peace or war is power... . (56)

Life, Hobbes maintains, is marked by 'a perpetual and restless desire of power after power, that ceaseth only in death' (64). Why? Because life is insecure: an individual who has accumulated power or wealth or a comfortable life cannot defend these 'without the acquisition of more power' (64). The drive for power, thus, is rooted in the impersonal logic of competition in an anarchic setting. This is what Hobbes means by 'the state of war' he sees as man's natural condition: 'it is manifest that during the time men live without a common power to keep them all in awe, they are in that condition which is called war; and such a war as is of every man against every man' (82). Life in such a world, Hobbes says in his most famous phrase, is 'solitary, poor, nasty, brutish, and short' (82). The only solution to such a world, Hobbes concludes, is to devise a common power – Leviathan, the state, with monopoly control on the use of force. But Hobbes could imagine no logical check on the power of the state that would not plunge society back into a state of nature, so his intellectual edifice, built on a foundation of radical individualism, ends up producing the first modern argument for absolutist or totalitarian political power.

'Political power,' Mao Zedong famously proclaimed, 'grows out of the barrel of a gun' (Mao 1954–56, 2:272). But it doesn't stop growing there. By the end of their analyses, both Machiavelli and Hobbes develop rich and complex conceptions of power. Even if power is rooted in force and violence, mastery of violence is not enough to build durable human societies. Frans de Waal, the primatologist, makes the same point about chimpanzee politics: 'Physical strength is only one factor and almost certainly not the critical one in determining dominance relationships' (de Waal 1998, 87). The ability to form coalitions and alliances is even more a part of the daily experience of chimpanzee society, and the job requirement for male and female alpha chimps. Machiavelli felt almost instinctively the power of relationships, but could not figure out how to achieve them in the modern world; for him the solution lay in the distant past, in the inspiring example of ancient, republican, pre-Christian Rome – and in one or two remarkable passages about the lively energy of modern free societies (e.g., *Discourses on Livy*, II.2). For his part Hobbes succeeded in laying out a complete if barren vision of life under a totalizing social contract in which the legitimized power of the state – a wholly realized Weberian 'monopoly of violence' – stands as the sole remaining, but panoptic, threat to individual freedom.

SOFT POWER

But let us not be too quick to presume that force, even a wholesale monopoly on violence, is an accurate gauge of power. Such kinds of power can be virtually futile in certain contexts – as George Orwell, a great student of power, expressed in his beautiful essay, 'Shooting an Elephant.' Orwell spent five miserable years in Burma as a young colonial police officer. As the representative of the empire, he had a kind of supreme power in the village of Moulmein – but as an outsider, a white man, he was utterly alone, hated, and, in a sense, powerless. One day, he writes, he gets report of a rogue elephant in the town. Feeling that he must deal with the situation, he picks up a rifle and marches off. A crowd gathers and follows him with amusement, excitement, and hostility. 'And it was at this moment, as I stood there with the rifle in my hands,' Orwell writes,

> that I first grasped the hollowness, the futility, of the white man's dominion in the East. Here was I, the white man with his gun, standing in front of the unarmed native crowd – seemingly the leading actor of the piece; but in reality I was only an absurd puppet pushed to and fro by the will of those yellow faces behind. I perceived in this moment that when the white man turns tyrant it is his own freedom that he destroys. He becomes a sort of hollow, posing dummy, the conventionalized figure of a sahib. For it is the condition of his rule that he shall spend his life trying to impress the 'natives,' and so in every crisis he has got to do what the 'natives' expect of him. He wears a mask, and his face grows to fit it. (Orwell 1956, 6–7)

What at first glance seems an image of power – a police officer with a gun, at the head of a crowd – is inverted into an image of weakness, or the anxiety of power. We cannot conclude that Mao was wrong, but there are other kinds of power than the power of the gun – and guns can only do so much.

Consider another Asian scene: *A hot, steamy day in Burma's Irawaddy River delta, six decades after Orwell served there. Half a dozen government soldiers block the road from the river into town. A woman walks toward the soldiers, with a small group around her. The soldiers train their rifles on the group. A woman in the group motions her companions aside and walks alone toward the line of armed men. A captain shouts an order. Suddenly a major runs up, shouting and waving his arms. The soldiers lower their guns. The woman, followed by the group, walk past the soldiers and into the town.* Who had power here? Who is the woman? Why didn't the soldiers shoot? The date was April 5, 1989, and the place was the town of Danubyu.[6] The woman was Aung San Suu Kyi, recently returned to her native Burma from private life and studies in England, now campaigning for democratic reforms in post-colonial Burma. With Aung San Suu Kyi, we encounter a very different kind of power; the power of charisma.

Suu Kyi is the daughter of a seminal leader in Burmese history, Aung San, who built and led Burma's army during the Second World War and negotiated independence from the British. He was assassinated in 1947, when his daughter was two years old. Since independence in 1948 the army has dominated Burmese politics – behind the scenes until 1962 and openly since then. In 1988 popular desire for freedom sparked into mass demonstrations, to which the army responded by declaring a state of emergency, establishing the State Law and Order Restoration Council (SLORC), and killing thousands of protesters. It was to this Burma that Suu Kyi returned from England, where she had spent years studying and starting a family. She helped organize the National League for Democracy (NLD) and at once became a prominent symbol of Burmese democracy. She began speaking across Burma on behalf of the NLD and the cause of freedom. But she has spent most of the years since her return to Burma in 1988 under house arrest, separated from her husband and two sons, and while under house arrest in 1991 won the Nobel Peace Prize. The men with guns who rule Burma dare not kill Suu Kyi, nor free her.

Charisma, according to Max Weber, the great German sociologist, is 'a certain quality of an individual personality by virtue of which he is considered extraordinary and treated as endowed with supernatural, superhuman, or at least specifically exceptional powers or qualities' (Weber 1978, 1:241). These qualities, often interpreted as a kind of magic or divinity, manifest in extraordinary strength and courage or in a prophetic or inspired message; the instruments of charisma, Weber says in a strikingly Machiavellian phrase, are 'revelation and the sword' (Weber 1946, 297; cf. *The Prince*, ch. 6).

But broadly speaking, charisma cannot merely be asserted by a leader. It arises, Weber says, 'from collective excitement produced by extraordinary events and from surrender to heroism of any kind' (Weber 1978, 2:1121). Thus charisma is bestowed on a leader by followers – who may withdraw their recognition at a moment's notice. The complex interplay between charismatic leaders and their uncertain followers is a major theme in history and literature from Moses and the 'stiff-necked' Israelites (Exodus 34) to the present day. Charisma as a source of power, Weber notes, 'is naturally unstable' (Weber 1978, 2:1114). It arises 'in moments of distress' (2:1111), when familiar or habitual solutions fail to address new crises, and it is associated with discontinuity and radical change. As the story of Suu Kyi illustrates, charisma is also associated with self-sacrifice and risk on the leader's part: 'Charismatic leaders make public demonstrations of their dedication to the cause, and in doing this, they communicate clearly that they are willing to engage in significant personal sacrifice and danger' (De Cremen 2003, 118). The essence of charisma is an emotional connection between leader and follower; its power goes deeper than physical force: 'Charismatic belief revolutionizes men "from within"' (Weber 1978, 2:1116).

But as scholars like Charles Lindholm (1990) have made clear, charisma has a dark side. There is nothing inherently genuine or moral about cultivating a strong emotional linkage to followers. Skillful leaders can exploit this emotional power for their own purposes. In Chinua Achebe's novel of post-colonial Nigeria, *A Man of the People*, the young and wary Odili finds himself overpowered by the practiced charisma of the canny politician, Kanga:

> Our hands met. I looked him straight in the face. The smile slowly creased up into lines of thought.... 'You are Odili.' 'Yes, sir.' Before the words were out of my mouth he had thrown his arms round me smothering me in his voluminous damask.... 'Odili, the great,' said the Minister boyishly, and still out of breath.... I became a hero in the eyes of the crowd. I was dazed. Everything around me became suddenly unreal; the voices receded to a vague border zone. I knew I ought to be angry with myself but I wasn't. (Achebe 1989, 8–9)

Charisma is a kind of authority, of power that is recognized as legitimate, that is accepted and willingly obeyed: Weber defines authority as 'power to command and duty to obey' (Weber 1978, 2:943). But authority can take form even when there is no explicit duty to obey, when obedience is a matter of habit. In his thoughtful study of power, Adolf Berle tells the story of a young man during the 1965 blackout in New York City who, like many other volunteers, stepped into the street and began directing traffic: 'He had no authority. Everyone nevertheless obeyed him as faithfully as if he had been a uniformed policeman.... Self-appointed, the power was momentarily illegitimate. It was recognized, and thus became legitimate on the instant' (Berle 1969, 44–45).

Weber perceived in history three distinct bases for authority: charisma, tradition, and rationality. Each of these three modes implies a different kind of social and political arrangement – and thus a different kind of power. Charisma is a 'revolutionary' power, Weber says (1978, 2:1115), associated with individuals (heroes, prophets, entrepreneurs, visionaries) who establish new customs, ask new questions, propose new answers. (Today the term 'charisma' is often used more loosely but less usefully, to signify personal magnetism and the power of personality.)

By contrast with charisma, the authority of tradition represents the routinization or institutionalization of power. Traditional authority rests 'on an established belief in the sanctity of immemorial traditions and the legitimacy of those exercising authority under them' (Weber 1978, 1:215); it is 'domination that rests upon ... piety' (Weber 1946, 296). Since, as Weber notes, most traditional forms of authority are patriarchal, one may see tradition as a common means by which men have transformed force into authority. (An orthodox view, of course, would see patriarchal rules as expressions of divine will. Thus a female professor of Islamic studies in Egypt denounces a woman's leading of Friday prayers in an Islamic service in New York City in March 2005: 'It is categorically forbidden for women to lead prayers if they include men worshippers.... . [T]he woman's body, even if veiled, stirs desire' [Associated Press 2005].)

In the modern world, patriarchal and other kinds of traditional authority have largely given way to Weber's third kind of authority; rational-legal or bureaucratic authority. Weber defines bureaucracy – literally, 'rule by offices' – as 'a permanent structure with a system of rational rules' (1946, 245). Bureaucracy is how the modern world legitimizes power into its social institutions. Schools, prisons, and workplaces operate by habits of power that we scarcely think about – their legitimacy makes them almost invisible. College courses, workdays, and prison sentences begin and end at set times, to the minute. In a school day, teachers and students move according to a schedule. Students follow a sequence of courses from their freshman to senior years, registering for courses by following complex scheduling rules. Faculty and departments follow guidelines in terms of what courses to offer, how many students to permit in a given course, what rooms to select. New courses may be tried out, but if they are to become habitual, they must run the gauntlet of curricular oversight – committees, divisions, deans, and faculty approval. The college itself must periodically be inspected and accredited by an expert external review team – all of this activity guided by and producing vast reams of records and documents. The power embedded in the system finds expression in a thicket of rules, policies, and procedures. Kafka's *The Trial* follows a nightmarish bureaucratic procedure to its absurd yet logical result. Václav Havel's play *The Memorandum* concerns a bureaucratic plan to achieve more precise communication by devising an artificial language. A memorandum written in the language causes confusion and anxiety – but since it seems to have been duly issued by the bureaucracy, no one who encounters the memo dares to point out the obvious, that no one can read it.

After Weber's three kinds of authority, the most influential recent effort to distinguish kinds of power comes from the psychologists John French and Bertram Raven. In a classic 1959 paper, French and Raven defined power as the ability of an 'agent' to alter the beliefs, attitudes, or behaviors of one or more 'targets,' and distinguished between five 'bases of power' to achieve this: rewards, coercion, legitimacy, expertise, and reference. Reward and coercive power refer to the agent's ability to bestow positive or negative outcomes on a target. Legitimate power depends on the target's belief that the agent has the authority to lead, and that the target has the duty to obey. Expert power stems from the agent's possession of special knowledge, or the target's belief about the agent's expertise. Finally, referent power (for which the term 'charisma' is often used in the literature) comes from the target's identifying with the agent in some dimension. (A sixth base of power, information power, was later added to the model [Raven 1965].)

As influential and useful as French and Raven's model has been, it does not provide an especially clear analytic framework. Despite the label of 'bases,' the five (or six) bases are not really distinct foundations or sources of power. Rewards and coercion are resources or outcomes controlled by the agent, while legitimacy and referent power are attributes of the agent as well as perceptions by the target. Referent power has elements of reward and coercion, as Raven has acknowledged: 'the personal approval of someone we respect can also be a very powerful reward, and a threat of rejection or disapproval from someone we value highly can serve as a source of coercive power' (Raven 2004, 1242). And information power and expert power trade in the same currency, access to valued information or experience (itself a kind of reward). French and Raven's third base of power, legitimacy, is a complex concept not really comparable to influence tactics like reward or coercion. As Weber suggested, there can exist different kinds of authority that make different claims about the legitimacy of leaders' power. In addition, a reward or a punishment, or any of the other bases of power, may be perceived as legitimate or illegitimate; the moral dimension of legitimacy runs across all assertions of power by leaders or agents. Any particular influence attempt, in short, is likely to represent the workings of several bases of power at once. A good deal of effort has gone into trying to bring more conceptual clarity to the French and Raven scheme, for instance by reducing it to clusters of 'personal' and 'position' power, or distinguishing between 'interpersonal' power (all the French and Raven bases) and structural power (a scheme that oddly ignores the structural–institutional dimension of legitimacy) – but these efforts (see for instance Yukl 2002 or Neider and Schriesheim 2004) have not yet succeeded in producing a clear and compelling reworking of the scheme.

A much simpler analysis of power comes from the political scientist (and Dean of the Kennedy School of Government) Joseph S. Nye, Jr., who distinguishes between 'hard' and 'soft' power. Beginning with a standard definition of power – 'the ability to influence the behavior of others to get the outcomes one wants,' Nye notes there are three main ways to achieve this: 'You can coerce them with threats; you can induce them with payments; or you can attract and co-opt them to want what you want' (Nye 2004, 2). The first two ways, threats and payments, are the usual tools of what Nye calls 'command power.' The third, attraction, is the tool of co-optive or 'soft power.' Its essence is the ability to make others 'want what you want.' Critical to this is that one's goals and values be desirable and legitimate by others. Thus the concept of soft power yokes together power-wielders and those they hope to act upon, so that the success of soft power depends on willing partners.

So what constitutes 'soft power'? There are two main approaches to 'making others want what you want.' First, one can articulate and emphasize one's values and goals, if these resonate with what others value. Nye sees liberal democracies like the USA as possessing vast amounts of soft power thanks to the wide appeal of prosperity and democracy. Second, one can seek to educate or change others to make one's own goals and values more attractive to them, as the USA did, with remarkable effectiveness, in Japan after the Second World War. A striking example of soft power comes from Xenophon's *Cyropedia*, one of the most remarkable ancient texts on leadership. Xenophon tells how, through assiduous image management, the Persian emperor Cyrus was able to transform hard power into soft power: 'And who, besides Cyrus, ever gained an empire by conquest and even to his death was called "father" by the people he had subdued? For that name obviously belongs to a benefactor rather than to a despoiler' (Xenophon, *Cyropaedia*, VIII.ii.9). Co-optation has an obvious dark side, and one of the worries about soft power is that it may depend on hidden reserves of hard power.

The idea of soft power is a very old one. It is the central leadership idea of Taoism, for instance. In the *Tao Te Ching*, Lao Tzu dismisses the power of weapons and armies, and says that the best rulers exert power indirectly and lightly, like water: 'Water is good; it benefits all things and does not compete with them' (Lao Tzu 2003, 177). Machiavelli himself, the father of modern hard-power doctrines, preferred, as noted earlier, the soft power of republics to the hard power of princes (and in chapter 20 of *The Prince* he cautions princes that fortresses are less useful than the good will of their subjects). In the 20th century, Mary Parker Follett dismissed 'power-over' – akin to Nye's 'command power' – as less useful to effective leadership than 'power-with,' the power of connections and mutuality (Follett 1951, 186). Robert Greenleaf buttresses his case for servant-leadership by noting the widespread existence of 'countervailing power' (Greenleaf 1977, 85) that arises against direct assertions of power.

The only real way to achieve lasting purposes, Greenleaf said, was for leaders to win the trust of their followers and gain their support. Thus for Greenleaf the ultimate leader is really a servant, like Leo in Herman Hesse's *Journey to the East*, who tends to followers' spiritual development and gives them what they truly need.

POWER AND KNOWLEDGE

But who decides what the people need, how they 'need' power to be used? Even if we answer 'the people themselves,' who has taught them? What lessons have they learned? It was necessary, the Bible says, for the generation of Israelites who accompanied Moses into the wilderness to perish during the journey so that a new generation could grow up, more obedient to Moses' leadership and new laws (Numbers 29–35). Plato makes a parallel statement in the *Republic* (540e–541b), when he has Socrates say that to establish an ideal commonwealth one would have to send out of the city all those over ten years of age, as only the young are capable of being radically re-educated. These passages suggest a relativistic nature of power: power is always deployed in particular cultural contexts, and different cultures may possess different understandings, and different kinds, of power.

A modern theorist of culture like Edgar Schein would wonder what took us so long to get to this basic point. Schein has devoted a career in leadership and management studies to the role of culture in shaping organizations and how power operates within them. To take one example, Schein spent decades studying the American computer firm DEC (Schein 2003, 2004). When Schein began attending senior staff meetings at DEC in the 1960s, he was astonished at how aggressive the executives were with one another. Schein initially tried to reduce the level of conflict between senior managers, 'trying to get the group to be "nicer" to each other' (Schein 2004, 47). But over time Schein came to understand that power worked in a particular way in DEC's culture – that managers and workers were expected to fight hard for their beliefs, that technological innovation required constant challenges to every new (and old) idea. What Schein had at first seen as pathological in-fighting was in fact the way power flowed in one cultural setting.

In similar fashion, the anthropologist Clifford Geertz employed what he called 'thick description' to study the cultural context of power. In *Negara*, his classic study of a 19th-century Balinese state, Geertz explores the workings of what he calls a 'theatre state,' which channeled its energies and powers not toward conquest or efficient rule, but toward a dramatization of its own virtues and status. In this culture, Geertz concludes, 'power served pomp, not pomp power' (Geertz 1980, 13). Geertz's approach has influenced how a generation of scholars frame the study of power. In literary studies, for instance, New Historicist scholars insist that the cultural and historical context is crucial to reading literary representations of power. The leading New Historicist, Stephen Greenblatt, ties Shakespeare's depiction of Hal/Henry V to the broader nature of power in Elizabethan England:

> To understand Shakespeare's conception of Hal, from rakehell to monarch, we need in effect a poetics of Elizabethan power, and this in turn will prove inseparable, in crucial respects, from a poetics of the theater. Testing, recording, and explaining are elements in this poetics, which is inseparably bound up with the figure of Queen Elizabeth, a ruler without a standing army, without a highly developed bureaucracy, without an extensive police force, a ruler whose power is constituted in theatrical celebrations of royal glory and theatrical violence visited upon enemies of that glory … . Elizabethan power … depends on its privileged visibility. (Greenblatt 1988, 64)

Culture-oriented theorists like Schein, Geertz and Greenblatt have had a great impact on how modern scholars think about power. But perhaps the most influential of such thinkers has been the French intellectual historian Michel Foucault. Power, Foucault argued, is not simply control of material resources or bodies or actions, but something that shapes who we are and how we think:

> [I]n thinking about the mechanisms of power, I am thinking … of its capillary form of existence, the point where power reaches into the very grain of individuals, touches their bodies and inserts itself into their actions and attitudes, their discourses, learning processes and everyday lives. (Foucault 1980, 39)

Here Foucault echoes Machiavelli's ideas about the inescapability of power relations in human identity. But whereas Machiavelli saw the workings of power – its penetration into daily life and human hearts – as a simple and immutable fact of human nature, Foucault, like most modern scholars of culture, argues that different historical eras produce, and are produced by, different kinds of power. There is a whiff of Weber in Foucault's characterization of power in the ancient world as 'magical and religious' (Foucault 2000a, 31) and of modern power as administrative and rationalistic. But while Weber saw modern rationalistic power as a kind of apotheosis or culmination of human development, Foucault sees it as one more historical turn: 'I don't think I am a Weberian, since my basic preoccupation isn't rationality considered as an anthropological invariant' (Foucault 2000a, 229). Rationality – or 'governmentality,' the broader label Foucault preferred, is simply the most recent historical turn that power has taken. Governmentality – a set of rationalizing procedures, statistical tools, and administrative disciplines assembled in 18th-century Europe – has shaped the modern world, which is to say us and how we see, experience, think about, and judge power. This modern kind of power, founded on surveillance, examination, and science, seems at first glance to be less coercive than the older power of the sword. Yet it is more intrusive, more totalizing, than past efforts to use power to control individuals and shape society:

> If one were to do a history of the social control of the body, one could show that, up through the eighteenth century, the individual body was essentially the inscription surface for tortures and punishments; the body was made to be tortured and punished. Already in the control authorities that appeared from the nineteenth century onward, the body acquired a completely different signification; it was no longer something to be tortured but something to be molded, reformed, corrected, something that must acquire aptitudes, receive a number of qualities, become qualified as a body capable of working. (Foucault 2000a, 82)

In *Discipline and Punish* Foucault called this new kind of power 'panoptic,' after Jeremy Bentham's Orwellian vision of the panopticon, the single central prison tower from which guards could monitor many inmates. Ceaseless surveillance is the foundation of modern power.[7]

Thus, while Robert Greenleaf drew on Hesse's novel *Journey to the East* as a spark for his ideas about servant-leadership, Foucault would cast a darker eye on the text. Hesse's mysterious Leo understands better than the protagonist, H.H., what his stage of spiritual development is, what he 'really' needs. Leo never explains or teaches H.H. in a conventional sense; instead the story traces the protagonist's uncertain, painful journey toward self-understanding – with a critical step being when Leo drops his servant's disguise, dons his impressive robes, and takes up the active role of judge of H.H.'s life and deeds. The very power that Greenleaf celebrates – Leo's ability to peer into H.H.'s soul – Foucault would be more cautious about:

> Christianity is the only religion that has organized itself as a Church. As such, it postulates in principle that certain individuals can, by their religious quality, serve others not as princes, magistrates, prophets, fortune-tellers, benefactors, educationalists, and so on, but as pastors. However, this very word designates a special form of power.
>
> 1. It is a form of power whose ultimate aim is to assure individual salvation in the next world.
> 2. Pastoral power is not merely a form of power that commands; it must also be prepared to sacrifice itself for the life and salvation of the flock. Therefore, it is different from royal power, which demands a sacrifice from its subjects to save the throne.
> 3. It is a form of power that looks after not just the whole community but each individual in particular, during his entire life.
> 4. Finally, this form of power cannot be exercised without knowing the inside of people's minds, without exploring their souls, without making them reveal their innermost secrets. It implies a knowledge of the conscience and an ability to direct it. (Foucault 2000b, 333)

Between Hesse's Leo and Dostoevsky's Grand Inquisitor, Foucault might point out, there may be as many similarities as differences.

But in a sense, Foucault says, we are all little Grand Inquisitors, implicated in the exercise of power even as we seek to study and understand it. Our very attempts to think about power, Foucault says, are freighted, or infected, with power. He dismisses as 'a great Western myth' the belief, dating back to Plato, that power and knowledge can be separated (2000b, 32). In this Foucault may be termed a postmodernist – but he is better understood as a faithful student of Nietzsche, as he himself readily acknowledged.[8] Such a stance, it has often been said, leaves Foucault no ground on which to make moral statements about power (though he frequently did, generally criticizing existing institutions of power and praising, more or less, 'resistance'). Certainly, when Foucault says that 'power is everywhere; not because it embraces everything, but because it comes from everywhere' (Foucault 1978–86, 1:93) or that 'in a certain way, one is always the ruler and the ruled.' (3:87), it does seem hard to find secure ground on which to build an ethics of power. One sympathetic scholar has tried to create space for an ethical dimension to Foucault's thought by emphasizing his interest in a 'dynamics of power' (Rouse 1994, 93), but even this gloss concedes that Foucault was ultimately more interested in questions or '*problematiques*' than in solutions (112). Like his teacher Nietzsche, Foucault succeeds in undermining our confidence in the modern world's chief forms of authority, of power-that-is-accepted – but fails to supply any more trustworthy basis for power. (Nietzsche at least imagined the outrageous figure of the Superman, whose will to power soared above the gray mediocrity of modern mass society.) Foucault, in his ability to ask piercing questions about power but his inability to develop a useful ethics of power, ends up, ironically, as yet another disciple of the 'great Western myth' about the separate domains of power and knowledge.

QUESTIONING POWER

We began with questions about power in Shakespeare's *Coriolanus*, and let us close by returning to that text. In 1682 Nahum Tate, a notorious 'improver' of Shakespeare and an unabashed propagandist for Charles II, reshaped Shakespeare's play to suit the political moment of Restoration England. The play's moral, Tate explained in a dedicatory epistle, was 'to Recommend Submission and Adherence to Establisht Lawful Power' (quoted in Ripley 1998, 55). Tate's dull version of the play, entitled *Ingratitude of a Commmon-wealth*, is useful for helping us better recognize Shakespeare's far more complex and thoughtful treatment of power. The lessons about power in *Coriolanus* are primarily negative. Shakespeare's haughty general never learns how to connect with other people, how to create and sustain any kind of socially productive power. The play's other grand figures – the people's tribunes, Coriolanus' aristocratic friends, the Volscian general Aufidius – are themselves power-hungry and not especially trustworthy or admirable. The commoners are a measure better – they actually labor, and do their best to think and act fairly. But they lack the rawest dimension of power, the ability to fight and defend their city. The closest the play has to a hero is Coriolanus' severe mother, Volumnia, who saves Rome by convincing her son to abandon the Volscian army – but this Roman mother saves Rome at the cost of her son's life.

In an essay on the meaning of military leadership, the equally formidable Burmese activist, Aung San Suu Kyi, confronts the ironies of her own life: the army that her father created to liberate Burma now keeps the country, and his daughter, imprisoned. Trying to teach her countrymen the meaning of real power, she quotes the 18th-century Burmese poet Let-We-Thondara:

> How superior
> The tactics of war
> How potent
> The weapons!
> Without gathering in
> The hearts of the people,
> Without relying on
> The strength of the people,
> The sword edge
> Will shatter,
> The spear
> Will bend. (Suu Kyi 1995, 189)

Our musings on power come back once again to seemingly simple things, to weapons and bodies. A Congolese woman's voice echoes: 'Who will protect me if I say who it was who raped me? The men with guns still rule here. The UN only protect a small part of town and they will not help me if these men come to my door' (Human Rights Watch 2005, 42). Shakespeare and the Burmese poet play on the same theme: the sword's edge, and the hearts of the people – two kinds of power, both essential, neither sufficient. Do we, one wonders, truly have the 'power in ourselves to do it'? – and what will we do? When the men with guns appear, will we recognize them?

NOTES

1. Quotations from Shakespeare are from *The Norton Shakespeare*, (ed.) 1997, Stephen Greenblatt. New York: W.W. Norton.
2. From an article in the *Washington Post*:

On the streets of Beirut, they call it the 'intifada for independence.' In the corridors of Washington, they prefer to call it the 'Cedar Revolution.' In a media age, such branding could be crucial. The name given to Lebanon's popular political movement is shorthand for its historical roots and its future direction. The label will help shape how the world understands Lebanon's small but telling part of the ongoing struggle for democracy throughout the Middle East. (Morley 2005)

3. Quotations from the Bible are from the King James Version.
4. *Gilgamesh* can be read as a lesson in how to domesticate the power of strong men. The gods fashion Enkidu, Gilgamesh's only physical equal, in response to the people's complaints. Gilgamesh and Enkidu wrestle and become friends; their friendship humanizes Gilgamesh. When Enkidu dies, Gilgamesh turns his lust for power into a lust for knowledge about death and immortality. When this project fails, he comes to realize that the most important use of his power is to build his city and to be remembered through its greatness.
5. One of the more influential recent studies of power in the field of management, McClelland and Burnham's 'Power Is the Great Motivator,' might be termed almost neo-Machiavellian in its willingness to embrace power – McClelland and Burnham conclude that the most effective managers have a high need for power – but also in its argument about how to yoke this strong individual drive: 'The manager's concern for power should be socialized – controlled so that the institution as a whole, not only the individual, benefits' (2003, 126).
6. In a bit of historical irony, it was at this town in 1824 that British forces used superior technology to win a key battle against a Burmese army 60,000 strong in the first Anglo–Burmese War. British shells killed the Burmese commander Bandula (his glittering gilt umbrella, which he refused to put away, made him an easy target). Two years later the British steamer *Diana*, the first steamship ever used in battle, defeated the Burmese navy's great teak war-boats (Thant 2001, 18).
7. News like this only makes Foucault's vision more persuasive:

> European Space Agency (ESA) officials commissioned a study to streamline driving in England and the Continent by allowing individual vehicles to pay road tolls via a direct satellite connection.
>
> The project builds on global positioning technology and is aimed at providing a unified approach to road tolling throughout Europe. In April, the European Union announced a proposal that would require all vehicles to pay tolls electronically with the use of a black box that would be tracked by satellites. That plan, ESA officials said, would track distance traveled, the class of road and the time of travel… .
>
> ESA officials envision a Europe-wide system that would provide automatic payment of road tolls for drivers travelling not only in their own country, but across borders as well. This means integrating existing satellite tolling systems in Germany and Switzerland and developing the intelligence required for a satellite to deduce distance-based tolls across multiple time zones… .
>
> ESA intends to incorporate the Europe-wide tolling system into Galileo, Europe's planned satellite navigation hoped to begin operation in 2008. Galileo would consist of 30 satellites arranged in three circular orbits to create a worldwide network. (Malik 2003)

8. See the first of Foucault's lectures given in Rio de Janeiro in 1973, collected in the essay 'Truth and Juridical Forms,' (Foucault 2000a, 1–16), as well as this passage from the same essay:

> With Plato there began a great Western myth: that there is an antinomy between knowledge and power. If there is knowledge, it must renounce power. Where knowledge and science are found in their pure truth, there can no longer be any political power.
>
> This great myth needs to be dispelled. It is this myth which Nietzsche began to demolish by showing, in the numerous texts already cited, that, behind all knowledge, behind all attainment of knowledge, what is involved is a struggle for power. Political power is not absent from knowledge, it is woven together with it. (Foucault 2000a, 32)

REFERENCES

Achebe, Chinua. 1989. *A Man of the People.* New York: Anchor.

Achebe, Chinua. 1994. *Things Fall Apart.* New York: Anchor.

Associated Press. 2005. 'New York Prayer Service Irks Mideast Muslims.' *New York Newsday.* March 19, 2005.

Bentley, Eric. 1954. *The Dramatic Event.* New York: Horizon.

Berle, Adolf A. 1969. *Power.* New York: Harcourt, Brace & World.

Brownmiller, Susan. 1975. *Against Our Will: Men, Women and Rape.* New York: Simon & Schuster.

De Cremen, David. 2003. 'A Relational Perspective on Leadership and Cooperation: Why it Matters to Care and Be Fair.' In Daan van Knippenberg and Michael A. Hogg, eds. *Leadership and Power: Identity Processes in Groups and Organizations.* London: Sage. 109–22.

DuPree, Max. 1997. *Leading Without Power: Finding Hope in Serving Community.* San Francisco: Jossey-Bass.

Follett, Mary Parker. 1951. *Creative Experience.* New York: Peter Smith.

Foucault, Michel. 1978–86. *The History of Sexuality*, 3 vols. Trans. Robert Hurley. New York: Pantheon Books.

Foucault, Michel. 1980. *Power/Knowledge: Selected Interviews and Other Writings, 1972–1977.* Ed. Colin Gordon. Trans. Colin Gordon, Leo Marshall, John Mepham, and Kate Soper. New York: Pantheon Books.

Foucault, Michel. 2000a. *Power.* Vol. 3 of *Essential Works of Foucault, 1954–1984.* Ed. James D. Faubion. Trans. Robert Hurley and others. New York: New Press.

Foucault, Michel. 2000b [1982]. 'The Subject and Power.' In Foucault, *Power*, vol. 3 of *Essential Works of Foucault.* Ed. James D. Faubion. New York: New Press. 326–48.

French, John R.P., Jr. and Bertram Raven. 1959. 'The Bases of Social Power.' In D. Cartwright, ed., *Studies in Social Power.* Ann Arbor: MI: Institute for Social Research. 150–67.

Fukuyama, Francis. 1998. 'Women and the Evolution of World Politics.' *Foreign Affairs*, 77:5 (September/October), 24–40.

Geertz, Clifford. 1980. *Negara: The Theatre State in Nineteenth-Century Bali.* Princeton, NJ: Princeton University Press.

Gilbert, Felix. 1984. *Machiavelli and Guicciardini: Politics and History in Sixteenth-Century Florence.* New York: W.W. Norton.

Gilgamesh: A New Rendering in English Verse. 1992. Trans. David Ferry. New York: Farrar, Straus & Giroux.

Goldstein, Joshua S. 2001. *War and Gender: How Gender Shapes the War System and Vice Versa.* Cambridge, England: Cambridge University Press.

Gordon, Colin. 2000. 'Introduction.' In Foucault, *Power.* Ed. James D. Faubion. New York: New Press. xi–xli.

Greenblatt, Stephen J. 1988. 'Invisible Bullets.' Ch. 2 of *Shakespearean Negotiations.* Berkeley: University of California Press. 21–65.

Greenleaf, Robert K. 1977. *Servant Leadership: A Journey into the Nature of Legitimate Power and Greatness.* New York and Mahwah, NJ: Paulist Press.

Guicciardini, Francesco. 1965. *Maxims and Reflections of a Renaissance Statesman (Ricordi).* Trans. Mario Domandi. New York: Harper & Row Torchbooks.

Havel, Václav. 1993. 'The Memorandum.' Trans. Vera Blackwell. In *The Garden Party and Other Plays.* New York: Grove Press.

Hesse, Herman. 1956. *Journey to the East.* New York: Picador.

Hillman, James. 1995. *Kinds of Power: A Guide to its Intelligent Uses.* New York: Currency Doubleday.

Hobbes, Thomas. 1960 [1651]. *Leviathan, or the Matter, Forme and Power of a Commonwealth Ecclesiasticall and Civil.* Ed. Michael Oakeshott. Oxford: Basil Blackwell.

Human Rights Watch. 2001. *No Escape: Male Rape in U.S. Prisons.* New York: Human Rights Watch.

Human Rights Watch. 2005. *Seeking Justice: The Prosecution of Sexual Violence in the Congo War.* New York: Human Rights Watch.

Kafka, Franz. 1992. *The Trial.* Trans. Willa and Edwin Muir. New York: Schocken.

Lao Tzu. 2003. Excerpt from the *Tao Te Ching.* In Joanne Ciulla, ed. *Leadership Ethics.* Belmont, CA: Wadsworth/Thomson. 174–85.

Lindholm, Charles. 1990. *Charisma.* London: Basil Blackwell.

McClelland, David C. and David H. Burnham. 2003 [1976]. 'Power Is the Great Motivator.' *Harvard Business Review*, 81:1 (January), 117–26.

Machiavelli, Niccolò. 1985. *The Prince.* Ed. and trans. Harvey C. Mansfield, Jr. Chicago: University of Chicago Press.

Machiavelli, Niccolò. 1996. *Discourses on Livy.* Trans. Harvey C. Mansfield and Nathan Tarcov. Chicago: University of Chicago Press.

Malik, Tariq. 2003. 'Your Future: Never Out of Touch.' Press release. Space.com: www.space.com/businesstechnology/technology/satcom_future_031126.html.

Mao Zedong. 1954–56. *Selected Works.* 4 vols. New York: International Publishers.

Maus, Katharine Eisaman. 1997. Introduction to *The Tragedy of Coriolanus.* In *The Norton Shakespeare*, gen. ed. Stephen Greenblatt. New York: W.W. Norton. 2785–92.

Morley, Jefferson. 2005. 'The Branding of Lebanon's "Revolution."' *Washington Post.* March 3.

Neider, Linda L. and Chester A. Schriesheim. 2004. 'Power: Overview.' In George R. Goethals, Georgia J. Sorenson, and James MacGregor Burns, eds, *Encyclopedia of Leadership.* 4 vols. Thousand Oaks, CA: Sage. 3:1248–51.

Nye, Joseph S., Jr. 1990. *Bound to Lead: The Changing Nature of American Power.* New York: Basic Books.

Nye, Joseph S., Jr. 2004. *Soft Power: The Means to Success in World Politics.* New York: Public Affairs.

Orwell, George. 1956. 'Shooting an Elephant.' In *The Orwell Reader*, introduction by Richard H. Rovere. New York: Harcourt Brace. 3–9.

Raven, Bertram. 1965. 'Social Influence and Power.' In I.D. Steiner and M. Fishbein, eds, *Current Studies in Social Psychology.* New York: Holt, Rinehart, Winston.

Raven, Bertram. 2004. 'Power, Six Bases of.' In George R. Goethals, Georgia J. Sorenson, and James MacGregor Burns, eds, *The Encyclopedia of Leadership.* 4 vols. Thousand Oaks, CA: Sage. 3:1241–8.

Ridolfi, Roberto. 1968. *The Life of Francesco Guicciardini.* Trans. Cecil Grayson. New York: Alfred A. Knopf.

Ripley, John. 1998. Coriolanus *on Stage in England and America, 1609–1994.* London: Associated University Presses.

Rouse, Joseph. 1994. 'Power/Knowledge.' In Gary Gutting, ed., *The Cambridge Companion to Foucault.* Cambridge, England: Cambridge University Press.

Rousseau, Jean-Jacques. 1973. *The Social Contract and Other Writings.* Ed. and trans. G.D.H. Cole, rev. and augmented by J.H. Brumfitt and John C. Hall. New York: Dutton.

Schein, Edgar H. 2003. *DEC Is Dead; Long Live DEC*. San Francisco: Berrett-Koehler.

Schein, Edgar H. 2004. *Organizational Culture and Leadership*. 3rd edn. San Francisco: Jossey-Bass.

Shakespeare, William. 1997. *The Norton Shakespeare*. Gen. ed. Stephen Greenblatt. New York: W.W. Norton.

Suu Kyi, Aung San. 1995. *Freedom from Fear and Other Writings*, rev. edn. London: Penguin.

Thant Myint-U. 2001. *The Making of Modern Burma*. Cambridge, England: Cambridge University Press.

United Nations. 2003. *Trends in Europe and North America: The Statistical Yearbook of the Economic Commission for Europe 2003*. Geneva: United Nations Economic Commission for Europe.

US Department of Justice. 1994. *Violence Against Women*. Washington, DC: Bureau of Justice Statistics.

US Department of Justice. 1997. *Correctional Populations in the United States, 1997*. Washington, DC: Bureau of Justice Statistics.

US Department of Justice. 2002. *Sourcebook of Criminal Justice Statistics, 2002*. Washington, DC: National Criminal Justice Reference Service.

de Waal, Frans. 1989. *Peacemaking among Primates*. Cambridge: Harvard University Press.

de Waal, Frans. 1998. *Chimpanzee Politics*, rev. edn. Baltimore: Johns Hopkins.

Wallechinksy, David. 1997. 'The Voice of Her People.' *Parade Magazine* (January 19).

Weber, Max. 1946. *From Max Weber: Essays in Sociology*. Ed. and trans. H.H. Gerth and C. Wright Mills. New York: Oxford University Press.

Weber, Max. 1978. *Economy and Society*. 2 vols. Eds. Guenther Roth and Claus Wittich. Berkeley: University of California Press.

Wrangham, Richard, and Dale Peterson. 1996. *Demonic Males: Apes and the Origins of Human Violence*. Boston: Houghton Mifflin.

Xenophon. 1914. *Cyropaedia*. Trans. Walter Miller. Loeb Classical Library. London: William Heinemann; New York: Macmillan.

Yukl, Gary. 2002. *Leadership in Organizations*, 5th edn. Upper Saddle River, NJ: Prentice Hall.

Yukl, Gary. 2004. 'Influence Tactics.' In George R. Goethals, Georgia J. Sorenson, and James MacGregor Burns, eds, *The Encyclopedia of Leadership*. 4 vols. Thousand Oaks, CA: Sage. 2: 711–14.

5. Leader–follower relations: group dynamics and the role of leadership

Crystal L. Hoyt, George R. Goethals and Ronald E. Riggio

'Man is by nature a social animal.' – Aristotle

Tom Wren's chapter detailing the deliberations of the general theory group quotes Burns as suggesting that one way of moving toward an integrated theory of leadership would be to examine the key 'elements' of leadership: power, motivation, leader–follower relations, context, and values (p. 17). Although the group has varied in its belief about the utility of concentrating on these elements, at our final joint meeting in May, 2004 we agreed that we needed to have chapters addressing power and leader–follower relations. Thus the previous chapter on power by Michael Harvey and the present chapter are included.

Of course the story of Professor Burns's interest in the dynamics of leader–follower relations, and the closely related topic of human motivation, goes back much further than the initiation of the general theory project. It can be traced to his earliest thinking about leadership more than 30 years ago and his insight that understanding psychology was essential to understanding leadership. In his 2003 book *Transforming Leadership: A New Pursuit of Happiness* Professor Burns describes the action stemming from this insight. He went to talk to a colleague in the Williams College psychology department who was interested in leadership – Al Goethals, one of the authors of this chapter (Burns, 2003, p. 9). After their conversation Burns delved into the psychology of motivation and other relevant topics. All three authors of this chapter fully agree that Burns's insight from the 1970s was and is still compelling. Appreciating the psychological aspects of leadership, particularly leader–follower relations, is essential to an integrated theory of leadership. In this chapter, then, the three of us, social psychologists all, attempt to spell out the basic theory and data from psychology that are most important in understanding leadership.

We begin with discussions of the impact of other people, particularly groups of other people, on the individual that go back to the very founding of social psychology at the end of the 19th century. Gustave Le Bon's disturbing and perceptive book, *The Crowd*, published in 1895, helped mark the founding of social psychology as a distinct discipline (Goethals, 2003). *The Crowd* served as the starting point for Sigmund Freud's 1921 *Group Psychology and the Analysis of the Ego*, one of the earliest systematic treatments of leadership. Freud, quoting at great length from Le Bon, emphasized the excited, violent, irrational, and mercurial side of crowds. For the most part, in group situations, Le Bon and Freud claimed, human beings regress to violent, instinctual behaviors. They act but do not think. Their analyses of group dynamics have been applied to lynch mobs, panics, and crowds at soccer matches and rock concerts but also to enduring organizations such as the Catholic Church and the army.

Despite their generally troubling account of group behavior, Freud also quotes Le Bon's assertion that 'under the influence of suggestion groups are also capable of high achievements in the shape of abnegation, unselfishness and devotion to an ideal' (Freud, 1921, p. 79). And he notes that 'Le Bon himself was prepared to admit that in certain circumstances the morals of a group can be higher than those of the individuals that compose it, and that only collectivities are capable of a high degree of unselfishness and devotion' (p. 82). In this chapter we explore the nature of groups and the role of leadership in transforming group chaos and potential group violence into constructive and ethical behavior that benefits humankind. How does leadership produce both the worst and the best from individuals in groups?

We begin with a discussion of some basic group phenomena in a section called Group Dynamics. In the most general sense, how do people in groups behave? How do they make decisions? Our focus here will be on the impact of the presence of others on collective processes. We will find that at this level group behavior is not particularly ethical, but neither is it irrational, savage, or regressed. Our next section, Social Influence and Persuasion, considers a phase in the life of groups and individuals where one person, or a small group of individuals, attempts to influence others, or the larger group. Sometimes the modes of influence are raw and coercive, sometimes they are gentle and subtle. Often, but not always, such influence leads to socially undesirable behavior. The third major section, Social Perception, focuses on followers rather than leaders. It considers what followers expect of leaders and examines their schemas and stereotypes of leaders and leadership, and how they perceive actual individuals in positions of leadership when expectation meets the reality of a specific person.

With these matters of group dynamics, interpersonal influence, and leader perception as a background, we then focus on the nature of leader–follower relationships. We capitalize on Burns's distinction between transactional and transforming leadership to consider both the tangible and psychological exchanges that are involved in leading, and also the ways transforming leaders lift others to a higher level of motivation and morality. Leaders and leadership processes make a tremendous difference in whether individuals within groups and groups within larger societies behave ethically or destructively.

GROUP DYNAMICS

We begin this section with a broad overview of individuals' behavior in the presence of others. One significant concern that arose in the general theory of leadership discussions involved levels of analysis. In this chapter we address varying levels of analysis; our examination of these general group processes considers how the presence of others affects individual performance, decision-making processes in groups, and behavior in large collectives.

The Effect of the Presence of Others on Individual Performance

Social facilitation
After observing that bicycle racers were fastest when competing with other cyclists than when racing alone or with a motorized pacer, noted bicycling enthusiast Norman Triplett proposed that the presence of others increases people's performance. Conducting the first experiment in social psychology, Triplett (1898) supported his hypothesis when he studied the effects of children winding fishing reels either alone or in a group. While initially the findings seemed to indicate that the presence of others leads to performance enhancement, further research revealed contradictory and equivocal findings. In 1965, Zajonc conducted a landmark review and analysis of the conflicting early literature in this area. He demonstrated that the presence of others, whether they are co-actors or mere observers, serves to enhance performance on well-learned, or dominant, responses (social facilitation) but impairs performance on novel, or subordinate, responses (social inhibition). This effect is quite universal, occurring among humans, other animals, and even insects. In classic research by Zajonc and colleagues (1969), cockroaches ran a simple, straight runway or a complex runway with a turn, and they ran either alone, in pairs, or with an 'audience' of cockroaches watching. As predicted, both running in pairs and running in front of spectator cockroaches facilitated performance on the easy runway (social facilitation) but it hindered performance on the more complex runway (social inhibition).

Zajonc's model of social facilitation and inhibition effects proposes that the mere presence of others is sufficient to produce these effects. Alternate and more cognitive interpretations of these effects have also received substantial support (see Baron et al., 1992 and Guerin, 1993 for reviews). For example, evaluation apprehension theorists proposed that individuals are motivated to make positive impressions on and receive positive evaluations from others. Alternatively, the distraction-conflict theorists proposed that the presence of others produces an attentional conflict in which individuals are torn between paying attention to the audience or the task. The various explanations are not necessarily in conflict indeed, it is likely that all mechanisms can affect performance in varying circumstances.

Social loafing

Another topic of particular importance to leaders of small groups is the potential for motivation loss and decreases in performance when individuals work collectively compared to when they work individually. In the 1880s, agriculturist Max Ringelmann gauged how hard individuals pulled on a rope when they worked alone compared with when they worked in groups of 7 or 14 people. Counter to commonsense, Ringelmann found that as group size increased individual group members pulled less hard (Kravitz and Martin, 1986). This reduction in individual motivation and effort when individuals work in a group, termed social loafing, has received significant empirical support for over 25 years and is quite robust and prevalent (Karau and Williams, 1993). A familiar example of social loafing occurs in restaurant settings: as the size of the dining group increases, the cheaper the individual patrons become at tipping time, thus explaining the familiar restaurant policy to automatically add gratuity to the bill for large parties.

Social loafing is often described using an expectancy–value framework. For example, Karau and Williams's (1993) collective effort model states that people's motivation within a group is dependent on their belief about how important/necessary their contribution is to group performance and how much they value the group's success. Thus, a student who believes that her input on a group project is valuable and who highly values receiving a good grade in the course is less likely to loaf on the project than a student who views his input as less valuable or who values the grade less. In general social loafing is more likely to occur when individual outputs cannot be evaluated, when people work on tasks they don't value, when people work with strangers, or when people expect others to perform well. The quality of the relationship between leader and follower also plays an important role in social loafing such that people are less likely to loaf when they have a high-quality relationship with their leader (Murphy et al., 2003).

Brainstorming

If a campaign manager is in charge of developing a memorable political slogan, should she ask her staff members to work on developing ideas individually or together as a group? Many people would suggest the staff should engage in brainstorming, a technique in which group members are encouraged to offer novel ideas in an environment devoid of criticism. Popularized by the work of

Osborn (1957), today many leaders continue this practice to facilitate the generation of ideas and solutions; however, ironically, brainstorming groups are illustrative of the problems groups face when working together. While brainstorming has intuitive appeal, the literature consistently reports that aggregates of individuals are more effective in generating more and better ideas than brainstorming groups (Mullen et al., 1991).

A number of explanations have been proffered to explain why brainstorming groups tend to underperform collections of individuals (Brown and Paulus, 1996). The production-blocking explanation emphasizes that group discussion tends to interfere with individuals starting and maintaining a train of thought (Nijstad, 2000). Also, although the environment is criticism-free some people may experience evaluation apprehension, which may inhibit creative thinking. Finally, through a process of social matching, group members may not produce a great deal if a low group productivity norm is established. Fortunately, recent research is beginning to highlight important measures that leaders can take to minimize production loss in brainstorming groups, such as minimizing production blocking and evaluation apprehension, reframing the problem to decrease 'derailment,' and encouraging the use of electronic brainstorming groups (Kerr and Tindale, 2004).

Group Decision Making

Leaders have to be aware of the forces that drive decision making in groups such as juries, security councils, party caucuses, and faculty meetings. We will discuss various group phenomena that undermine the effectiveness of group decision making including oversampling shared information, the tendency to make extreme decisions (group polarization) and an extreme concurrence-seeking that results in potentially disastrous decisions (groupthink).

Biased information sampling

By pooling the knowledge and information from all the individual members, groups can potentially take into account significantly more information in making their final decision than any single individual could. However, groups have a tendency to focus primarily on shared information and neglect information known to only one or a few members, especially when the task is perceived to have a correct solution. This biased sampling can result in poor decisions when the unshared information is particularly important (Stasser and Titus, 1985). For example, if a hiring committee focuses their discussion on shared information that points to candidate A as the strongest candidate, they would make a poor decision in the situation where all of the information together (unshared and shared) identified candidate B as the strongest job applicant. Fortunately, the leader can play an important role in assisting information management in groups by encouraging group members to disclose unshared information and by ensuring that the unshared information is included in the discussion (Larson et al., 1996).

Group polarization

Research revealing that group decisions tended to be riskier than individual decisions challenged the widely held assumption that group recommendations are less extreme than individual positions (Stoner, 1961). Discovery of this risky shift phenomenon sparked considerable research, some of which contradicted the initial findings by showing that groups sometimes make more conservative decisions than individuals. Further investigations reconciled these equivocal findings by elucidating a larger process of group polarization. Group polarization refers to the tendency for group discussion to lead to more extreme decisions, opinions, and judgments in the direction that was initially preferred by the group members (Levine and Moreland, 1998). In a classic example of polarization, secondary school French students' attitudes toward both Charles de Gaulle (initially positive) and Americans (initially negative) were assessed both alone and after they discussed the issue in a group (Moscovici and Zavalloni, 1969). Group discussion resulted in polarization of attitudes such that post-discussion attitudes were significantly more positive toward de Gaulle and more negative toward Americans.

Polarization effects are extremely reliable and robust and occur across a wide variety of issues. For example, prejudiced people become more prejudiced and people who favor either a 'guilty' or 'not guilty' verdict become even more confident in their position after talking with like-minded individuals (Myers and Bishop, 1971; Myers and Kaplan, 1976). A number of explanations have been proffered to help explain the group polarization effect (Levine and Moreland, 1998). The social identity perspective asserts that as individuals identify with the group they feel pressure to conform to the extreme perceived norm of the group. Alternatively, the persuasive arguments explanation contends that the shift results from exposure to new and persuasive arguments during the group discussion. Yet another approach suggests that when comparing themselves to other group members, individuals perceive that others have similar yet more extreme positions than they do and thus they shift in the direction of extremity to be viewed favorably, to be 'better' than average. All of these explanations have empirical support and group polarization is likely a multiply determined phenomenon.

Groupthink

Not only must leaders be cognizant of the potential for group decisions to be polarized, it is also important to understand how strong desires for group consensus can harm the decision-making process. Groupthink occurs when dynamics within a group result in group members engaging in a distorted mode of thinking that ultimately results in serious errors of judgment and poor decisions (Janis, 1972, 1982). In groupthink, group processes cause members to suspend their normal critical decision-making processes and arrive at a potentially flawed, premature decision. Examples of groups that succumbed to groupthink include Nixon's White House staff deciding to cover-up the Watergate break-in and the team of government and industry officials deciding to launch the space shuttle *Challenger*. Some likely causes of groupthink include high group cohesiveness, isolation from outside scrutiny, a strong, directive leadership style, lack of procedures to evaluate alternatives, and high levels of stress or external threat. These antecedents lead members to rationalize the correctness of their group's actions and believe stereotypes of opposing groups, to maintain an illusion of invulnerability and an exaggerated belief in their group's morality, and to feel extreme pressure to conform to the group and sustain group cohesiveness (Janis, 1972).

One clear outcome from investigations into groupthink is that the leader plays a pivotal role in determining the quality of the decision making and in navigating the group through potentially disastrous decision-making scenarios (Tetlock et al., 1992). This crucial role of the leader is clearly illustrated in two prominent decisions made by the Kennedy administration that resulted in dramatically different outcomes. Kennedy's ad hoc policy-making group's decision to send a group of commandos to invade Cuba at the Bay of Pigs is a classic example of how a group of excellent individual decision makers can make a disastrous decision. However, Kennedy was determined not to make a similar mistake when, a year and a half later, he oversaw the executive committee of the National Security Council addressing the Soviet Union's construction of a missile base in Cuba. With a focus on using effective decision-making techniques, correcting misperceptions and limiting concurrence-seeking, Kennedy's group made effective decisions and the Cuban missile crisis was successfully resolved. While these two examples point to the important role of the leader, they also call attention to potential problems with Janis's theory. Arguably, stress and cohesiveness were higher during the Cuban missile crisis, indicators of more groupthink rather than less. Research into the groupthink process is somewhat equivocal; it appears that the processes that cause groupthink may be more complicated than indicated by Janis. While sometimes a seemingly reasonable and intelligent group will make a disastrous decision, there are also times where cohesive groups with strong leaders make good decisions.

Behavior in Large Collectives

Deindividuation
As noted at the beginning of this chapter, special problems arise in large groups and crowds. Large collectives have left a trail of brutality throughout history

including the persecution of Jews in Europe, the lynchings of blacks in America, and the massacre of Tutsis by the Hutu in Rwanda. In Le Bon's (1969) discussion of the impact of collective influence on the individual he identified the concept of social contagion: the notion that the behavior of individuals in crowds is infectious. Social contagion is marked by a loss of a sense of responsibility for actions and a breakdown of normal control mechanisms such as values, ethics, and social rules that normally inhibit antisocial behaviors. Beginning with Festinger and colleagues (1952), social psychologists have sought to explain antinormative and disinhibited behavior within social groups through decades of research into deindividuation theory.

According to Zimbardo's (1969) framework, a number of circumstances contribute to deindividuation including arousal, sensory overload, anonymity, novel or unstructured situations, and reduced feelings of individual responsibility. Refining and expanding this theory, other researchers have explained deindividuation in terms of self-awareness, where in crowd situations individuals' attention is drawn away from the self (values, behaviors, internal standards of conduct) to the external environment (Diener, 1980). However, a recent review of the deindividuation literature found little support for either antinormative behaviors or a deindividuated state (Postmes and Spears, 1998). Rather their results support the explanation that 'deindividuation' heightens individual's identity with the group and thus conformity to the situation-specific group norms is increased. Importantly, this social identity perspective highlights the potential for deindividuated acts to be prosocial. This model also underscores the potential for leaders to positively impact the group norms in deindividuating circumstances thereby harnessing the collective energies for good rather than evil. In Le Bon's terms the leader can provide the 'influence of suggestion' to impel groups toward principled achievements.

SOCIAL INFLUENCE AND PERSUASION

The group level dynamics discussed above largely concern forces that govern the group as a whole, and thus all the individuals in a group. Now we turn our attention to examining how individual group members influence and persuade one another; that is, we begin our discussion of the leader–follower relationship as it relates to influence and persuasion. We begin with a general discussion of social influence processes and how individuals impact others in a group. Next, we discuss obedience to legitimate authority, conformity to group norms and the influence that minorities can have on the larger group. Finally, we distinguish between three forms of influence and we address persuasion processes. Power, one of the key elements of leadership that is explicitly addressed in the previous chapter by Michael Harvey, takes a prominent role in this section.

Social Influence

Social influence can be defined generally as the ability to affect another's behavior. In everyday life, people use social influence to try to persuade, convince,
induce, or cajole others to provide assistance, change an opinion, offer support,
or engage in certain behaviors. A great deal of research has focused on identifying specific tactics of social influence and trying to understand their dynamics
(Kipnis et al., 1980; Yukl & Falbe, 1990). Influence tactics can be perceived as
'positive,' 'negative,' or 'neutral', and include: reciprocity/exchanges, assertiveness, ingratiation, rational persuasion, appeals, threats, sanctions, and forming
coalitions.

Effective leadership can be seen as the successful application of influence
to move followers to achieve the leader's and the group's objectives. Yet, social
influence works both ways, with leaders attempting to influence followers and
followers using their own influence tactics to affect their leaders. For example,
a transactional leader in Burns's sense might rely primarily on using social
exchange tactics (money and recognition in exchange for loyalty and performance). A tyrannical leader makes liberal use of threats and sanctions. Followers
may be more likely to use rational persuasion or form coalitions with like-
minded peers in order to try to influence the leader. In fact, Ansari and Kapoor
(1987) found that followers were more likely to use ingratiation and blocking
tactics (e.g., threatening a work slowdown) with authoritarian leaders, while
followers tried to influence their more participative leaders via rational
persuasion.

Effective leaders are typically, consciously or unconsciously, masters of social
influence tactics. They know how to influence followers' attitudes and behaviors
and may have a better understanding of the underlying processes. Leaders can
develop this tacit knowledge or 'common sense' understanding of how to influence individuals and groups. Research has found positive relationships between
tacit knowledge for certain leadership positions and ratings of leader effectiveness (Hedlund, et al., 2003; Sternberg and Horvath, 1999).

Social Impact Theory

One useful approach to thinking about how individuals in a group affect others
is Social Impact Theory (Jackson, 1987; Latane, 1981). This theory draws
analogies to the impact that physical stimuli have on objects, and states that that
impact is a function of the strength, immediacy, and number of the stimuli. For
example, the amount of light that falls on a table is a function of how many
lamps are pointed toward it, how strong each one is, and how close they are. In
human terms, the amount of impact that one or more people as sources of influence have on an individual varies with the number of people, their strength, and

each one's immediacy to the individual. For example, the impact that a group of drill instructors has on an individual officer candidate during boot camp in the Marine Corps is a function of how many of them are shouting at the young soldier, how loud each one is, and how close they are. Let's consider the case of a single drill instructor leading a small group. The intensity of his impact will be determined in part by his strength, but not just the loudness of his voice. Various dimensions of his power are relevant, including his physical strength, his rank, how much he is admired, and his capacity to reward or punish (see Chapter 4 of this volume; also, cf. French and Raven, 1959). The more 'strength' he has according to these characteristics, the greater his impact. As a single leader he must combine his strength with immediacy, and be very 'up front and personal' with his officer candidates.

According to social impact theory, it is not only the number of sources of influence that matters. We must also consider the number of individuals those sources are trying to affect. The impact of one or more sources is diffused across one or more influence targets. If there is one drill instructor yelling at three officer candidates, the instructor's impact will be diffused across the three. It will have less impact than if he were yelling at just one or two.

For a single leader trying to influence a group, her impact will vary according to her power or strength, how many targets her influence is diffused across, and how close she is to each target. Strong leaders who have close personal contact with a small number of followers, other things being equal, have more impact. We will see how important strength and immediacy are in some classic studies of obedience to authority.

Obedience to Authority

A special instance of influence concerns the tendency for humans to obey those who are deemed to be authority figures. This often 'blind' obedience to authority was demonstrated in Stanley Milgram's (1975) well-known shock experiments. Under the guise of studying the effects of punishment on learning, study participants, who were always assigned the teacher role, were required to provide increasingly stronger electric shocks to a learner (actually a confederate) each time he failed to correctly identify a previously learned word pair. Milgram found that the majority of participants would obey the experimenter – the authority figure in the experiment – and continue to shock the helpless learner over his protests, cries of pain, and requests to be released.

In the initial experiments, the teacher was placed in another room, providing distance between him and the mistreated learner. In these instances, rates of obedience were quite high. In fact, nearly two-thirds of the participants continued to shock the helpless learner (even after the learner screamed in agony, pounded on the walls, and eventually stops responding completely) until the experiment was terminated. In subsequent experiments the learner was brought into the same room, and in another condition the teacher had to force the learner's hand onto a shock plate. As expected, as the teacher–learner distance lessened, obedience decreased – but a substantial minority of participants continued to obey the experimenter and force shocks on the helpless learner. Additionally, as social impact theory predicts, these experiments also showed that the closer the authority figure was to the teacher, the more the teacher obeyed.

These studies, and others conducted by Milgram and other social scientists, clearly demonstrate that people will obey authority figures even when there is no pre-existing relationship between the individual and the person of authority. Furthermore, obedience occurs even when the authority figure has questionable credentials. For example, Milgram demonstrated that people would readily obey the directions of an individual wearing a generic security guard uniform. Imagine then, the power wielded by a legitimate leader over followers, particularly if the leader is one of unquestionable authority and if the relationship between leader and followers is a long-standing and close one.

Majority vs. Minority Influence

There is a strong tendency for group members to change their opinions, behaviors, or perceptions to be consistent with group norms. In a classic conformity experiment, participants were asked to focus on a dot of light 15 feet in front of them in a pitch black room and they were asked to indicate the distance that the dot moved. Unbeknownst to the participants, the dot was stationary and only appeared to move due to the visual illusion known as the autokinetic effect. In groups of three, group members' judged how far the dot moved and their judgments gradually converged over time illustrating conformity to the developing group norm (Sherif, 1936). Substantial research has shown that conformity, or majority influence, occurs primarily for two reasons: people look to others for information and people want to avoid appearing deviant.

Processes of conformity and obedience might lead one to believe that followers are at the mercy of the group majority and their leaders. Fortunately, that is not the case. Research by Moscovici (1985) has demonstrated that a group minority can resist conforming to the majority and can influence the group's processes and outcomes if the minority presents a realistic alternative viewpoint and if the minority is consistent in advocating it.

In Solomon Asch's (1955) well-known conformity studies that involved having groups of students judge the length of lines, each group contained only a single participant, with the rest of the group consisting of confederates who gave predetermined incorrect responses. The measure of conformity was whether the lone participant would give in to the group pressure and also give an incorrect response even though the correct answer was obvious. Under this subtle, but strong, conformity pressure, the majority conformed. However, the presence of only one other group member who consistently gave correct responses was enough to enable the participant to overcome the conformity pressure.

This suggests that a minority – even a relatively small one – can have considerable impact on group decision making and group processes. As in the famous film about a jury, *Twelve Angry Men*, the lone dissenter is able to eventually persuade the entire jury to his point of view by being persistent and consistent in advocating the defendant's innocence. This illustrates the reality that small groups of followers can play an important part in leading the larger group. In this regard, the boxer Muhammad Ali provides an interesting example of using effective nonconformity to achieve social change. He insisted that he be called by his Muslim name, he refused to be inducted into the armed services, and he consistently embodied a different way for African-Americans to behave in a White-dominated society. The nation caught up with his initially reviled point of view. It took 30 years for his image to appear on boxes of Wheaties cereal, but by the late 1990s that seemed unremarkable. The notions of commitment and consistent advocacy are important strategies for the leader. Political leaders are often valued for being consistent in advocating particular plans or courses of action. In fact, too little consistency on the part of a leader can be attacked as evidence that the leader is 'wishy-washy' or a 'flip-flopper.'

Compliance and Persuasion

In Milgram's studies of obedience, the experimenter has great influence, depending on such variables as his proximity to the subject. Many participants obey the experimenter's orders, or comply with them. However, it is obvious that they are not in any way persuaded that what they are doing is right, or even that it makes any sense. Understanding leadership involves understanding obedience or compliance to powerful individuals, such as authority figures, in the context of other forms of influence that potential leaders might have on potential followers. Herbert Kelman (1958) usefully distinguished three 'processes of opinion change' that compare compliance with other forms of influence.

Kelman first discusses compliance as a kind of influence that is produced by pure coercion. Leaders or authorities, such as Milgram's experimenter, must have power to produce compliance, but they need no other attribute. Compliance is a form of influence that is relatively short-lived. It depends on constant surveillance by the authority to make sure that the target of influence is complying with whatever directive he or she has issued. In this volume we do not think of leadership as having taken place when an individual or group is merely complying with the coercive power wielded by an authority. Leadership happens when people go along with an influence attempt with some degree of volition. Kelman identifies two other forms of influence in which the targets of influence do have a degree of volition in going along.

The first of these volitional forms of influence is identification. In this case a person is influenced because he or she wants to be like or form a relationship with an attractive leader. The leader's influence is based on attractiveness rather than power. A young musician might imitate his piano teacher because he admires her, or a resident physician might take on the attitudes of the chief surgeon because she admires the surgeon's success. Identification produces influence that is longer lasting than compliance. It does not require surveillance. On the other hand, the behavior or attitude that results from identifying with a source of influence may not be fully integrated into the person's overall view of the world or overall standards for behavior. Thus the behavior or attitude may change when attraction to the source ends and the identification ceases. Several authors (Bass, 1997; Freud, 1921; Gardner, 1995) believe that identification with a leader is a key element of leadership. We will discuss its role later in the chapter.

Kelman's third form of influence, and the second volitional form, is internalization. Internalization results from influence sources who are credible rather than powerful or attractive. Internalization involves the person integrating an attitude into his or her overall value system. This kind of influence is the longest lasting. It doesn't depend on any continued contact, actual or psychological, with the influence source. It is fully integrated into the person's way of thinking and will last a long time.

Central vs. Peripheral Routes to Persuasion

Kelman's distinction between internalization and identification is related to an important approach to persuasion called the Elaboration Likelihood Model, or the ELM (Petty and Cacioppo, 1986). The ELM distinguishes two routes to persuasion. First, with the 'central route to persuasion' attitude change results from thoughtful consideration of the arguments in a communication. In contrast, with the 'peripheral route to persuasion' attitude change results from signals or cues, other than arguments themselves, which lead the target to believe the communication. For example, the influence target might believe that the communicator is honest, or the target may be in a receptive mood, or may be impressed that the message is long and contains lots of bulleted points. In all three cases, persuasion happens not because of a full consideration of the actual arguments, but because of peripheral cues that suggest that the message should be believed. Leaders can persuade followers by good arguments, or 'stories' (cf. Gardner, 1995). But other elements also matter greatly. Is the leader someone with whom followers might identify, or trust and believe? Has the leader

presented his or her message in a manner that encourages receptivity and cre-
dulity? Personal characteristics are important here, but so are contextual
features, such as illustration, easily remembered slogans, and impressive-look-
ing documentation.

Induced Compliance, Self-persuasion and Internalization

Kelman's distinction between compliance and internalization seems very clear.
The two are very different forms of influence. This should not blind us to the
fact that compliance can be an extremely useful tool in leadership, and if used
properly, can produce internalization. Decades of experiments testing cognitive
dissonance theory (Festinger, 1957) using the so-called 'forced compliance'
paradigm have shown that under some conditions people who have been induced
to comply with pressure to behave in a particular way subsequently internalize
the attitude implied by their behavior (Cooper and Fazio, 1984). In one classic
study students at Yale University were asked, with some gentle nudging, to write
essays in exchange for money, supporting the actions of the New Haven, Con-
necticut, police who had rather brutally broken up a riot on campus (Cohen,
1962). Students who were paid the smallest amounts for writing the essay actually came to believe what they wrote more than those given larger amounts of
money. When students were well paid for writing essays, they were unbothered
by any contradiction between their essay-writing behavior and their negative
attitudes toward the police. But students who were paid very little really didn't
have sufficient justification for their behavior, so they reduced the 'cognitive
dissonance' produced by their contradictory behavior and actually came to believe that the police action probably made sense. Their own behavior served as
a cue that the police action was justified, and it seems that they actually internal-
ized that belief. When people are subtly coerced into certain actions, they often
perceive themselves as having chosen freely, and justify the behavior by inter-
nalizing attitudes that support it. Adept leaders will apply just enough pressure
to get followers to behave in ways they might not act without pressure, and then
to take responsibility for their actions by coming to believe it was right.

SOCIAL PERCEPTION

Now we turn our attention to the followers and we take a social-cognitive approach to understanding people's perceptions of leaders. Many recent theorists
have argued that leadership emerges from various cognitive and attributional
processes; that is, leadership is, at least in part, in the eye of the beholder. Indeed
Lord and Maher define leadership as 'the process of being perceived by others
as a leader' (1991, p. 11). This perspective is consistent with the constructionist

approach brought forth by members of the general theory group wherein leadership is described as 'a result of both constructing reality and negotiating roles within that reality' (Chapter 1, p. 24). According to Hickman and Couto (Chapter 7), 'constructionists believe that humans construct or create reality and give it meaning through their social ... interactions' (p. 152). In this section we will review the role of schemas, stereotypes or role expectations, and social identities as they relate to leadership.

Leader Categorization Theory

In a foundational paper, Hollander and Julian (1969) highlighted the importance of the perceiver in leadership processes by maintaining that the individual who best fits the followers' shared conceptions will emerge as the group leader. Implicit leadership theories refer to individuals' preconceptions regarding leaders' traits, abilities, and behaviors and these implicit theories are influenced both by individual factors, such as personality traits and individual's values, as well as cultural values and beliefs. Empirical research on implicit leadership theories has demonstrated that there are widely shared beliefs about leader behavior and traits that focus around both task skills and people skills (Kenney et al., 1996). For example, leaders are generally thought to be active, determined, influential, and in-command while also being caring, interested, honest, and open to others' ideas.

Building on the implicit leadership theories research, Lord et al., (1982) proposed leader categorization theory, which asserts that individuals have both general and task-specific cognitive schemas of types of leaders that are developed through past experience with leaders. According to this theory, leader schemas act like other schemas in that individuals are categorized as a leader to the extent their traits and/or behaviors are perceived to match the prototypic attributes (i.e., schema) of a preexisting leader category (Lord and Maher, 1991). Thus, by observing the behaviors and traits of all group members, people compare those observations to their leader schemas and the individual who best matches their schemas is preferred as the group leader. Once individuals are categorized as leaders, the relevant schemas affect how followers both encode and recall information about leaders and how they perceive and evaluate leaders. For example, if followers think that leaders should be assertive they may remember only the times when their leader was behaving assertively and forget the times their leader was more timid. Indeed, followers' ratings of leaders oftentimes reflect the followers' leadership schemas more so than they reflect the leaders' actual behaviors, and the effectiveness of the leader is often judged from the fit of the leader's attributes and behaviors to those of the salient leader prototype (Lord, 1985).

Role Congruity Theory

Now we turn our focus to a particularly pernicious effect of these leader schemas, in particular, how these preconceptions conflict with other cognitive preconceptions such as gender stereotypes. According to role congruity theory (Eagly and Karau, 2002) the agentic qualities considered necessary in the leadership role (e.g., independence, competence, assertiveness, competitiveness, aggressiveness, and decisiveness) are incompatible with the largely communal qualities associated with women (e.g., sensitivity, warmth, expressiveness, helpfulness, sympathy, and nurturance; Heilman, 2001). There is considerable empirical evidence suggesting that successful leaders are often thought to require and/or possess stereotypically male attributes and that people combine both gender and leader role expectations when perceiving leaders. For example, people perceive male politicians as better suited for pursuing the more agentic tasks of public policy, such as directing the military, the economy, and foreign relations, whereas female political leaders are perceived as more appropriately suited for more communal tasks such as helping the poor and working for peace (Eagly and Karau, 2002). Also, research demonstrates that in order to be influential leaders, women must delicately combine communal qualities (e.g., warmth and friendliness) with agentic qualities (e.g., competence and directiveness; Carli, 2001).

This perceived incongruity between the leadership role and the female gender role results in two forms of prejudice against women leaders. First, the descriptive aspect of the gender stereotype (beliefs about how women and men are) results in the perception that women are highly communal and thus less qualified for leadership positions than men. Second, the prescriptive component of the stereotype (beliefs about how women and men ought to be) suggests that women are perceived negatively when demonstrating favorable leadership characteristics because those behaviors do not meet the expectations of appropriate and desirable female behaviors. For example, a successful female CEO may be viewed effective as a leader but she will be disliked on a personal level, and may be conferred an epithet, such as battleaxe, for her violations of stereotypical feminine behaviors. Taken together, these forms of prejudice help explain a considerable number of research findings: in spite of empirical evidence suggesting no actual leadership effectiveness differences between women and men, people tend to hold less favorable attitudes toward female than male leaders and women have greater difficulty attaining, and being viewed as effective in, top leadership roles (Eagly and Karau, 2002).

Not only can this discrepancy between gender and leadership role expectations affect others' perceptions and evaluations of women leaders, it can also affect the women leaders themselves. Recent research is starting to uncover factors that determine the extent to which the 'think leader–think male' stereotype affects women leaders. For example, when stereotypes are subtly activated women assimilate to the stereotype and are less likely to desire a leadership position whereas blatant stereotype activation results in a heightened desire to assume a leadership position (Stoddard et al., 2003). Additionally, women who are not confident in their leadership abilities demonstrate deleterious responses to the stereotype whereas confident women show more positive responses (Hoyt and Blascovich, 2005).

Social Identity Theory of Leadership

While leader categorization theory views leadership as a product of individual information processing and role-congruity theory addresses shortcomings of this information processing, another recent perspective views leadership as emerging from normal social-cognitive processes associated with group membership. The primary thesis behind the social identity analysis of leadership is that as group members identify more strongly with the group, the perception, evaluation, and effectiveness of the leader is increasingly based on how representative, or how prototypical, of the group the leader is (Hogg, 2001). Hence, in a group where intellectual and analytic ability is highly valued, the more group members begin to identify with the group, the more the members will look to highly analytical and intelligent members to be their leader. Importantly, this social identity perspective acknowledges that leader schemas also play a role in leader perception, but as group membership becomes more salient the relative influence of leadership schemas to group prototypicality decreases (Duck and Fielding, 1999).

In addition to affecting perceptions, group prototypicality also affects group members' liking for one another (Fielding and Hogg, 1997). More prototypical members are more popular and more liked than less prototypical members and thus they have the status and ability to gain compliance from the other members. Additionally, highly prototypical members are more likely to behave in a group-serving manner than less prototypical members, which not only increases social attraction but also allows for the other members to begin trusting the leader. This increased social attraction and perceived legitimacy gives the prototypical members the latitude to be pioneering and nonconformist in their social influence and it imbues them with many attributes of leadership. The important role of legitimacy in leader–follower relations is discussed further in the next section.

While social contextual changes may change group prototypicality, the leader can attempt to prevent a redistribution of influence within the group by trying to change the prototype in a self-serving manner. Methods for doing this include emphasizing the current prototype, ridiculing deviant group members, or condemning an appropriate outgroup. These tactics are often observed in national leaders including Margaret Thatcher who, during the Falklands War, 'accentuated her nationalistic prototype of Britain, pilloried deviant groups within Britain who did not represent her prototype, and demonized the Argentinian outgroup' (Hogg, 2001, p. 191). Likewise, George W. Bush engaged in similar strategies, vowing to rid the world of evil-doers, to secure his prototypicality during the 2003 war with Iraq. As alluded to in the last point, the prototypicality approach to leadership also takes into account the intergroup dimension of leadership. The very notion of a leader being prototypical of their group is based, in part, on a comparison to other groups. Oftentimes leaders not only lead their group toward goals but also against other groups. For example, when considering various political leaders, we often conceptualize them in intergroup terms; that is, we consider how they achieve their group goals as well as how they lead their constituents against opposing political parties. These intergroup interactions are examined further in Terry Price and Doug Hicks's chapter (Chapter 6), as they focus on the ethics of treating one's own group with more consideration than outsiders.

LEADER–FOLLOWER RELATIONS

In this final section we explicitly focus on one of the major discussion themes evident throughout the general theory of leadership conversations: the nature of leader–follower relationships. From a social scientific perspective we address leader–follower relations by examining exchanges between leaders and followers, the importance of followers identifying with the leader and perceiving her or his procedures as just, and we end with a discussion of the transforming aspects of leadership.

The Exchange Perspective

Some kind of leadership structure emerges or already exists in most groups, and within that structure leaders and followers engage in a psychological exchange. Leaders satisfy a number of needs for followers, including vision and direction, protection and security, inclusion and belongingness, and followers give leaders commitment, focus, gratitude, loyalty and cooperation, among other things (Messick, 2005). One overarching element in the exchange is legitimacy. Hollander notes that followers 'accord or withdraw support to leaders' and thereby have a key role in 'defining the latitudes of a leader's actions.... Influence and power flow from legitimacy, which is in several ways determined or affected by followers, and their response to leaders' (Hollander, 1993, p. 29). In exchange for competency, esteem and recognition, help in achieving group goals, and providing meaning and vision, followers grant leaders legitimacy and follow their direction.

A central element in Hollander's social exchange theory, and a central concept in understanding leadership, is the notion of idiosyncrasy credit. By bringing rewards to the group and by demonstrating competence and conformity to group norms, leaders are given 'credit to deviate', which allows later nonconformity and innovation to be accepted (Hollander, 1993, p. 33–34). This idea is similar to the one noted previously that social attraction and perceived legitimacy give prototypical group members degrees of freedom in leading. In 1972 when President Richard Nixon announced that he was going to visit Communist China, his Republican followers went along with little objection. Nixon had paid his dues by competence, conformity, and success, and he had credit to deviate. A Democratic president might have been accused of treason by Congressional Republicans for giving the same opening to the 'Reds.'

The concept of idiosyncrasy credit suggests that leaders spend their capital down when they deviate or innovate, but in fact leaders are expected to deviate to some degree, and if a novel departure brings the group success, the leader is likely to build up further idiosyncrasy credit, rather than deplete it. One implication of this analysis is that leaders who have little or no credit may well propose new initiatives to deafening silence. Their suggestions fall flat. Followers no longer regard them as legitimate. Legitimacy, like charisma, is a quality that is 'invested by followers and accorded or withdrawn by them' (Hollander, 1993, p. 41). This idea resonates with Freud's claim, borrowed from Le Bon (1969 [1895]), that 'all prestige, however, is dependent on success, and is lost in the event of failure' (Freud, 1921, p. 81). Had Nixon's China initiative failed, he would have lost a great deal of credit with his followers, and his legitimacy would have been seriously jeopardized.

The power of self-interest underlies the social exchange approach to understanding leader–follower relations, and it has been challenged by a number of recent approaches to leadership. First, scholars of charismatic and transformational leadership have argued that there is more to leadership than exchange or transaction, or brokerage (Bass, 1998; Burns, 1978). There's more to the leader–follower relationship than mutual back-scratching. Followers respond to moral, motivational, and emotional uplift. In return, Hollander argues that there is no essential difference between transformational vs. exchange or transactional leadership, and that the former is an extension of the latter 'with greater leader intensity and follower arousal' (Hollander, 1993, p. 41). We will address these issues shortly.

Procedural Justice

Another challenge to the social exchange model grows out of Tyler and Lind's (1992) relational model of authority in groups. Tyler and Lind's work is fundamentally concerned with legitimacy and the psychological factors that produce it. They argue that more important than followers' specific outcomes are their perceptions of a leader's fairness. Furthermore, they found that a form of fairness called procedural justice is considerably more important than its counterpart, distributive justice. Leaders and authorities who make decisions fairly gain more voluntary compliance than leaders who simply distribute rewards fairly. It is more important that your outcomes are allocated through just procedures than that they seem just in relation to what has been distributed to others. A leader might not give you what you think you deserve, but if he or she has used fair procedures in deciding what you get, he or she is perceived as legitimate, and is likely to be followed.

During the construction of the Panama Canal, chief engineer George W. Goethals won over the initially hostile labor force with a novel use of procedural justice. He met with individual members of the work force starting early every Sunday morning on a first-come, first-served basis without regard to rank, race, or nationality. Their concerns were heard, and matters were resolved expeditiously. 'The new approach was in fact wholly unorthodox by the standards of the day. In labor relations Goethals was way in advance of his time, and nothing that he did had so discernable an effect on the morale of the workers or their regard for him.' As a result they gave him 'the best service within their power' (McCullough, 1977, p. 538).

What creates procedural justice, and why is it so important? If people are given a chance to make their case, if they are treated with dignity and respect, and if the leader is honest and unbiased in making decisions, followers will feel that they have been treated fairly, that they have had procedural justice. 'Above all, the leader must be concerned with the appearance of fairness, with convincing followers that he or she is willing to consider their point of view, and that he or she will be even-handed and nondiscriminatory in decision-making' (Tyler and Lind, 1992, p. 161). When the leader accords followers procedural justice, they feel validated as members of the group by the most prominent and credible person in the group. The leader speaks for the group in treating individuals or groups of followers in a way that shows that they are in good standing. Thus it is people's need for validation within a valued group, rather than narrow self-interest, that is central in getting them to willingly follow from a procedural justice viewpoint. 'The belief that the authority views one as a full member of the society, trust in the authority's ethicality and benevolence, and belief in the authority's neutrality – these appear to be the crucial factors that lead to voluntary compliance with the directives of authority' (Tyler and Lind, 1992, p. 163).

Thus, rather instrumental concerns and exchanges between leaders and followers are important in their relationship, but there are other motives, including crucial needs for self-validation and self-worth, that strongly affect followership. These and other important motives are activated by charismatic and transformational leaders.

Charisma and Identification with the Leader

Charisma, as first defined by Weber (1947) and discussed earlier by Harvey (Chapter 4), involves the collective perception of followers that an individual possesses certain extraordinary characteristics that make her or him worthy of leadership. Therefore, according to Weber, leadership is a form of social influence that comes partly from the leader's extraordinary qualities, but primarily from followers' collective identification with and willingness to follow a chosen person. Leaders of national or social movements, such as Mohandas Gandhi and Martin Luther King, Jr., who were able to mobilize huge numbers of followers without formal authority, are good examples.

While this view of charisma relates to our earlier discussion of social perception in that it views charisma as a leader personality constructed from social-cognitive processes of followers, subsequent research has focused more on the characteristics and behavior of charismatic leaders. Conger and Kanungo (1998), and others emphasize the abilities of charismatic leaders to inspire followers through a compelling vision, strong commitment to the vision, and perceptions of the leader's competence to achieve it. Followers therefore must strongly identify with the chosen leader in order for him or her to remain in power.

Conger (2004) argues that charismatic leaders build strong follower identification through being truly concerned with and responsive to follower needs and through self-sacrifice, such as the decision of Chrysler's CEO, Lee Iacocca, to take a one dollar salary when he came on board to try to turn the company around. It also helps if the charismatic leader shows exceptionally strong devotion to the vision he or she articulates for the organization, even to the extent of taking great personal risks to prove his or her dedication to 'the cause.'

Other scholars have focused on personal characteristics of charismatic leaders that play a part in inspiring followers and in building follower commitment. For example, charismatic individuals are emotionally expressive and use their expressiveness to energize, inspire, and motivate followers (Riggio, 2004). Charismatic individuals are often exceptionally gifted speakers, using words to inspire and to clearly and persuasively articulate their visions. A recent study demonstrated that charismatic US presidents used more inspirational metaphors in their inaugural addresses than did non-charismatic presidents (Mio et al., 2005). Charismatic leaders can be exceptionally persuasive and wield great influence over followers through their use of inspirational and motivating speech as well as emotional expressiveness.

Transformational/Transforming Effects of Leadership

In 1978 James MacGregor Burns introduced the concept of the transforming leader – one who empowers followers to produce profound and fundamental change. Burns argues that transformational leadership goes beyond the straight-forward social exchange relationship offered by transactional leadership, to provide deeper levels of connection and higher levels of commitment, perform-ance, and morality on the part of both follower and leader.

The fact that transformational leaders are extraordinarily effective in many leadership situations can be better understood by an analysis of group dynam-ics. Building from Burns's conception of transforming leadership, Bass (1998) argues that truly effective leaders are both transactional and transformational, with transactional leadership representing the social exchange elements inher-ent in the leader–follower relationship, and transformational leadership accounting for the more extraordinary levels of follower commitment and motivation. In the Bass and Avolio model (Bass, 1985, 1998; Bass and Avolio, 1994), transformational leadership is made up of several components. Two of these components, Idealized Influence and Inspirational Motivation, are ele-ments of charismatic leadership. Idealized Influence relates to the leader's ability to 'walk the talk' – to be a role model for followers and to truly lead the way. Notions of embodying the prototypical, effective leadership role, as dis-cussed in role congruity and social identity theories, come into play here. Inspirational Motivation is the leader's ability to create and articulate the vision in a way that inspires followers and builds their loyalty and commitment. The elements of building strong follower identification with the leader and com-mitment to the leader's vision have already been discussed.

According to Shamir et al., (1993), leader charisma is particularly effective because it raises followers' collective sense of self-esteem and self-efficacy. A transformational leader, for example, conveys confidence in followers and holds high expectations for their performance. By articulating a shared vision, the transformational/charismatic leader raises both the intrinsic value of the collec-tive goal and followers' sense of being able to accomplish the goal. For example, Franklin Delano Roosevelt demonstrated this element of transformational/char-ismatic leadership in his efforts to lead the USA out of the Great Depression. He was successful in painting a vision of a better future and persuading the citi-zenry that they had the means and ability to accomplish it.

The remaining components of Bass's transformational leadership are Indi-vidualized Consideration and Intellectual Stimulation. Understanding of these elements is also enhanced by knowledge of group dynamics and processes. Individualized Consideration relates to the leader's ability to develop a strong relationship with each follower – one that goes beyond the mere exchange relationship and is characterized by the leader's genuine concern for the fol-lower's individual needs, perspective, and personal development. Through this process, leaders can develop followers into leaders. Intellectual Stimula-tion is the transformational leader's ability to intellectually challenge followers to go the extra mile, to be innovative and creative, and to become an active and a constructively critical participant in group decision making and processes.

CONCLUSION

One point that was generally agreed upon in this quest for a grand theory of leadership is that to understand the nature of leadership we must understand the human condition. One aspect of the human condition that has long intrigued those from the humanities and the social sciences alike is the social facet. In this largely descriptive chapter we present a social scientific perspective on understanding the social animal as it relates to leadership.

We have seen that group life is marked with many dynamics that challenge leadership. Groups can become extreme, they can produce nearly blind conformity, and they can permit or even encourage antisocial behavior. Individuals in groups can become remarkably thoughtless, in both a literal cognitive sense and a figurative moral sense, and they can be very lazy, thereby exploiting the good will of others. Nevertheless, leaders can use their personal resources and their persuasiveness to mobilize groups toward effective, moral ends and to bring out Lincoln's 'better angels of our nature.' Using both transactional and transformational behaviors, leaders throughout history – Mohandas Gandhi, Nelson Mandela, and Eleanor Roosevelt, for example – have attempted to transform themselves and their followers in the service of goals or causes we applaud. The world is a better place for their contributions.

There may be times when it is easier to judge whether leaders and their followers were successful than to judge whether their goals were moral. Morality is often debatable, in the present and in historical hindsight. Of his famous meeting with Robert E. Lee, when Lee surrendered his Army of Northern Virginia, effectively ending the Civil War, Ulysses S. Grant wrote 'I felt like anything rather than rejoicing at the downfall of a foe who had fought so long and valiantly, and had suffered so much for a cause, though that cause was, I believe, one of the worst for which a people ever fought, and one for which there was the least excuse. I do not question, however, the sincerity of the great mass of those who were opposed to us' (Grant, 1886, pp. 489–90). Do we understand Lee's leadership differently depending on whether we agree with Grant's assessment of the morality of Lee's cause? While we believe that questions of morality are central to understanding leadership, our chapter on leader–follower relations does not much help address them. However, all of the contributors to this volume believe that they must never be allowed to get too far from view.

REFERENCES

Ansari, M. and A. Kapoor (1987), 'Organizational context and upward influence tactics', *Organizational Behavior and Human Decision Processes*, **40** (1), 39–49.

Asch, S.E. (1955), 'Opinions and social pressure', *Scientific American*, **193** (5), 31–35.

Baron, Robert, Norbert Kerr, and Norman Miller (1992), *Group Process, Group Decision, Group Action*, Pacific Grove, CA: Brooks/Cole.

Bass, Bernard M. (1985), *Leadership and Performance Beyond Expectations*, New York: Free Press.

Bass, Bernard M. (1997), 'Does the transactional–transformational leadership paradigm transcend organizational and national boundaries?', *American Psychologist*, **52** (2), 130–39.

Bass, Bernard M. (1998), *Transformational Leadership: Industrial, Military, and Educational Impact*, Mahwah, NJ: Lawrence Erlbaum Associates.

Bass, Bernard M., and Bruce Avolio (eds) (1994), *Improving Organizational Effectiveness through Transformational Leadership*, Thousand Oaks, CA: Sage.

Brown, V. and P. Paulus (1996), 'A simple dynamic model of social factors in group brainstorming', *Small Group Research*, **27** (1), 91–114.

Burns, James M. (1978), *Leadership*, New York: Harper & Row.

Burns, James M. (2003), *Transforming Leadership: The Pursuit of Happiness*, New York, NY: Atlantic Monthly Press.

Carli, L.L. (2001), 'Gender and social influence', *Journal of Social Issues*, **57** (4), 725–41.

Cohen, Arthur R. (1962), 'An experiment on small rewards for discrepant compliance and attitude change', in Jack W. Brehm and Arthur R. Cohen (eds), *Explorations in Cognitive Dissonance*, New York: Wiley, pp. 73–8.

Conger, Jay A. (2004), 'Charismatic theory', in George R. Goethals, Georgia J. Sorenson, and James M. Burns (eds), *Encyclopedia of Leadership*, Thousand Oaks, CA: Sage Press, vol. 1, pp. 162–7.

Conger, Jay A. and Rabindra N. Kanungo (1998), *Charismatic Leadership in Organizations*, Thousand Oaks, CA: Sage.

Cooper, Joel and Russell H. Fazio (1984), 'A new look at dissonance theory', in Leonard Berkowitz (ed), *Advances in Experimental Social Psychology*, New York: Academic Press, vol. 17, pp. 229–64.

Diener, Ed (1980), 'Deindividuation: The absence of self-awareness and self-regulation in group members', in Paul B. Paulus (ed.), *The Psychology of Group Influence*, Hillsdale, NJ: Lawrence Erlbaum, pp. 209–42.

Duck, J.M. and K.S. Fielding, (1999), 'Leaders and subgroups: One of us or one of them?', *Group Processes & Intergroup Relations*, **2** (3), 203–30.

Eagly, A.H. and S.J. Karau (2002), 'Role congruity theory of prejudice toward female leaders', *Psychological Review*, **109** (3), 573–98.

Festinger, Leon (1957), *A Theory of Cognitive Dissonance*, Palo Alto, CA: Stanford University Press.

Festinger, L., A. Pepitone, and T. Newcomb (1952), 'Some consequences of de-individuation in a group', *Journal of Abnormal & Social Psychology*, **47**, 382–9.

Fielding, K.S. and M.A. Hogg (1997), 'Social identity, self categorization, and leadership: A field study of small interactive groups', *Group Dynamics: Theory, Research, and Practice*, **1** (1), 39–51.

French, John R.P., Jr. and Bertram Raven (1959), 'The bases of social power', in Dorwin

Cartwright (ed.), *Studies in Social Power*, Ann Arbor, MI: Institute for Social Research, pp. 150–67.

Freud, Sigmund (1921), 'Group psychology and the analysis of the ego', in James Strachey (ed.), *The Standard Edition of the Complete Works of Sigmund Freud, V. 28: Beyond the Pleasure Principle, Group Psychology and Other Works*, London: Hogarth Press, pp. 65–143.

Gardner, Howard (1995), *Leading Minds: An Anatomy of Leadership*, New York: Basic Books.

Goethals, George R. (2003), 'A century of social psychology: Individuals, ideas, and investigations', in Michael A. Hogg and Joel Cooper (eds), *The Sage Handbook of Social Psychology*, London: Sage, pp. 3–23.

Grant, Ulysses S. (1886), *The Personal Memoirs of U.S. Grant*, New York: Charles L. Webster & Company.

Guerin, Bernard (1993), *Social Facilitation*, New York, NY: Cambridge University Press.

Hedlund, J., G.B. Forsythe, J.A. Horvath, W.M. Williams, S. Snook, and R.J. Sternberg (2003), 'Identifying and assessing tacit knowledge: Understanding the practical intelligence of military leaders', *The Leadership Quarterly*, **14** (2), 117–40.

Heilman, M.E. (2001), 'Description and prescription: How gender stereotypes prevent women's ascent up the organizational ladder', *Journal of Social Issues*, **57** (4), 657–74.

Hogg, M.A. (2001), 'A social identity theory of leadership', *Personality and Social Psychology Review*, **5** (3), 184–200.

Hollander, Edwin P. (1993), 'Legitimacy, power, and influence: A perspective on relational features of leadership', in Martin M. Chemers and Roya Ayman (eds), *Leadership Theory and Research*, San Diego: Academic Press, pp. 29–48.

Hollander, E.P. and J.W. Julian (1969), 'Contemporary trends in the analysis of leadership processes', *Psychological Bulletin*, **71** (5), 387–97.

Hoyt, C.L. and J. Blascovich (2005), *Leadership Efficacy of Women and Activation of Female Leader Stereotypes*, manuscript submitted for publication.

Jackson, Jeffrey M. (1987), 'Social impact theory: A social forces model of influence', in Brian Mullen and George R. Goethals (eds), *Theories of Group Behavior*, New York: Springer-Verlag, pp. 112–24.

Janis, Irving (1972), *Victims of Groupthink*, Boston, MA: Houghton-Mifflin.

Janis, Irving (1982), *Groupthink: Psychological Studies of Policy Decisions and Fiascoes*, Boston, MA: Houghton-Mifflin, 2nd edn.

Karau, S.J. and K.D. Williams (1993), 'Social loafing: A meta-analytic review and theoretical integration', *Journal of Personality and Social Psychology*, **65** (4), 681–706.

Kelman, H.C. (1958), 'Compliance, identification, and internalization: Three processes of opinion change', *Journal of Conflict Resolution*, 2, 51–60.

Kenney, R.A., B.M. Schwartz-Kenney, and J. Blascovich (1996), 'Implicit leadership theories: Defining leaders described as worthy of influence', *Personality and Social Psychology Bulletin*, **22** (11), 1128–43.

Kerr, N.L. and R.S. Tindale (2004), 'Small group decision making and performance', *Annual Review of Psychology*, **55**, 623–56.

Kipnis, D., S.M. Schmidt, and I. Wilkinson (1980), 'Intraorganizational influence tactics: Explorations in getting one's way', *Journal of Applied Psychology*, **65** (4), 440–52.

Kravitz, D.A. and B. Martin (1986), 'Ringelmann rediscovered: The original article', *Journal of Personality and Social Psychology*, **50** (5), 936–41.

Larson, J.R., Jr., C. Christensen, A.S. Abbott and T.M. Franz (1996), 'Diagnosing groups:

Charting the flow of information in medical decision making teams', *Journal of Personality and Social Psychology*, **71** (2), 315–30.

Latane, B. (1981), 'The psychology of social impact', *American Psychologist*, **36** (4), 343–56.

Le Bon, Gustave (1969, [1895]), *The Crowd*, New York: Ballantine.

Levine, John M., and Richard L. Moreland (1998), 'Small groups', in Daniel Gilbert, Susan Fiske and Gardner Lindzey (eds), *The Handbook of Social Psychology*, Boston: McGraw-Hill, 4th edn, vol. 2, pp. 415–69.

Lord, Robert G. (1985), 'An information processing approach to social perception, leadership, and behavioral measurement in organizations', in Barry Staw and Larry L. Cummings (eds), *Research in Organizational Behavior*, vol. 7, Greenwich, CT: JAI Press, pp. 87–128.

Lord, Robert G. and Karen J. Maher (1991), *Leadership and Information Processing: Linking Perceptions and Performance*, Boston, MA: Unwin Hyman.

Lord, Robert G., Roseanne J. Foti and James S. Phillips (1982), 'A theory of leadership categorization', in James G. Hunt, Uma Sekaran, and Chester Schriesheim (eds), *Leadership: Beyond Establishment Views*, Carbondale: Southern Illinois University Press, pp. 104–21.

McCullough, David (1977), *The Path between the Seas: The Creation of the Panama Canal, 1870–1914*, New York: Simon & Schuster.

Messick, David M. (2005), 'On the psychological exchange between leaders and followers', in David M. Messick and Roderick M. Kramer (eds), *The Psychology of Leadership*, Mahwah, NJ: Lawrence Erlbaum Associates, pp. 81–96.

Milgram, Stanley (1975), *Obedience to Authority*, New York: Harper Colophon.

Mio, J.S., R. E. Riggio, S. Levin, and R. Reese (2005), 'Presidential leadership and charisma: The effects of metaphor', *The Leadership Quarterly*, **16** (2), 287–94.

Moscovici, Serge (1985), 'Social influence and conformity', in Gardner Lindzey and Elliot Aronson (eds), *The Handbook of Social Psychology*, New York: Random House, 3rd edn, vol. 2, pp. 347–412.

Moscovici, S. and M. Zavalloni (1969), 'The group as a polarizer of attitudes', *Journal of Personality and Social Psychology*, **12** (2), 125–35.

Mullen, B., C. Johnson, and E. Salas (1991), 'Productivity loss in brainstorming groups: A meta-analytic integration', *Basic and Applied Social Psychology*, **12** (1), 3–23.

Murphy, S.M., S.J. Wayne, R.C. Liden and B. Erdogan (2003), 'Understanding social loafing: The role of justice perceptions and exchange relationships', *Human Relations*, **56** (1), 61–84.

Myers, D.G. and G.D. Bishop (1971), 'Enhancement of dominant attitudes in group discussion', *Journal of Personality and Social Psychology*, **20** (3), 386–91.

Myers, D., and M. Kaplan (1976), 'Group-induced polarization in simulated juries', *Personality and Social Psychology Bulletin*, **2** (1), 63–6.

Nijstad, Bernard A. (2000), 'How the group affects the mind: effects of communication in idea generating groups', unpublished doctoral dissertation, Utrecht University.

Osborn, Alex F. (1957), *Applied Imagination: Principles and Procedures of Creative Thinking*, New York: Charles Scribner's Sons.

Petty, Richard E. and John T. Cacioppo (1986), 'The elaboration likelihood model of persuasion', in Leonard Berkowitz (ed.), *Advances in Experimental Social Psychology*, New York: Academic Press, vol. 19, pp. 123–205.

Postmes, T. and R. Spears (1998), 'Deindividuation and anti-normative behavior: A meta-analysis', *Psychological Bulletin*, **123** (3), 238–59.

Riggio, Ronald E. (2004), 'Charisma', in George R. Goethals, Georgia J. Sorenson, and

James M. Burns (eds), *Encyclopedia of Leadership*, Thousand Oaks, CA: Sage, vol. 1, pp. 158–62.

Shamir, B., R.J. House and M.B. Arthur (1993), 'The motivational effects of charismatic leadership: A self-concept based theory', *Organization Science*, **4** (4), 577–94.

Sherif, Muzafer (1936), *The psychology of social norms*, New York: Harper & Row.

Sternberg, Robert J., and Joseph A. Horvath (eds) (1999), *Tacit Knowledge in Professional Practice*, Mahwah, NJ: Lawrence Erlbaum Associates.

Stoddard, T., T. Kliengklom and T. Ben-Zeev (2003), 'Stereotype threat, assimilation, and contrast effects, and subtlety of priming', paper presented at the annual Society for Personality and Social Psychology conference, February, 2003. Los Angeles, California.

Stoner, J.A.F. (1961), 'A comparison of individual and group decisions involving risk', unpublished master's thesis, Massachusetts Institute of Technology.

Stasser, G. and W. Titus (1985), 'Pooling and unshared information in group decision making: Biased information sampling during discussion', *Journal of Personality and Social Psychology*, **48** (6), 1467–78.

Tetlock, P.E., R.S. Peterson, C. McGuire, S. Chang and P. Feld (1992), 'Assessing political group dynamics: A test of the groupthink model', *Journal of Personality and Social Psychology*, **63** (3), 403–25.

Triplett, N. (1898), 'The dynamogenic factors in pacemaking and competition', *American Journal of Psychology*, **9** (4), 507–33

Tyler, Tom R. and E.A. Lind (1992), 'A relational model of authority in groups', in Mark Zanna (ed.), *Advances in Experimental Social Psychology*, San Diego: Academic Press, vol. 25, pp. 115–91.

Weber, Max (1947), *The Theory of Social and Economic Organizations*, A.M. Henderson and T. Parsons translation, New York: Free Press.

Yukl, G.A. and C.M. Falbe (1990), 'Influence tactics and objectives in upward, downward, and lateral influence attempts', *Journal of Applied Psychology*, **75** (2), 132–40.

Zajonc, R.B. (1965), 'Social facilitation', *Science*, **149**, 269–74.

Zajonc, R.B., A. Heingartner and E.M. Herman, (1969), 'Social enhancement and impairment of performance in the cockroach', *Journal of Personality and Social Psychology*, **13** (2), 83–92.

Zimbardo, P.G. (1969), 'The human choice: Individuation, reason, and order versus deindividuation, impulse, and chaos', *Nebraska Symposium on Motivation*, **17**, 237–307.

6. A framework for a general theory of leadership ethics

Terry L. Price and Douglas A. Hicks

INTRODUCTION

The phenomenon of leadership presents a problem for moral philosophers and social critics alike. Leadership is so central a response to the human condition that it is difficult to imagine what we might do without it.[1] Yet this relationship is distinctive in its tendencies toward hierarchy and inequality.[2] First, role differentiation between leaders and followers is something of a descriptive truth about leadership. There are obvious disparities between the capacities and behaviors of leaders, on the one hand, and the capacities and behaviors of followers, on the other. For example, leaders generally exert greater influence than followers on the group, usually by means of the greater power and privileges derived from their positions of leadership. Second, associated with leadership are standard assumptions about the permissibility of differential treatment between groups. Leadership often demands giving special attention to the group of which one is a leader or – for that matter – a follower, even when so doing comes at the expense of outsiders. The problem, then, is to make moral sense of a ubiquitous human relationship that cuts against some of our best intuitions and commitments, in particular, about the ethical importance of equality.

This problem derives from the more general proposition that unequal treatment requires justification. Acceptance of this proposition is at least partially constitutive of what it is to be a reasonable participant in an argument. For example, if an individual holds that two claims are similar in all relevant respects but that one ought to be accepted and the other rejected, then he or she is being unreasonable. In such a case, the individual would rightly be subject to a charge of arbitrariness. Moral argumentation about persons is hardly different on this score. If an individual holds that two persons are similar in all morally relevant respects but that one ought – morally – to be treated differently than the other, then he or she is being unreasonable. More strongly, given the potential moral costs of unequal treatment of persons, the argument against treating these two persons differently has greater force than it would have from the more basic requirement of reasonableness alone. We might go so far as to say that the two individuals should be treated equally, unless and until we can identify some morally relevant distinction between them. In other words, equality is the status quo in morality, and deviations from the status quo require special justification.[3]

Applied to the phenomenon of leadership, the presumption in favor of equality generates a special task for moral philosophers and social critics. Specifically their task is to analyze the features of this relationship for morally relevant distinctions that would potentially justify particular inequalities, perhaps within a wider frame of equality. The result of any such analysis would fall into one of three types, which we can refer to as the conservative approach, the radical approach, and the moderate approach, respectively. First, the conservative approach maintains the inequalities we are inclined to associate with leadership by showing that they are fully justified in the end. Second, the radical approach holds that some or all of these inequalities are unjustified and that we must rework leadership, perhaps forging it into a tool against inequality. On this approach, leadership should combat inequality, not embody it.[4] Third, the moderate approach articulates the grounds for justified inequality in a way that sets clear limits on differential treatment of followers and outsiders, all the while maintaining a general frame of equality, specifically, the moral equality of citizens. Although it might be expected that a general theory of leadership would resolve the tensions between leadership and equality, our goal in this chapter is not to adjudicate among these options. It is rather to pull together the strands of ethical thinking that arrive at the conservative, radical, and moderate approaches and, in so doing, create a framework for future analysis in leadership studies.

A framework for a general theory of leadership ethics thus offers a conceptual organization of normative responses to inequality, not a determination of how much inequality can be justified in the relation between leaders and followers or between groups and outsiders.[5] The first three substantive sections of the chapter serve as historical background for this debate, focusing exclusively on traditional social, political and moral theory. Sections II and III consider historical understandings of inequalities in the leader–follower relation.[6] Section IV turns to historical understandings of inequalities between groups and outsiders or, to borrow the language of social psychologists, ingroups and outgroups. Section V then looks at contemporary moral debates about inequalities between leaders and followers as well as inequalities between ingroups and outgroups. Section VI examines these questions in light of three current approaches to leadership. The conclusions of this chapter articulate some of the preconditions for understanding ethical leadership, including the important task of naming different assumptions and perspectives in competing moral frameworks.

TRAIT AND SITUATIONAL APPROACHES TO INEQUALITIES IN THE LEADER–FOLLOWER RELATIONSHIP

The idea that leaders and followers merit equal treatment rests on the assumption that leaders and followers are – in fact – equals. Those who do not accept this assumption need not see inequalities in treatment between leaders and followers as any kind of affront to morality. As Aristotle articulates the formal principle of equality, '[J]ustice seems to be equality, and it is, but not for everyone, only *for equals*. Justice also seems to be inequality, since indeed it is, but not for everyone, only *for unequals*' (Aristotle 2001, 1280a10–13). In the *Republic*, Aristotle's teacher, Plato, utilized the assumption that there are differences between leaders and followers to develop what can be read as a conservative approach to the inequalities of leadership. According to Plato, leaders in the just state are drawn from a special class of highly educated guardians or 'philosopher kings'. Individuals in this class are 'fitted by nature both to engage in philosophy and to rule in a city, while the rest are naturally fitted to leave philosophy alone and follow their leader' (Plato 2001, 474b–c). Unsuited for rule, followers contribute to the division of labor as part of the auxiliary and money-making classes. Given the inequalities between leaders and followers (e.g., the guardians are 'by nature good at remembering, quick to learn, high-minded, graceful, and a friend and relative of truth, justice, courage, and moderation' [Plato 2001, 487a]), there is no need to treat leaders and followers equally. In fact it would be an injustice to do so: 'exchange and meddling is injustice … For the money-making, auxiliary, and guardian classes each to do its own work in the city, is the opposite. That's justice … ' (Plato 2001, 434c).

For Plato, trait differences between leaders and followers justify the inequalities in education and training as well as the resulting inequalities in power inherent in leader–follower relations. But the particular traits Plato extols cannot be used to justify other commonplace inequalities between leaders and followers, e.g., inequalities in wealth.[7] In fact Plato argues that the guardians should be strictly limited in their private property. Similarly, they must live in common, publicly accessible places and survive on taxes from citizens. For 'if [the guardians] acquire private land, houses, and currency themselves, they'll be household managers and farmers instead of guardians' (Plato 2001, 417a–b). Yet Plato thinks it is no mark against a theory of leadership that leaders do not get material benefits from their positions. This is because we are not 'aiming to give them the greatest happiness' but, rather, 'to see that the city as a whole has the greatest happiness' (Plato 2001, 421b). Here the more general point, one that recurs in the history of social and political theory, is that leadership is not for the good of the leader. Even the philosopher who wants nothing more than to contemplate the forms, which are the objects of knowledge for Plato, must 'go down again to the prisoners in the cave' (Plato 2001, 519d). The guardians rule, then, not for any kind of benefit to themselves. The most that they can expect is to avoid 'the greatest punishment', which is 'to be ruled by someone worse than oneself' (Plato 2001, 347c).

Aristotle agrees with Plato that the superiority of some individuals can constitute a good reason to entrench hierarchy between leaders and followers. Aristotle writes,

> [W]hen there happens to be someone who is superior in virtue ... , people would not say ... that they should rule over him. For that would be like claiming that they deserved to rule over Zeus, dividing the offices. The remaining possibility – and it seems to be the natural one – is for everyone to obey such a person gladly, so that those like him will be permanent kings in their city-states. (Aristotle 2001,1284b28–34)

But Aristotle's reference to Zeus betrays his skepticism that there might be an individual so superior in virtue. Such an individual would be a god, not a human being. This means that Aristotle accepts the trait approach to leadership in theory but not in practice. In practice, rulership must be 'based on things from which a city-state is constituted. Hence the well-born, the free, and the rich reasonably lay claim to office. For there must be both free people and those with assessed property, since a city-state cannot consist entirely of poor people, any more than of slaves' (Aristotle 2001,1283a15). Aristotle thus moderates Plato's conservative approach to the inequalities of leadership.

So for Aristotle the justification of inequalities inherent in leadership must attend to a variety of real-world differences between leaders and followers. Of course not just any differences will do. For example, 'if some are slow runners and others fast, this is no reason for the latter to have more [power] and the former less [power]' (Aristotle 2001,1283a10). Such differences between individuals are plainly irrelevant to political leadership (but perhaps not, say, to athletic or military leadership). Yet Aristotle holds that any of several other differences between individuals (e.g., whether one is well-born, free or rich) can be sufficient to justify the rule of some individuals over others. Different constitutions can be 'correct', that is, regardless of whether they make the 'authoritative element ... one person, or few, or many' (Aristotle 2001,1279a25). The correctness of the constitution is based on its contribution to the common benefit, which depends on the actual makeup of the citizenry. The actual makeup of the citizenry determines whether a constitution in the form of kingship, aristocracy or polity would make the greatest contribution to the city-state. It is for this reason that '[w]ithin each of [these] constitutions ... the decision as to who should rule is indisputable' (Aristotle 2001,1283b5). Things are more difficult, however, when 'all these [with a claim to rule] are present simultaneously' (Aristotle 2001,1283b8–9). In these circumstances, '[N]one of the definitions on the basis of which people claim that they themselves deserve to rule, whereas everyone else deserves to be ruled by them, is correct' (Aristotle 2001,1283b25). Here the most we get from Aristotle is that in the best constitution, the citizen takes his turn at both ruling and being ruled. He is 'the one who has the power and who deliberately chooses to be ruled and to rule with an eye to the virtuous life' (Aristotle 2001,1284a1–4).

Niccolò Machiavelli (1469–1527) was also sensitive to the fact that no qualities are sufficient to differentiate leaders and followers in all circumstances. Machiavelli's commitment to the situational component of leadership comes out in his oft-cited advice to leaders in *The Prince*: since we do not live an ideal world, 'you should be constantly prepared, so that, if these [positive qualities] become liabilities, you are trained and ready to become their opposites' (Machiavelli 2001 [1532], p. 452). In this work Machiavelli is primarily concerned with leadership behavior that is conducive to holding onto power, and he claims that 'it is necessary for a ruler, if he wants to hold on to power, to learn how not to be good' (Machiavelli 2001 [1532], p. 448). In important passages in his *Discourses on the First Ten Books of Titius Livius*, however, Machiavelli is less concerned with the situational ethic that leaders must exercise to hold onto power than with a general kind of behavioral flexibility necessary for effective leadership. According to Machiavelli, '[W]hether men have good or bad fortune depends on whether they adjust their style of behavior to suit the times' (Machiavelli 2001 [1531], p. 486). Here Machiavelli has in mind more morally neutral leadership qualities such as cautiousness and impetuousness.

Machiavelli is hardly optimistic that individual leaders might adapt to changing circumstances. He writes,

> There are two reasons why we are unable to change when we need to: In the first place, we cannot help being what nature has made us; in the second, if one style of behavior has worked well for us in the past, we cannot be persuaded we would be better off acting differently. The consequence is that one's fortune changes, for the times change, and one's behavior does not. (Machiavelli 2001 [1531], p. 487)

Both nature and experience, that is, conspire against a leader's ability to respond to changing circumstances. As a consequence Machiavelli prefers republics to monarchies: 'a republic should survive longer and should more frequently have fortune on its side, than a monarchy, for a republic can adapt itself more easily to changing circumstances because it can call on citizens of differing characters' (Machiavelli 2001 [1531], p. 486). Like Aristotle, then, Machiavelli thinks that we will be hard pressed to find particular differences between leaders and followers that justify the inequalities of leadership in all situations. Justification is a function of the ways in which individual qualities manifest themselves in different situations and, as we shall see, the ways in which these qualities can be combined in leader–follower relations to offset the influences of each.

Social and political thinkers often begin with a creation story or a description of the 'state of nature' to evaluate the morality of inequalities between leaders and followers. Machiavelli's creation story, which also explains why leadership is a necessary part of social life, indexes the differentiating qualities of leaders to the needs of a society at a particular time:

> When the world began, it had few inhabitants, and they lived for a while apart from one another as the animals do. As their numbers multiplied they gathered together, and in order to be better able to defend themselves, they began to defer to one among their number who was stronger and braver than the rest. They made him, as it were, their leader and obeyed him. (Machiavelli 2001 [1531], p. 472)

Soon their needs evolved to include more than mere survival, and 'when they had to choose a ruler, they no longer obeyed the strongest, but he who was most prudent and most just' (Machiavelli 2001 [1531], p. 472). In both cases, then, the fact that the rule of the monarch was for the common benefit justifies the resulting inequalities. The same is true for the distribution of power that characterizes the other constitutions that Machiavelli considers to be 'correct': aristocracy and democracy. Rule by the elite or the masses is justified when leaders put 'their own interests second and the public good first' (Machiavelli 2001 [1531], p. 472).

Despite the fact that monarchy, aristocracy and democracy are justified when they work for the common good, Machiavelli ultimately dismisses them on grounds of their instability. All three correct constitutions put too much faith in a single set of attributes, those of a person, a class of elites or the masses. As a result, each of the correct constitutions readily degenerates into its 'pernicious' counterpart: tyranny, oligarchy or anarchy. Monarchy becomes tyranny, and aristocracy becomes oligarchy, primarily because both depend upon hereditary succession. Similarly, democracy evolves into anarchy 'once the generation that had established it [has] passed away' (Machiavelli 2001 [1531], p. 472). The problem with the first two correct constitutions is that the descendents of the monarchs are often 'inferior to their ancestors' (Machiavelli 2001 [1531], p. 472) and the descendents of the aristocrats were not alive to experience the excesses of tyranny. Being unfamiliar with these evils, this new generation of aristocrats oversteps the bounds of its proper authority and is 'unwilling to continue treating their fellow subjects as their equals' (Machiavelli 2001 [1531], p. 472). As oligarchs, they ignore relevant equalities between leaders and followers, thus moving beyond the justified inequalities in power that characterize this constitution. In contrast, democracy-cum-anarchy suffers not from a lack of equality between leaders and followers but, rather, from too much of it: 'neither private individuals nor public officials could command any respect. Each person did as he chose, with the result that every day innumerable crimes were committed' (Machiavelli 2001 [1531], p. 472).[8]

Machiavelli concludes that 'all these forms of government are pestilential: The three good ones do not last long, and the three bad ones are evil' (Machiavelli 2001 [1531], p.473). Justified inequalities are a function of individual attributes in particular circumstances, but circumstances change to make the attributes of particular individuals irrelevant. Moreover, the individuals with the relevant attributes are replaced over time to make particular constitutions dangerous. The result is perpetual cycling between constitutions: monarchy to tyranny to aristocracy to oligarchy to democracy to anarchy and back to monarchy. Still, there may be a solution that draws on the attributes of the citizens in each of the correct constitutions. According to Machiavelli,

> Those who know how to construct constitutions wisely have identified this problem and have avoided each one of these types of constitution in its pure form, constructing a constitution with elements of each. They have been convinced such a constitution would be more solid and stable, would be preserved by checks and balances, there being present in the one city a monarch, an aristocracy, and a democracy. (Machiavelli 2001 [1531], p.473)[9]

TRANSACTIONAL AND TRANSFORMATIONAL APPROACHES TO INEQUALITIES IN THE LEADER–FOLLOWER RELATIONSHIP

The moral doctrine *volenti non fit injuria* holds that individuals cannot be wronged by that to which they have consented. Drawing on this line of argument, social contract theory focuses on consensual transactions among individuals in order to justify standard inequalities between leaders and followers. For social contract theorists such as Thomas Hobbes (1588–1679), the justified inequalities can be quite severe. Followers willingly transfer all power to an absolute sovereign, 'that great Leviathan', to replace the 'warre of every man against every man' that characterizes the state of nature (Hobbes 1991 [1651], p.90) with the peace and security that only strong leadership can provide: 'For by this Authoritie, given him by every particular man in the Common-Wealth, he hath the use of so much Power and Strength conferred on him, that by terror thereof, he is inabled to conform the wills of them all, to Peace at home, and mutuall ayd against their enemies abroad' (Hobbes 1991 [1651], pp.120–21). In fact on Hobbes's view, no treatment of followers can be properly deemed unjustified, regardless of how unequal the treatment might be,

> because every Subject is by this Institution Author of all the Actions, and Judgments of the Soveraigne Instituted; it followes, that whatsoever he doth, it can be no injury to any of his Subjects; nor ought he to be by any of them accused of Injustice. For he that doth any thing by authority from another, doth therein no injury to him by whose

> authority he acteth: But by this Institution of a Common-wealth, every particular man is Author of all the Soveraigne doth; and consequently he that complaineth of injury from his Soveraigne, complaineth of that whereof he himselfe is Author; and therefore ought not to accuse any man but himselfe; no nor himself of injury; because to do injury to ones selfe, is impossible. (Hobbes 1991 [1651], p. 124)

In other words consent makes followers the ultimate source of the unequal treatment. They have no one but themselves to blame for the treatment they receive from leaders.

It would be a mistake, however, to think that social contract theory puts no limits on justified inequalities between leaders and followers. Even Hobbes holds that '[t]he Obligation of Subjects to the Soveraign, is understood to last as long, and no longer, than the power lasteth, by which he is able to protect them. For the right men have by Nature to protect themselves, when none else can protect them, can by no Covenant be relinquished' (Hobbes 1991 [1651], p. 153). John Locke (1632–1704), also in the social contract tradition, was much more cautious than Hobbes about justified inequalities between leaders and followers, expressing his reservations about absolute sovereignty this way:

> As if when Men quitting the State of Nature entered into Society, they agreed that all of them but one, should be under the restraint of Laws, but that he should still retain all the Liberty of the State of Nature, increased with Power, and made licentious by Impunity. This is to think that Men are so foolish that they take care to avoid what Mischiefs may be done them by *Pole-cats*, or *Foxes*, but are content, nay think it Safety, to be devoured by *Lions*. (Locke 1988 [1690], p. 328)[10]

Accordingly Locke can be seen as advocating a moderate approach to the inequalities of leadership: '[T]he power of the Society, or *Legislative* constituted by them, *can never be suppos'd to extend farther than the common good*; but is obliged to secure every ones Property' (Locke 1988 [1690], p. 353), where *property* is understood in a broad sense to include life and liberty, in addition to estate. Still, within these limits, leaders are clearly differentiated from followers on the Lockean view, in that only the former have the power to act as indifferent judges and executioners of established law. Moreover, according to Locke, rulers should be granted the *prerogative* 'to do several things of their own free choice, where the Law was silent, and sometimes too against the direct Letter of the Law, for the publick good' (Locke 1988 [1690], p. 377).

Of the social contract theorists, no one expresses greater reservations about the inequalities between leaders and followers than Jean-Jacques Rousseau (1712–78). In his *Discourse on the Origin of Inequality*, Rousseau claims that the individuals in the state of nature were essentially duped into accepting the inequalities of political society: 'They all ran to chain themselves, in the belief that they secured their liberty, for although they had enough sense to realize the advantages of a political establishment, they did not have enough experience to foresee its dangers' (Rousseau 2001 [1755], p. 747). Worst among these dangers were those arising from the system of property rights advocated by thinkers such as Locke. According to Rousseau, '[T]he origin of society and laws ... gave new fetters to the weak and new forces to the rich, irretrievably destroyed natural liberty, established forever the law of property and of inequality, changed adroit usurpation into irrevocable right, and for the profit of a few ambitious men henceforth subjected the entire human race to labor, servitude and misery' (Rousseau 2001 [1755], p. 747). Far from allowing inequalities between leaders and followers in an effort to combat injustice, political society simply entrenches unjust inequalities.

How did leaders and followers find themselves in this condition? On Rousseau's creation story, as on Machiavelli's creation story and in the Hobbesian state of nature, individuals were forced into social units by the harsh realities of existence. But Rousseau holds that inequality arises not as a direct response to these realities, as – for example – when a leader is selected because he is 'stronger and braver than the rest' (Machiavelli 2001 [1531], p. 472). Rather, it has its roots in 'the petulant activity of our egocentrism' (Rousseau 2001 [1755], p. 743).

> People grew accustomed to gather in front of their huts or around a large tree; song and dance, true children of love and leisure, became the amusement or rather the occupation of idle men and women who had flocked together. Each one began to look at the others and to want to be looked at himself, and public esteem had a value. The one who sang or danced the best, the handsomest, the strongest, the most adroit or the most eloquent became the most highly regarded. And this was the first step toward inequality and, at the same time, toward vice ... as soon as men had begun mutually to value one another, and the idea of esteem was formed in their minds, each one claimed to have a right to it, and it was no longer possible for anyone to be lacking it with impunity. (Rousseau 2001 [1755], p. 743)

Leadership, then, is not a sacrifice of equality for the common good. Social and political organization provides little more than a context for people to make morally suspect expressions of status: 'they consent to wear chains in order to be able to give them in turn to others. It is very difficult to reduce to obedience someone who does not seek to command' (Rousseau 2001 [1755], p. 752). In other words, it is the desire to rule that first puts people in a position to be ruled by others.

Given Rousseau's seeming preference for the state of nature over political society, it might be hard to see why he would be characterized as a social contract thinker. After all, Rousseau sees natural man 'satisfying his hunger under an oak tree, quenching his thirst at the first stream, finding his bed at the foot of the same tree that supplied his meal; and thus all his needs are satisfied' (Rousseau 2001 [1755], pp. 726–7), whereas he sees social man living the life of a fraud. But it is important to notice that natural man might nevertheless be missing something valuable. Rousseau alludes to this possibility in his discussion of 'the faculty of self-perfection' (Rousseau 2001 [1755], p. 730). The desires of savage man 'do not go beyond his physical needs. The only goods he knows in the universe are nourishment, a woman and rest; the only evils he fears are pain and hunger' (Rousseau 2001 [1755], p. 731). The problem, Rousseau thinks, is that social and political arrangements as we know them do not engage the faculty of self-perfection. Not only do they fail to engage this faculty, but they also destroy natural instincts, putting man in a state of existence 'even lower than the animal itself' (Rousseau 2001 [1755], p. 730). Rousseau makes this point clear in his *On the Social Contract*. Under proper social and political arrangements,

> His faculties are exercised and developed, his ideas are broadened, his feelings are ennobled, his entire soul is elevated to such a height that, if the abuse of this new condition did not often lower his status to beneath the level he left, he ought constantly to bless the happy moment that pulled him away from it forever and which transformed him from a stupid, limited animal into an intelligent being and a man. (Rousseau 2001 [1762], p. 778)

This transformation, Rousseau thinks, ultimately requires leadership. Rousseau describes the true function of leadership this way:

> He who dares to undertake the establishment of a people should feel that he is, so to speak, in a position to change human nature, to transform each individual (who by himself is a perfect and solitary whole), into a part of a larger whole from which this individual receives, in a sense, his life and his being; to alter man's constitution in order to strengthen it; and to substitute a partial and moral existence for the physical and independent existence we have all received from nature. (Rousseau 2001 [1762], p. 786)

Ultimately this kind of leadership rests not in a person but in the citizenry. The point of this radical approach to the inequalities of leadership is that all citizens are legislators: 'the sovereign is formed entirely from the private individuals who make it up' (Rousseau 2001 [1762], p. 777). Sovereignty is exercised through expression of the general will, which prioritizes the common interest over the private interest of each particular citizen. The citizen who must sacrifice his private interest has no grounds for complaint because the moral liberty that characterizes obedience to the general will represents the highest form of freedom, higher even than the natural liberty he had in the state of nature. Where there is a conflict between his private interest and the common interest 'he will be forced to be free' (Rousseau 2001 [1762], p. 778). As a complete equal with other citizens, it only seems that this is a case of unequal treatment, when – in fact – he is acting on his better self, a self transformed through social and political organization.

UTILITARIAN AND KANTIAN APPROACHES TO THE RELATIONSHIP BETWEEN GROUPS AND OUTSIDERS

All of the social and political theories discussed in the previous sections agree that good leadership must be in the interests of followers. Where they disagree is on how much inequality between leaders and followers can be justified in pursuit of the common interest. Thus far we have equated the common interest with the interests of leaders and followers alone.[11] We turn now to a second main question about inequality that arises when we notice that outsiders also have interests, which sometimes compete with the interests of leaders and followers. Liberal moral theory, of which utilitarianism and Kantianism are paradigm examples, is committed to the claim that individuals count equally, regardless of group membership. On these theories at least, it is hard to see how leaders and followers might be justified in putting their interests and projects ahead of the interests and projects of members of the outgroup. For example, utilitarianism holds that the capacity for happiness and suffering is the only morally relevant characteristic, and we can assume that this capacity does not differ with membership in social groups.[12] The same can be said for the central characteristic that Kantians find morally relevant, namely, the capacity for rationality. On the face of it, then, both moral theories conflict with what many see as a defining characteristic of leadership as we know it: leaders and followers must be willing to put the interests and projects of group members ahead of the interests and projects of outsiders. In most cases, without this kind of unequal consideration, leadership would not be recognizable to us (Price 2006, ch. 4).

Utilitarian moral theory, as developed by philosophers such as Jeremy Bentham (1748–1832), John Stuart Mill (1806–73), R.M. Hare (1919–2002) and Peter Singer (1946–), holds that the morality of an action is determined by the overall happiness or well-being produced by that action. The right action is the one that maximizes happiness over suffering and pain. Utilitarians have a very straightforward answer to the question of whose happiness is the object of maximization. Although leadership exercised in the interests of followers is often described as 'utilitarian', such a description deviates from standard utilitarian moral theory. According to utilitarianism, leaders should consider the happiness of the whole, where this includes not just group members but members of the outgroup as well. In fact, the moral concern of contemporary utilitarians typically extends to all sentient beings. So it is not enough to add only the effects on the members of one's group, society or country into the utilitarian calculus. The morally correct action is the action that maximizes overall utility, which can sometimes result in a decrease in utility for leaders and followers.

Of course there can be utilitarian reasons for a leader to privilege the interests of group members. For instance, short-term attention to follower happiness and well-being may be necessary for long-term increases in overall utility. In other words, privileging the ingroup can be instrumental to achieving utilitarian goals, as when making sure that members of the group are well fed, rested and satisfied is a means to getting them to work in service to others needier than they. Moreover it is sometimes the case that attention to follower happiness and well-being is justified on utilitarian grounds because there is no one needier than followers, or it would be an inefficient use of resources to attend to the happiness or well-being of those who are in fact the neediest. The point, however, is that utilitarianism cannot allow leaders to favor some individuals merely on the grounds they are part of the ingroup.

John Stuart Mill may have made it sound as though this kind of behavior would be permissible for leaders. In *Utilitarianism* he suggests that there are few occasions on which a person can be 'a public benefactor' and that 'private utility, the interest or happiness of some few persons, is all he has to attend to' (Mill 1979 [1861], p. 19). But Mill's point is a practical implication of 19th-century social circumstances. As Peter Singer puts it,

> This may once have been a justification for being more concerned with the poor in one's own town than with famine victims in India. Unfortunately for those who like to keep their moral responsibilities limited, instant communication and swift transportation have changed the situation ... There would seem, therefore, to be no possible justification for discriminating on geographical grounds. (Singer 1972, p. 232)

In this respect the demands of utilitarianism are very much dependent on facts about the world. Mill and Singer are in basic agreement about the principles of morality, but the application of these principles will vary according to changes in social circumstances. Their disagreement, that is, is empirical.

One might object that the argument for equal consideration ignores stronger utilitarian reasons for giving special attention to the interests of group members. Support for this objection would point to what might be called 'the moral division of labor'. It makes good utilitarian sense, so this objection goes, to ask people to attend to the happiness and well-being of the ingroup, not humanity as a whole. After all it would hardly maximize utility to spread our moral concern too thinly. For example, there is greater overall happiness and well-being in a world in which parents attend to the interests of their own children, as compared with a world in which parents give equal attention to the interests of all children. The same might be said for giving exclusive attention to the interests of one's group, society or country. But this is a plausible utilitarian objection only in circumstances in which the moral division of labor does not leave too much room for members of the outgroup to have high utility deficits. If many outsiders are completely ignored by the division of moral labor, perhaps because they have bad leaders or disadvantaged economic opportunities, then overall utility would be maximized by giving more attention to outsiders and less attention to one's group, society or country. A similar point can be made with respect to the utility of children. Many children do not have parents to attend especially to them, or their parents are unable to give them the kind of attention they need. In these real-world circumstances, overall utility would be maximized if other parents would shift some of the moral concern they show for their own children to much needier children.[13]

A second line of objection draws on a variant of utilitarianism called 'rule utilitarianism' to justify special attention for the ingroup. Rule utilitarianism holds that rules, not acts, are the proper object of moral deliberation. We should act according to rules that, if followed by everyone, would maximize utility. The argument for rule utilitarianism is simply that we do not want people determining whether, for example, lying in a particular case would maximize utility. Giving this kind of discretion to moral actors would ultimately lead to a decrease in overall utility. Accordingly the second objection to the claim that utilitarianism does not allow leaders and followers to privilege the interests of members of the ingroup is as follows: Although there are particular cases in which giving greater consideration to the interests of outsiders would lead to an overall increase in utility, the kind of flexibility moral actors would need to make these determinations risks undermining the obvious utility gains achieved by unwavering commitment to the group.

Now this general way of thinking about rule utilitarianism often makes perfect sense. In some cases lying would certainly maximize utility, but allowing individuals to make exceptions when exceptions are justified opens the door to their making exceptions when exceptions are not justified. But the more particular worry is that individuals will make exceptions of themselves not for the sake of overall utility but for the sake of self-interest. There is no analogy to the cases in which leaders and followers might need to show less than exclusive concern for the interests of the ingroup. Exception making in the first set of cases thus feeds on the psychological tendency of individuals to care more about themselves than they care about others. This is why it is dangerous to give them moral discretion. In contrast, behavior that shows greater concern for the interests of the outgroup at the expense of ingroup competes with a different psychological tendency of individuals, namely, to care more about group members than about outsiders. This is what social psychologists call 'ingroup bias'. As a consequence there should be little worry that by asking leaders and followers to consider more than the interests of group members, we will somehow undermine the utilitarian payoffs of group membership.

Kantianism is more able than utilitarianism to justify the much greater attention that leaders and followers give to group members. This is not to deny that morality sometimes requires strictly equal treatment. According to Immanuel Kant (1724–1804), we must respect the rational faculties of all persons, treating them *'never simply as a means, but always at the same time as an end'* (Kant 1956 [1785], p. 96). By way of example, this implies that lying is always unjustified, regardless of whether it is to ingroup or outgroup members.[14] Lying bypasses the rational faculties of persons and, in so doing, treats them as instruments or objects in the liar's plans. But it does not follow from this basic moral demand that leaders and followers have all the same obligations to outsiders that they have to group members. Like lying, promise breaking is also always unjustified because it treats the person to whom the promise was made as a mere means. But notice that we can break promises only to those people to whom we have made promises. Therefore, to whatever extent leadership can be understood to embody promises between leaders and followers, leaders and followers can have obligations to each other and to other group members that they do not have to outsiders.

The moral demand that individuals not treat others as mere means is strong in the sense that it applies in all circumstances, but it is relatively weak in the sense that it does not require any positive consideration of others. This is because it tells us only what behaviors we are morally *not to do*, not what behaviors we morally *ought to do*. However the Kantian rider that we must treat others *'always at the same time as an end'* (Kant 1956 [1785], p. 96) makes the demand significantly stronger. By this Kant means that part of respecting the rational capacity of others is to see their plans and goals as worthy of support and to help them in the pursuit of their plans and goals, even when we have met all of our negative duties to them. One Kantian argument for giving serious consideration to the plans and goals of those to whom we do not have special obligations, e.g., outsiders, is that failing to do so constitutes a *contradiction in will* (Kant 1956 [1785], p. 91). If I refuse to help outsiders with their plans and goals, then I must be willing to accept seeing my behavior universalized. But I cannot accept seeing my behavior universalized because I will at some point in my life need the help of someone who has no special obligations to me. It is unreasonable to will that I not provide help and, at the same time, to will that others help me. The point here is not that my getting help as an outsider in the future depends on my helping an outsider now. It is rather that I contradict myself when I will both that outsiders not be helped and that I be helped when I am an outsider.

Still, for Kant, these duties are relatively weak. He calls them 'wider' or 'meritorious' duties to distinguish them from the 'strict or narrow' duties that apply in all circumstances (Kant 1956 [1785], p. 91). When it comes to the wider or meritorious duties, Kant holds that we have a fair amount of flexibility in carrying them out. This makes perfect sense on Kant's account. After all, any Kantian duty we might have, for example, to help others in the pursuit of their plans and goals, is ultimately traceable to the fact that we have our own plans and goals to pursue. Without these plans and goals, the contradiction in will cannot be generated. There is thus a sense in which our plans and goals, as well as the plans and goals we pursue with others in groups, are conceptually prior to any duty we might have to help outsiders pursue their plans and goals. It is for this reason that it is easier for Kantians than for utilitarians to justify the much greater attention that leaders and followers give to the ingroup. Leadership is the social counterpart to individual rationality. People use this process to achieve plans and goals that could not otherwise be achieved. Since these plans and goals are conceptually prior to any duty they might have to help outsiders achieve their plans and goals, the corresponding inequalities in treatment between group members and outsiders lend themselves to Kantian moral justification.

LEADERSHIP IN GOOD AND JUST SOCIETIES: CONTEMPORARY PHILOSOPHICAL APPROACHES

The perspectives outlined thus far deeply influence contemporary moral debates about leadership in good and just societies. The two central questions raised in the historical analysis – namely, inequality within leader–follower relations and inequality between ingroup and outgroup members – remain foci for moral analysis. In an era marked by increasing facility of communication and coordination (and hence fewer practical difficulties, such as those described by Mill, of extending one's reach beyond immediate neighbors), questions of the boundaries of political, social and economic groups and of how much inequality is tolerable between those groups have an increasingly prominent place in the analysis of ethics and leadership. Technological advances and the phenomenon of globalization add new ethical complexities to both leader–follower relations and identification with so-called outsiders.

Drawing on social contract theory and Kantianism, the political and moral philosopher John Rawls (1921–2002) framed contemporary questions of inequality and political society with his landmark book, *A Theory of Justice*. Arguing that the subject of justice is institutions, not individuals, Rawls sees the first act of leadership as establishing a 'just basic structure' of society based upon freedom and equality. Within his approach of justice-as-fairness, *fair equality of opportunity* assures that leadership positions should be open to everyone on an equitable basis. Coupled with the principle of *equal liberty*, Rawls creates a framework that sets the limits of permissible political and economic inequality among group members. Rawls's *difference principle* does allow for certain types of inequalities, as long as they benefit the least well-off in society.[15] In overall terms justice-as-fairness allows for leader–follower disparities, but only under strict conditions meant to maintain political and moral equality. Thus, on the first question of permissible inequalities, Rawls advocates the moderate approach within our framework.

As we turn to the question of inequalities between ingroups and outgroups, it is important to note that the ideal framework of Rawls's justice-as-fairness is that of a well-ordered nation state. Accordingly Rawls's principles of justice do not apply directly to international arrangements because, as he argues in his essay *The Law of Peoples*, the social contract applies to one's principal political community, and there are not sufficient political or moral ties beyond the national level to enact or maintain such strong agreement (Rawls 1999). Thus Rawls argues for a morally relevant difference between ingroups and outgroups. Justice-as-fairness is developed by looking at a particular society as 'a closed system isolated from other societies' (Rawls 1971, p. 8). Rawls's account of the law of peoples extends his theory 'outward' to consider justice in a more international or transnational context. Despite objections that would have Rawls *begin* at the global level, Rawls takes as his starting point the work he has already undertaken, which begins with the domestic level and can be 'extended' to the global level as a second step. Rawls thus places primary emphasis on leader–follower relationships within societies, treating as a second-level analysis the question of relations between ingroups (citizens of nation states) and outgroups (non-citizens).

Because justice-as-fairness builds upon the standard assumption of liberalism that citizenship in a nation state is a person's primary political identity, Rawls permits significant levels of inequalities between the leaders and followers of one nation, on the one hand, and people from other nations, on the other hand. The very restrictive difference principle that operates within a well-ordered society cannot be applied internationally. Societies that make 'better' economic decisions need not compensate persons in other societies, and there is currently no international body that could enforce this principle without becoming unjustifiably coercive. Rawls also notes that often the most serious problems of deprivation in less developed societies are grounded in political culture and public values; the difference principle would simply be the wrong way of going about redressing such difficulties. Just as important, the requisite guarantees of equal liberty and the fair equality of opportunity could not be established across national boundaries.

Under the law of peoples, then, the stringent difference principle would not be applied across societies. For this reason critics have charged that Rawls's approach to international affairs is overly conservative in its approach to inequalities. Not unlike Kantianism in this regard, the additional obligations to members of one's own community can permit significant inequality between the ingroup and outgroups. Nonetheless, nation states do have some obligations to one another. Rawls's account of the *duty of assistance* extends to assuring basic human rights and to meeting basic needs. Rawls argues that his presentation of the law of peoples would at least compel wealthier societies and their citizens to play a part – though Rawls does not specify exactly what part – in assuring that persons in poorer societies are not left destitute. While not nearly as strict as the limits of leader–follower inequalities, this does place some constraint on the tolerable inequality between citizens of one country and another.

In a second response to questions about our responsibility to outgroups, Rawls envisions a particular role for the enlightened leader – the *statesman* – to help his followers transcend narrow national self-interest in their involvements in the international arena. These '[s]tatesmen are presidents or prime ministers or other high officials who, through their exemplary performance and leadership in their office, manifest strength, wisdom, and courage [and] ... guide their people in turbulent and dangerous times' (Rawls 1999, p. 97). Statesmen help their followers build the 'affinity' or solidarity among people within one's society and in other societies so that some degree of social bonds will be established and antipathies will be sufficiently reduced in order to allow mutual or one-way assistance. This latter point suggests that good leadership tends to reduce extreme inequalities between nations in ways not developed in earlier social contract theories.

While Rawls's political liberalism has set the parameters of the moral debate about leadership and inequality, communitarian and cosmopolitan critics alike have questioned many of Rawls's assumptions and conclusions. Communitarian critics assert the problematic nature of liberalism's foundations. Specifically, they name what they see as a bias toward individualism over community, as well as a bias toward autonomy over identity and commitment. Michael Sandel (1982), for instance, criticizes Rawls for his methodology in which subjects design a just basic structure from behind 'the veil of ignorance', which ensures that the contracting parties do not know fundamental aspects of their identity. In the eyes of his communitarian critics, Rawls views all commitments as 'associative', or voluntary, rather than as 'constitutive', or non-voluntary. Some aspects of identity are not, however, subject to one's own choice. Indeed, to view commitments as voluntarily made by individuals, as if they are isolated from family members and other accidents of birth, is to lose any sense of a social whole that may be greater than the sum of its individual citizens.

Communitarians suggest that justice cannot be determined in the way that Rawls imagines, via a thought experiment by which any rational individual behind a 'veil of ignorance' would find justice-as-fairness to be a compelling conception. While Rawls intended his theory to be employed to condemn identity-based disparities, critics have maintained that his approach cannot provide adequate critique of oppression based upon factors of identity (such as gender, race/ethnicity and religion) in actual societies. On this point feminists have joined the critics of Rawls in viewing liberalism as incapable of denouncing some of the inequalities that it claims to reject.[16]

A different type of communitarian critique has been leveled against Rawls's justice-as-fairness – namely, that the liberal biases *in favor of equality* are built into his starting assumptions. Critics allege that there is no way to make the case that the egalitarianism of Rawls's justice-as-fairness is superior to well-ordered hierarchy apart from assumptions that are inherent to liberalism itself. That is, if a given society holds the general belief that women are morally inferior to men, then nothing from Rawls's approach to the contrary will be convincing. On this point a group of economists and anthropologists argues that Western-influenced economic development brings with it Western ideologies and necessarily destroys local worldviews that tend to be hierarchical; this process does not happen because the Western worldview is morally superior but, rather, only because it has more economic, political and sometimes military power (Apffel-Marglin and Marglin 1990). Liberals have responded to such criticisms with their own analysis of power – asserting that freedom, equality and democracy are not exclusively Western concepts. Amartya Sen, for example, suggests that thinkers in many so-called 'Asian cultures' have articulated strong visions of gender-based equality and human freedom, even if they have often been silenced by authoritarian voices (Sen 1999).

In general terms, then, liberalism holds a central place for equality; this is not necessarily the case in communitarianism. Admittedly some utopian communities – and their advocates – have held at their core a vision of radical egalitarianism as a means, and as an integral part, of realizing a strong community. More often, however, advocates of communalism over individualism favor a conservative approach to inequalities, often in the strong-handed form, such as Lee Kuan Yew's Singaporean regime and its justifiers. While communitarianism can range from equality to hierarchy – and hence from the radical approach to the conservative approach – it provides strong reason for permitting inequalities between ingroups and outgroups. Indeed, as Michael Walzer (a critic of both unbridled liberalism and zealous communitarianism) asserts, membership is the key good that comprises political society, and if there were no way for a society to enforce its borders, it would not have an identity (Walzer 1983). While Walzer and others caution against the excesses of parochialism (which can justify superiority), communitarians permit the exclusive (or nearly exclusive) focus upon one's own people. For example, in Alasdair MacIntyre's view, political morality 'requires that I strive to further the interests of my community and you strive to further those of yours' (MacIntyre 1994 [1984], p. 309).[17] This focusing on one's own membership and differentiating oneself from other persons and groups can have the effect of justifying inequality between the ingroup and outgroups.

In contrast to the communitarians, cosmopolitans criticize political liberals for being too parochial – and thus too conservative in their outlook on international inequalities. Specifically they criticize Rawls and others for taking the nation state as the starting point for analysis of politics and morality. Cosmopolitans, those who take world citizenship or membership as a principal unit and proper scope for moral analysis, argue that national boundaries have little or no moral significance. As noted in section IV, Peter Singer argues that proximity and distance have no relevance when assessing utility. The only reasons to favor utility gains or losses of one person over another would be, first, practical concerns about ability to affect persons 'far' from one's sphere of influence or, second, a related argument for universal preference for 'nearby' persons (this is the 'moral division of labor' considered above). The foundational claim is that the political starting point for both liberals and communitarians – namely, the nation state – has little moral relevance. Outcomes that are permissible in these two approaches – enabling vast inequalities with perhaps a weak duty of assistance to save outgroup members from absolute destitution – would clearly not be morally acceptable in full-fledged utilitarianism.

A few further notes are in order regarding utilitarianism. First, for Singer the analysis of utility extends beyond the human race to all sentient beings. To analyze the impact of leadership on the pain and pleasure of sentient beings would be radical indeed, including a fuller examination of the 'environmental impacts' (in which all non-human forms of life are standardly cast) of particular policies and practices.

Another issue that arises for a utilitarian such as Singer is how strictly to adhere to what he understands morality to require. In his classic article, 'Famine, Affluence, and Morality', Singer offers both a strong and a weak form of what morality requires in a worldwide case of vast resource disparity – in which one group of persons suffers from acute hunger and another group enjoys prodigal affluence (Singer 1972). The strong form of the principle requires assistance from the richer person up to the point that giving any more would place his or her marginal utility below that of the poorer person; this position is clearly a radical approach to inequalities. The weaker form of the principle – which Singer finds little reason to prefer to the stronger form – requires 'merely' giving up those things that are not of moral significance in order to assist the person who is clearly suffering. In a recent work Singer significantly weakens the position he takes in 'Famine, Affluence, and Morality', and he does so for what is a second-order utilitarian reason. In order to maximize overall utility by factoring in that persons will not respond well to overly demanding moral dicta, the demands upon persons can be reduced. In this case Singer calls for the affluent to contribute – as a minimum for an adequate moral life – 1 percent of their incomes toward the assistance of persons in needier cultures and contexts. This is a far cry, to be sure, from equalizing marginal utilities, but it is still a move in the direction toward reducing inequality between human beings and between countries (Singer 2002, pp. 185–95).

Presumably Singer would use similar thinking to justify those inequalities between leaders and followers that tend to increase overall utility. Particularly in his more recent writings Singer acknowledges the motivational problems of convincing persons to uphold the demands of morality, and his recent shifts on the duty of assistance can also justify significant privileges for leaders, as long as they contribute to an overall rise in utility. Hence this shift opens Singer up to the classic criticism of consequentialism – viz., that nearly any kind of privilege can be justified in such calculations.

While pure utilitarians tend to be cosmopolitans, to be a cosmopolitan does not require one to be a utilitarian. In her supportive analysis of cosmopolitanism, Martha Nussbaum explains at least two types of possible motivations for cosmopolitanism. First, when a person has compassion for others and thus experiences empathy for other human beings and other sentient beings, she or he can be led to respond with aid. Exercising the moral imagination – seeing the predicament that other persons face in their particular circumstances – can allow persons to transcend their own narrow interests or the interests of their nearest neighbors. Alternatively, cosmopolitanism can be based upon commitment to abstract principles, such as respect for the equal human dignity of all persons (Nussbaum 2003). On this point Nussbaum has in mind, above all, Kantianism. This is for good reason. For its part, utilitarianism could be supported by a motivational argument from compassion, but it is more convincingly a principle-based application of the capacity of all persons and other sentient beings to experience pleasure and pain. Singer, for example, is critical of the whimsical nature of compassion.

Upholding a commitment to dignity or some other value, regardless of one's emotions or sentiments or imagination, thus appears to be the more reliable of the two kinds of motivation. While it can extend to all persons or beings, imaginative compassion tends to allow persons to focus on those like themselves. It takes extraordinary virtue to imagine the moral value of persons and beings near and far away. Nussbaum herself criticizes the misapplication of compassion that can readily turn into jingoism and care for only 'one's own kind'. At the same time, adherence to abstract principles, whether equal dignity or maximization of utility, may not generate the kind of motivation required to complete the task. Perhaps this motivational problem helps explain Rawls's call for the statesman to act, communitarians' retreat into their own group and Singer's need to weaken the moral demands of international assistance. Nussbaum's own position is to temper compassion with moral education about equality and respect for people of diverse cultures. For her the motivation of compassion must be harnessed by the constraints of dignity in order to achieve a sense of moral community beyond the local or national level.

In its various forms cosmopolitanism is highly egalitarian in its approach both to leader–follower relationships and to international relations among nation states. The compassion-based view would call, as Rawlsianism does, for leaders who are set apart by their capacity to spark the moral imagination of their followers. Howard Gardner, emphasizing the need to spark imagination and vision through narrative, calls these persons 'leading minds' who reach the 'five-year-old mind' of followers (Gardner 1995, pp. 25–9). It is reasonable to surmise that Nussbaum and other advocates of enlightened compassion would allow special privileges for such leaders, with the important constraint that privileges must not violate the foundational ethos of equality among leaders and followers. Thus cosmopolitans lean toward the radical position among our three approaches, although some limited inequalities that promote overall equality among ingroup and outgroup members can be allowed.

ETHICAL APPROACHES IN LEADERSHIP STUDIES

This section examines three approaches to the study of leadership in terms of the central questions explored in this essay: inequality within the leader–follower relationship and inequality between ingroups and outsiders. Approaching ethics and leadership by asking these two questions provides a fresh framework for highlighting the distinctions among the approaches as well as ambiguities inherent in each of them.

Arguably the most influential recent theory of leadership is James MacGregor Burns's account of 'transforming leadership', which was set forth in his 1978 classic text, *Leadership*, and subsequently developed in his own writings and in the work of other scholars. Transforming leadership is an alternative to, and is more demanding than, transactional leadership, in which two parties come together for an exchange of valued goods and, while they respect each other as persons, they form no lasting bond or relationship. Traditional social contract theorists, including Hobbes and Locke, have transactional leadership do most of the work in maintaining a just society. Leadership by transactions addresses issues of inequality principally in terms of commutative justice: the parties must both have agency enough to come to the transaction of their own accord, without coercion. At certain levels of political or economic inequality among a population, this requirement is difficult to attain.[18] Thus it remains minimalist compared with transforming leadership, which – in contrast – presumes a level of significant, mutual engagement by leaders and followers. In Burns's view, the transformational process has the effect of increasing the level of motivation and morality of both leader and follower. This account of transforming leadership echoes the depth of commitment in the social order articulated in most detail in the Western canon by Rousseau. Similar to Rousseau, Burns describes the highly positive impact that being part of such a relationship can have upon leader and follower. And not surprisingly this relationship is highly egalitarian at its core. The ideal of the transformational process is that followers are raised up to the level of leaders; followers, that is, become leaders.

This is not to say, however, that some forms of exceptions cannot be made for leaders that create certain inequalities between them and their followers. On the contrary, Burns leaves significant room for leaders to justify their privileges by appeal to what he calls end-values; he places special emphasis on the pursuit of liberty that could allow a leader to overlook standard requirements of morality that are otherwise equally applicable to leaders and followers alike. His examination of Franklin D. Roosevelt's use of deception during World War II is one such case in point. Although Burns's approach is at bottom egalitarian, transforming leaders are set apart – at least temporarily – from followers by the special insight they have into the needs and values of followers.

It is through transforming leadership that lasting, significant social change occurs. The heroes of Burns's writing are those figures who risk their careers, and their very lives in many cases, in order to achieve social transformation. Mohandas K. Gandhi and Franklin D. Roosevelt are paradigmatic transforming leaders. Enlightenment philosophers and politicians, who ushered in an era of fundamental political change, also receive Burns's praise. Conversely Burns is brutally critical of leaders who approach leadership only in transactional terms; even those broadly viewed as successful at transactional exchange, such as Bill Clinton, earn Burns's scorn for their failure to risk genuine progress and for their concession to the status quo (Burns and Sorenson 1999).

Burns's commitment to social change as well as his strong conviction about the rights of all people as enumerated in the Universal Declaration of Human Rights (1948) place stringent constraints on the inequality that his frame permits between group members and outsiders. To the degree that being an agent within the transformational process is a positive good for Burns, this does create one kind of inequality between participants and non-participants in the leadership process. Yet Burns's reply to this possible critique is that he would open the leadership process to all persons as quickly as is practical. His recent call for international 'freedom leaders' to work alongside local agents in the fight against poverty in the developing world is one example of his desire to overcome serious inequalities of material status as well as of participation (Burns 2003, pp. 231–40). Although his vision is more egalitarian than Rawls's law of peoples in the international arena, his standard acceptance of the nation-state system does not qualify him as a cosmopolitan. This fact, combined with his justification of certain forms of special status and function for leaders, makes Burns more moderate than fully radical in his approach.

Robert K. Greenleaf's servant leadership offers interesting answers to our two central questions, but his account is not precise enough to provide detailed philosophical answers (Greenleaf 1977). Greenleaf promises to turn some aspects of the inequality questions on their heads, by suggesting that the leader should make himself lower than the follower – and, potentially – lower than other persons as well. This basic idea is communicated in an oft-quoted passage:

The servant-leader *is* servant first … [One] begins with the natural feeling that one wants to serve, to serve *first*. Then conscious choice brings one to aspire to lead. That person is sharply different from one who is *leader* first, perhaps because of the need to assuage an unusual power drive or to acquire material possessions. (Greenleaf 1977, p. 13)

Greenleaf suggests that the motivation of the leader should not be material or other privileges. While he does not denounce leaders for holding significant possessions (a point that undoubtedly makes it simpler than it perhaps should be for CEOs and other privileged persons to dub themselves 'servant leaders'), Greenleaf implies by his examples that the leader should eschew privileges, live modestly and lead quietly. Not unlike transforming leadership in this regard, the test of good servant leadership is 'Do those served grow as persons? Do they, *while being served*, become healthier, wiser, freer, more autonomous, more likely themselves to become servants?' (Greenleaf 1977, pp. 13–14) The growth in agency of followers is a key measure of servant leadership. Yet, unlike transforming leadership, the mutual benefits to the leader are not emphasized. Servant leadership in its most literal form implies that inequalities run in favor of the followers over the leaders. Critiques of servant leadership often focus on the failure of an earnest servant leader to attend to his or her own legitimate needs as a result (e.g., Hill 1991; Hicks 2005). While in practice would-be servant leaders may not typically go this far, a strong reading of Greenleaf would seem to justify inequalities that demean the servant leaders themselves.

What about the relationship between the participants (leaders and followers) in the servant-leadership process and outsiders? One might surmise that Greenleaf's strong view of servant leadership suggests that leaders and followers alike should subordinate their interests and well-being to those of the neediest persons in society. In other words leaders and followers are together servants to the wider society's most basic needs. If Greenleaf were to take such a line, his approach would be subject to the same kind of critique about subservience just noted. Yet Greenleaf takes a surprisingly reserved approach to this question. His second test of servant leadership asks: 'What is the effect on the least privileged in society; will they benefit, or, at least, not be further deprived?' (Greenleaf 1977, p. 14). To be sure, the question of the benefit to the least privileged is suggestive of the Rawlsian difference principle, whereby the measure of success is increasing the well-being of the least well-off. But the additional phrase, 'at least not be further deprived', seems to allow near indifference toward the neediest. If this latter condition applies, then servant leadership can permit, counter-intuitively, a significant increase in inequality between the ingroup and outsiders.[19] This feature of servant leadership makes the theory difficult to classify. Greenleaf's approach to leader–follower relations is certainly radical, but his approach to the inequalities between the ingroup and outgroups is moderate at best.

Several accounts of spiritual leadership suggest that goodness, truth and justice will be increased when the spiritual dimension, variously described, of leaders and followers is welcomed in the leadership process. There is no scholarly consensus on the definition of spiritual leadership; indeed, a survey of the literature indicates that it is defined to include elements from self-discovery and wholeness to creativity, community and interdependence. Consistently, however, models of spiritual leadership, like transforming and servant leadership, place high value on the full participation of leaders and followers. Indeed, advocates of this approach assert that secular leadership processes generally force leaders and followers to divorce important aspects of their identity – namely, their spiritual or religious values – from their role in the leadership process. As we will see, the different definitions of spiritual leadership can justify either significant equality or inequality of various kinds.[20]

In theory, the spiritual leadership approach should tend to create equality among leaders and followers, allowing them each to bring their 'whole person' to the leadership process.[21] Secular forms of leadership, according to advocates of the spiritual approach, entail unequal treatment of spiritual or religious persons who are forced to make undue sacrifices of identity in order to engage in the group and its process. While these discussions are often couched in terms of spiritual expression or even religious freedom, they tend to have an equalizing effect. One problem with this view, however, is that some persons, including atheists, will believe that the prevalence and influence of spiritual views makes them less than full participants.

Religious and spiritual worldviews, as strong aspects of identity formed over time among like-minded persons, are in many ways communitarian. Although they can be based partly or wholly on rationality, religious convictions can be seen as constitutive aspects of identity that are beyond moral analysis. As noted above, if a religious person believes that women simply are inferior to men, it is difficult to convince that person otherwise. Yet religious and spiritual convictions can also be sources of egalitarian social struggle (including along gender-based lines). The key point is that welcoming a plethora of spiritual and religious views into a leadership process may increase the importance of effective communication and healthy negotiation of conflict.

In practice, the challenges of spiritual leadership are compounded by at least two factors. First, while all spiritual and religious views may be welcome in theory, the beliefs and practices of the leader can take a predominant place. Spirituality or religion in leadership is often translated into a nearly exclusive focus upon the faith of the leaders themselves.[22] The beliefs and practices of followers or subordinates are much less studied or emphasized in practice. Second, the spirituality or religion of the majority can receive undue attention or a privileged status. In the USA, for example, spiritual leadership often translates into Christian-based leadership, which can lead to an acceptance of one religious worldview as the official worldview of a group or organization. This can have the clear effect of privileging persons from that background and of marginalizing persons from minority traditions. This preference for one perspective over another contributes to inequality. One measure of equality, then, is the degree of respect afforded to leaders, and especially followers, from spiritual or religious minorities.

Spirituality and religion in leadership are often strong aspects of group cohesion and identity. As critics of religion in public life frequently note, traditional political liberalism, for its part, had its rise in response to the 16th- and 17th-century wars of religion in Europe. Like other types of strong community, religiously or spiritually influenced groups may well find conservative justifications for treating themselves as different from – and in many cases, superior to – outsiders. At the same time, however, the type of spiritually *diverse* groups described above can model mutual respect amongst themselves. If this mutual respect is based upon a fundamental conviction of the dignity of all persons, then that same commitment can encourage equal treatment toward outsiders and thus a more radical approach to inequalities. Yet as in other cases – such as Kantianism, communitarianism and transforming and servant leadership – the value of participation itself and deep obligations toward fellow group members tend to justify inequalities that give preference to ingroup members over outsiders.

CONCLUSIONS

While there are many ways to frame an analysis of ethics and leadership, this chapter has suggested that historical and contemporary approaches can be fruitfully dissected and distinguished from one another by focusing on how they justify or condemn hierarchy and inequality. A background issue that often goes unquestioned is the composition of the leaders and followers in the first place. Who is included as a participant? Who is left out? From the ancient Greeks, who had specific requirements for citizenship in the *polis* (excluding many men as well as women, children and slaves), to contemporary cosmopolitans, who argue there is no morally relevant reason not to include all human beings, the issue of participation in the leadership process has been fundamental.

Within the leader–follower relationship, the classic answer has been one of presumed equality unless and until inequalities of power, status and privileges can be justified. Some communitarian critiques of liberalism have suggested that inequality can be justified by simple reference to tradition, but this type of hierarchicalism is increasingly hard to defend in the present era. The difficulties of maintaining monarchy – beyond mere ceremony – in western European countries (and, arguably, in the Middle East) is just one example. At the other extreme servant leadership opens the possibility that leaders would actually subordinate themselves to followers.

Disparities between group members and outsiders raise a question with a wider array of answers among leadership perspectives. And since theorists tend to focus exclusively on the leader–follower relationship, they also leave more ambiguity in their particular answers to this second question. In most approaches in which significant inequality is allowed, it is not because one group is considered morally superior to the other. Rather it has to do with claims about special obligations of leaders and followers to one another. It can also simply be an unintended result of a preoccupation with treating followers appropriately. As we have asserted, practical developments under the broad phenomenon of globalization may lessen some, but perhaps not all, of the reasons for upholding special obligations. At the other end of the spectrum, for the cosmopolitans (whether their motivation is based in compassion or moral principle), the relationship between group members and outsiders can be seen as the more foundational question. How leaders and followers relate to one another must then be addressed within the context of the answer to this question.

To assert that moral philosophers and social critics alike generally begin from a presumption of equality, and that inequalities must be justified, is not to say that both theorists and practitioners of leadership have not perennially bent over backwards to justify exceptions not only for themselves, but for 'their own kind' within ingroups. The emphasis on equality in this chapter suggests that while leadership often embodies hierarchy and inequality, leaders (and followers) who would justify privileges for themselves bear the burden of proof.

NOTES

1. For the general theory group's discussion of the question 'What is it about the human condition that makes leadership necessary?', see J. Thomas Wren's contribution to this volume 'A Quest for a Grand Theory of Leadership'.
2. This aspect of the problem is in the background of most all discussions within the general theory group, and it serves as part of the justification of the place within leadership studies of what James MacGregor Burns refers to as 'the key elements of leadership': power, motivation, leader–follower relations, and values. Again, see Wren, 'A Quest for a Grand Theory of Leadership'.
3. To be sure, a key question for moral analysis is 'equality of what?' While modern Western thinkers generally accept a premise of equality, the currency of equality – whether utility, primary goods, opportunity, etc. – is under debate. See Hicks (2000), ch. 2.
4. It is possible for an approach to leadership to be strongly hierarchical as a means toward achieving the end of increased equality. See, for example, W.E.B. Du Bois's account of the 'Talented Tenth' among African-Americans, the aim of which was to elevate African-Americans as a whole and to create a more equal America (W.E.B. Du Bois 1996 [1903]).
5. In fact, a determination of acceptable inequalities may require context-dependent analyses of particular cases.
6. These two sections draw on the basic framework of Terry L. Price (2004b), pp. 1195–99.

7. Plato also believed that women should be part of the guardian class and that they should be educated as the men are educated. This egalitarian gesture is qualified by his claim that men are admittedly superior to women in most things (Plato 2001, p. 455d).

8. Notice the similarities to Judges 21:25, the conclusion of that book: 'In those days there was no king in Israel; all the people did what was right in their eyes'.

9. Machiavelli favors the Roman constitution, in which 'two consuls ... played the same role as the kings', the senate played the role of the aristocrats and the tribunes of the people provided the democratic element (Machiavelli 2001 [1531], p. 473). See also Machiavelli's claim in his *Discourses* that

   [f]or a people that governs and is well regulated by laws will be stable, prudent, and grateful, as much so, and even more, according to my opinion, than a prince, although he be esteemed wise; and, on the other hand, a prince, freed from the restraints of the law, will be more ungrateful, inconstant, and imprudent than a people similar situated. The difference in their conduct is not due to any difference in their nature ... ; but to the greater or less respect they have for the laws under which they respectively live. (Machiavelli 2004 [1531], p. 220)

10. Commentators see Hobbes or, more likely, Filmer, as being the object of Locke's critique in this passage.

11. We have left to the side the important questions about non-participants within the same society – for example, children, slaves and often, women – who were not considered citizens.

12. Admittedly, some have believed that class differences and even slavery can be justified on differences in the capacity for happiness and suffering.

13. This is not to say that parents are not justified in attending primarily, or even solely, to the interests of their own children. It is rather to say that if this kind of behavior is justified, it is probably not on utilitarian grounds.

14. For a discussion of the contrasts between Kantianism and utilitarianism, see Price (2004a), pp. 462–70.

15. In his *Political Liberalism* (1993), Rawls expresses his skepticism about the ability to attain consensus among citizens holding diverse worldviews on a principle as strong as the difference principle.

16. For one generally appreciative feminist reading of Rawls, see Okin (1989).

17. For a discussion of this point, see Price (2006), ch. 4.

18. Note that for Rawls a stronger basic structure would need to be in place – beyond merely assuring no brute coercion takes place – in order to assure commutative justice.

19. See Price (2006), pp. 99–100.

20. The approaches to spirituality and leadership are analyzed in more detail in Hicks (2003).

21. See, for example, Robinson (1988) and also Mitroff and Denton (1999).

22. As one example, see Nash (1994).

REFERENCES

Apffel-Marglin, Frédérique and Stephen A. Marglin (eds) (1990), *Dominating Knowledge: Development, Culture, and Resistance*, Oxford: Clarendon Press.

Aristotle, *Politics*, in Michael L. Morgan (ed.) (2001), *Classics of Moral and Political Theory*, 3rd edn, Indianapolis: Hackett, pp. 301–56.

Burns, James MacGregor (1978), *Leadership*, New York: Harper & Row.

Burns, James MacGregor (2003), *Transforming Leadership: A New Pursuit of Happiness*, New York: Atlantic Monthly Press.

Burns, James MacGregor and Georgia J. Sorenson (1999), *Dead Center: Clinton–Gore Leadership and the Perils of Moderation*, New York: Scribner.

Du Bois, W.E.B. (1903), *The Souls of Black Folk*, with an introduction by Donald B. Gibson (1996), New York: Penguin.

Gardner, Howard (1995), *Leading Minds: An Anatomy of Leadership*, New York: Basic Books.

Greenleaf, Robert K. (1977), *Servant Leadership: A Journey into the Nature of Legitimate Power and Greatness*, New York: Paulist Press.

Hicks, Douglas A. (2000), *Inequality and Christian Ethics*, Cambridge, UK: Cambridge University Press.

Hicks, Douglas A. (2003), *Religion and the Workplace: Pluralism, Spirituality, Leadership*, Cambridge, UK: Cambridge University Press.

Hicks, Douglas A. (2005), 'Self-Interest, Deprivation, and Agency: Expanding the Capabilities Approach', *Journal of the Society of Christian Ethics*, **25** (1), (spring/summer), 147–67.

Hill, Thomas E., Jr. (1991), 'Servility and Self-Respect', in his *Autonomy and Self-Respect*, Cambridge, UK: Cambridge University Press, pp. 4–18.

Hobbes, Thomas (1651), *Leviathan*, in Richard Tuck (ed.) (1991), *Leviathan*, Cambridge, UK: Cambridge University Press.

Kant, Immanuel (1785), *Groundwork of the Metaphysic of Morals*, in H.J. Paton (trans. and ed.) (1956), New York: Harper & Row.

Locke, John (1690), *Two Treatises of Government*, in Peter Laslett (ed.) (1988), *Two Treatises of Government*, Cambridge, UK: Cambridge University Press.

Machiavelli, Niccolò (1531), *Discourses on the First Ten Books of Titius Livius*, excerpts reprinted in Michael L. Morgan (ed.) (2001), *Classics of Moral and Political Theory*, 3rd edn, Indianapolis: Hackett, pp. 467–87.

Machiavelli, Niccolò (1531), 'Discourses on Livy', excerpt reprinted in J. Thomas Wren, Douglas A. Hicks and Terry L. Price (eds) (2004), *International Library of Leadership 1: Traditional Classics on Leadership*, Cheltenham, UK and Northampton, MA, US: Edward Elgar, pp. 219–22.

Machiavelli, Niccolò (1532), *The Prince*, reprinted in Michael L. Morgan (ed.) (2001), *Classics of Moral and Political Theory*, 3rd edn, Indianapolis: Hackett, pp. 422–66.

MacIntyre, Alasdair (1984), 'Is Patriotism a Virtue?' reprinted in Markate Daly (ed.) (1994), *Communitarianism: A New Public Ethics*, Belmont, CA: Wadsworth, pp. 307–18.

Mill, John Stuart (1861), *Utilitarianism*, in George Sher (ed.) (1979), *Utilitarianism*, Indianapolis: Hackett.

Mitroff, Ian I. and Elizabeth A. Denton (1999), *A Spiritual Audit of Corporate America: A Hard Look at Spirituality, Religion, and Values in the Workplace*, 1st edn, San Francisco: Jossey-Bass.

Nash, Laura L. (1994), *Believers in Business*, Nashville, TN: Thomas Nelson.

Nussbaum, Martha (2003), 'Compassion and Terror', *Daedalus*, **132** (1), 10–26.

Okin, Susan Moller (1989), *Justice, Gender, and the Family*, New York: Basic Books.

Plato, *Republic*, in Michael L. Morgan (ed.) (2001), *Classics of Moral and Political Theory*, 3rd ed., Indianapolis: Hackett, pp. 28–191.

Price, Terry L. (2004a), 'Ethics: Overview', in George R. Goethals, Georgia Sorenson and James MacGregor Burns (eds), *Encyclopedia of Leadership*, volume 1, Thousand Oaks, CA: Sage, pp. 462–70.

Price, Terry L. (2004b), 'Philosophy', in George R. Goethals, Georgia Sorenson and James MacGregor Burns (eds), *Encyclopedia of Leadership*, volume 3, Thousand Oaks, CA: Sage, pp. 1195–9.

Price, Terry L. (2006), *Understanding Ethical Failures in Leadership*, New York: Cambridge University Press.

Rawls, John (1971), *A Theory of Justice*, Cambridge, MA: Belknap Press of Harvard University Press.

Rawls, John (1993), *Political Liberalism*, New York: Columbia University Press.

Rawls, John (1999), *The Law of Peoples with 'The Idea of Public Reason Revisited'*, Cambridge, MA, US and London, UK: Harvard University Press.

Robinson, Gill D. (1988), 'Person-Centered Management', *Black Women of Achievement Magazine*, **1** (1), p. 1.

Rousseau, Jean-Jacques (1755), 'Discourse on the Origin and Foundations of Inequality among Men', in Michael L. Morgan (ed.) (2001), *Classics of Moral and Political Theory*, 3rd edn, Indianapolis: Hackett, pp. 717–70.

Rousseau, Jean-Jacques (1762), 'On the Social Contract, or Principles of Political Right', in Michael L. Morgan (ed.) (2001), *Classics of Moral and Political Theory*, 3rd edn, Indianapolis: Hackett, pp. 771–830.

Sandel, Michael (1982), *Liberalism and the Limits of Justice*, Cambridge, UK and New York, US: Cambridge University Press.

Sen, Amartya (1999), *Development as Freedom*, 1st edn, New York: Alfred A. Knopf.

Singer, Peter (1972), 'Famine, Affluence, and Morality', *Philosophy and Public Affairs*, **1** (1), 229–43.

Singer, Peter (2002), *One World: The Ethics of Globalization*, New Haven, CT and London: Yale University Press.

Walzer, Michael (1983), *Spheres of Justice: A Defense of Pluralism and Equality*, New York: Basic Books.

7. Causality, change and leadership[1]

Gill Robinson Hickman and Richard A. Couto

This chapter includes the invaluable contributions of our late colleague and friend, Fredric M. Jablin, who provided his seminal insights during the conceptualization and outlining phase of this project.

CONCEPTUAL PERSPECTIVES ON LEADERSHIP AND CHANGE

During the early stages of discussions at Mount Hope, we realized that scholars in the project were working from different assumptions about human nature and the conditions that give rise to leadership and change. Project leaders divided the group into three teams – Purple, Red and Gold – to discuss our assumptions and write a short paper summarizing each group's perspectives.

Our different viewpoints roughly corresponded to essentialist and constructionist beliefs. In general essentialists maintain that social and natural realities exist apart from our perceptions of reality and that individuals perceive the world rather than construct it (Rosenblum and Travis 2003, p. 33). Conversely, constructionists believe that humans construct or create reality and give it meaning through social, economic and political interactions. Specifically, reality cannot be separated from the way people perceive it (Rosenblum and Travis 2003, p. 33). According to the constructionist view, therefore, people can change reality by changing their perceptions of it. Gold Team members, including the two authors of this chapter, took a relatively constructionist position in contrast to the other teams. We contended that:

Humans make sense of their world and seek meaning through processes of imagination and interpretation, which are situated within social constructions of reality and affirmed through language and inter-subjective encounters. These processes enable humans to conceptualize space, time, and conditions beyond their immediate context and to employ linguistic discourses such as narrative to express and communicate those alternative realities. As social beings, humans depend on others not only for survival but also in the construction of frames of social reality through which people understand their everyday experiences, collaborations, and conflicts. (Couto et al., 2002, p. 1)

We argued that understanding differences in the perspectives of scholars and practitioners is important to the study of leadership because these perspectives shape the way we view problems, ask questions, conduct research, construct theories and create solutions. If we posit, for example, that there are essential and innate human differences among people that we categorize in certain racial groups, then we formulate hypotheses, assign meaning and draw conclusions about these differences that have a significant impact on the way each group is valued and treated in society. If as humans we construct social differences in power, status or opportunity based on variations in factors such as physical distinctions in appearance or group characteristics, then we can change these constructions to reflect new or different arrangements. Accordingly, the Gold team asserted:

> From birth, each human is unique in terms of physical characteristics, dispositions, social histories and environments, and cultural contexts. Through socio-cultural categories and language, humans organize and assign value to some attributes (e.g., along lines of sex, skin pigmentation, or age) and construct systems of social relations in order to distinguish among individuals of the group and among groups. (Couto et al., 2002, pp. 1–2)

Differences in perspectives affect the views of scholars and students of leadership studies and practitioners who endeavor to lead. Most do not adopt a strict essentialist or constructionist view; rather, they synthesize the two perspectives in a way that makes sense to them. Even Karl Marx, whom most scholars would consider a constructionist given his championing of humans as change agents, made some concessions to the essentialist view, observing that 'men make their own history, but they do not make it as they please; they do not make it under self-selected circumstances, but under circumstances existing already, given and transmitted from the past' (Marx 1869).

We start from the constructionist perspective in this chapter, framing the discussion of change, causality and leadership around it. Based on this perspective, we define *change* as a collective effort by participants to intentionally modify, alter or transform human social systems. This is not to assert that conditions change merely because a group of people wants them to change. As we shall see, social reality is subject to historical conditions that can either foster or hinder change beyond any single person's or group's ability to effect change.

A Case Approach

Scholars in the General Theory of Leadership Project provided our annual update on the group's progress at the 2002 International Leadership Association Conference using a different format from past presentations. Project leaders James

McGregor Burns, Georgia Sorenson and Al Goethals asked us to engage the conference participants in our thinking and discussions by exploring the elements and conditions for leadership in the 1955 Montgomery bus boycott case.

Similarly, we have chosen to present our thinking in this chapter by using a case from the civil rights movement in Prince Edward County, Virginia. Through this case we hope to uncover general concepts about the relationship among causality, change, and leadership that are relevant to multiple contexts including organizational, community, political, and social movements among others.

Barbara Rose Johns's actions as a high school junior in 1951 contributed to the end of public school segregation in the USA. She led a school boycott in Prince Edward County, Virginia, which culminated in the federal court case of *Davis v. County School Board*. Upon appeal to the US Supreme Court, this case joined four other school desegregation cases as *Brown v. Board of Education*. A review of both her actions and the profound consequences of school desegregation offers the opportunity to look at the conduct and causality of change. To what extent did Barbara Rose Johns end school desegregation? The question seems absurd, but it conveys how people often attribute change to the actions of a single individual, such as crediting Rosa Parks's actions with sparking the Montgomery bus boycott that triggered the civil rights movement in a three-link chain of causality or, even simpler, crediting Martin Luther King Jr. with leading the civil rights movement.

If we change contexts, causality often becomes a two-link chain of cause and effect. Airport book racks, for example, display titles that explain how corporate leaders brought about profit, excellence or some other worthwhile outcome. And too often we perceive the actions of nations as the decisions of a single leader with good or bad consequences; for example, consider the book *Bush at War* which details the war in Afghanistan. Change is frequently portrayed as the effect of a leader – a person in a position of formal or informal authority – acting heroically.

We take a different approach to leadership and change in this chapter. We describe and analyze Johns's actions as a cause of school desegregation and related changes. But instead of focusing on change as it pertains to leaders, their actions and outcomes, we address change in the context of the interdependence and interaction of many actors, all of whom we may regard as leaders in light of the consequences of their actions. Their actions, if intended to bring or hinder change, we will call *leadership*.

By placing Johns's actions in a broader field of change related to school desegregation, we are better able to see the domain of her intended change – thus leadership – and its interactions and interrelatedness with other leaders and domains of leadership. Considering her actions within a broader field of race relations suggests myriad influences upon her and myriad influences of her actions upon others in a field of change. The chapter offers a synthesis on causality from theories in the social sciences, the natural sciences and philosophy. Although grounded in social change, the case offers context-free generalizations of leadership, change and causality.

Barbara Rose Johns

As a junior at Robert R. Moton High School in Farmville, the county seat of Prince Edward County, Virginia, Barbara Rose Johns knew that the segregated, all-black school that she attended in 1951 was separate but certainly not equal. She saw the same markers of inequality familiar to African-American school children and their parents throughout the South at the time: textbooks handed down from the white students and, most of all, overcrowded facilities. In Johns's case, a school built in 1939 to serve 180 students instead housed 450 students. The school accommodated some of the overflow students in three buildings hastily erected in 1949. Built of 2 × 4s, plywood and tar paper, they were dubbed 'shacks' or 'chicken coops.'

At the constant prodding of the Moton PTA and its president, the Reverend L. Francis Griffin, pastor of the First Baptist Church, the all-white school board offered regular assurances but no action on a new high school for African-American children. Progress slowed and the assurances became so broad that in April 1951, the school board suggested that the Moton High School PTA not come back to the school board's meetings. Johns shared her concerns about the poor facilities and her frustration with the board's delaying tactics with her favorite teacher, Inez Davenport. Davenport replied, 'Why don't you do something about it?'

So Johns did. During a six-month period she enlisted student leaders a few at a time to take action themselves. Finally on April 23, 1951, following the PTA's failed efforts, the students put their plans in motion. They started by luring M. Boyd Jones, the African-American principal of the school, away from the premises with a false alarm about students making trouble at the bus station. He had received such complaints before and was anxious to put a stop to whatever was going on. As soon as he left, Johns and the other student leaders sent a forged note to every classroom calling for a school assembly at 11:00 a.m.

When the students and teachers arrived in the auditorium, the stage curtain opened on Johns and other student strike leaders. She asked the two dozen teachers to leave, and most of them did. She then laid out the already well-known grievances and said that it was time for the students to take matters into their own hands by striking. No one was to go to class. If they stuck together, she explained, the whites would have to respond. Nothing would happen to them, because the jail was not big enough to hold all of them. Principal Jones returned to school to find the student assembly in full swing. He pleaded with the students not to strike and explained that progress on the new school was being made. Johns asked him to go back to his office, and he did.

Flush with their initial success, the student strike committee asked Rev. Griffin to come to the school that afternoon and give them some advice. They asked him if the students should ask their parents' permission to strike. The African-American adult population in Prince Edward County was 'docile' in the view of Rev. Griffin, who had spent time trying to organize an NAACP chapter in the county. He suggested that the matter be put to a vote, which ultimately determined that the students should proceed without getting their parents' approval. At Griffin's urging, Johns and Carrie Stokes, student body president, wrote a letter to the NAACP attorneys in Richmond asking for their assistance.

The next afternoon the strike committee met with the superintendent of schools, T.J. McIlwaine, who was serving a fourth decade in that position. He represented the softer side of Jim Crow – accepting things as they were and doing his best to be fair and evenhanded in a system of injustice and oppression. At the meeting, the opposing sides hardened their stances. McIlwaine insisted on African-American subordination and made numerous promises – assuring the students that much had already been done and that more would be done in time. He also previewed a gauntlet of reprisals – warning the students that unless they went back to class, the teachers and the principal would lose their jobs. The students left dismayed by McIlwaine's elusive and evasive manner but encouraged by their performance in the confrontation. They had held their own in the face of white power.

On Wednesday, two days into the strike, NAACP attorneys Oliver Hill and Spottswood Robinson III came by to talk with the strike leaders and their supporters in response to the letter they had received from the students. Both Hill and Robinson were high-profile civil rights lawyers who regularly engaged in lawsuits. They had studied at Howard University, a training ground for advocacy lawyers, and had joined the network of African-American lawyers working to redress racial inequality across the country. On the state and national level, the premise of the NAACP's advocacy had been that as long as *Plessy v. Ferguson* was the law of the land, the government had to make equal what it insisted remain separate. They had already won several lawsuits for equal pay and facilities around the state of Virginia. Hill had even won a case for equal salaries for Prince Edward County teachers before World War II.

Hill and Robinson were not encouraging on this day, however. They and other NAACP members had grown tired of equalization suits which, although plentiful, only succeeded in changing the subordination of African-American teachers and students at the margins. They were interested in shifting their strategy to confront school desegregation directly and were paying close attention to a case from Clarendon County, South Carolina, that was moving toward the US Supreme Court. In fact, when Hill and Robinson stopped to speak to the Farmville student strike organizers, they were en route to Pulaski County, Virginia, to determine if the plaintiffs in a case there were willing to transform their suit from equalization to desegregation. They counseled the students to go back to class.

The students, however, were adamant in their refusal to end the strike. Impressed by their determination and not wanting to dampen their spirits, Hill and Robinson offered to help if the students would agree to return to school and change their case from one of equalization to one of desegregation.

The next evening, April 26, one thousand students and parents attended a mass meeting in Farmville. The secretary of the state NAACP urged the parents to support their children. Without parental support, he said, the NAACP would not initiate what it knew would be a long, hard suit that would require considerable endurance. Initial assessments suggested that 65 percent of parents supported the students and the NAACP intervention; 25 percent opposed it; and 10 percent had no opinion. No opponents spoke that night.

On April 30, the school board sent out a letter signed by Principal Jones, urging parents to send their children back to school. The strange wording, which stated that Jones and the staff 'had been authorized by the division superintendent' to send the letter, suggested that Jones was acting under duress. Rev. Griffin, however appreciative of Jones's difficult position, nevertheless understood that the principal's prestige and authority could influence many parents to change or waver in their support of the strike and court action. Consequently, Rev. Griffin sent out his own letter calling for another mass meeting on Thursday, May 3, and underscoring the significance of what the students were trying to accomplish: 'REMEMBER. The eyes of the world are on us. The intelligent support we give our cause will serve as a stimulant for the cause of free people everywhere' (Smith 1965, p. 58). John Lancaster, Negro county farm agent, helped Griffin get out the mass mailing.

On May 3 Hill and Robinson petitioned the school board for the desegregation of the county's schools. The meeting that night took the form of a rally and served as a real turning point. J.B. Pervall, the former principal of Moton High School, spoke in favor of the standard of equality but not integration and gave many people in the packed church reason to pause and reassess what they were supporting. The NAACP officials attempted to regain the momentum, but it was Barbara Johns who succeeded in restoring the crowd's support. She reminded members of the audience of their experience and the students' action. In concluding, she effectively recounted the many small and large insults suffered by African-Americans in the history of race relations, challenging Pervall with unmistakable metaphors of white oppression and black accommodation to it. She admonished the huge gathering: 'Don't let Mr. Charlie, Mr. Tommy, or Mr. Pervall stop you from backing us. We are depending on you' (Smith 1965, p. 59). Rev. Griffin took the cue and asserted Pervall's right to speak but implied cowardice of anyone who would not match the students' courage and back them.

The students consented to return to school on Monday, May 7. Hill and Robinson promised that they would file suit in federal court unless the school board agreed to integrate by May 8.

The walkout becomes a federal case

On May 23, one month after the strike, Robinson followed through on the NAACP's promise in light of the board's inaction and filed suit in federal court in Richmond, Virginia, on behalf of 117 Moton students. In *Davis v. County School Board of Prince Edward County* he argued that Virginia's law requiring segregated schools be struck down as unconstitutional. The attorney general, looking at the facts, counseled that an equalization suit was indefensible for the state but that integration was too radical a remedy. The state immediately began improving the facilities in an effort to render the suit moot.

The prestigious Richmond law firm Hunton, Williams, Anderson, Gay & Moore represented the school board. Two senior partners, Archibald Gerard Robertson and Justin Moore, prepared a vigorous defense of segregation. During the five-day trial, which began on February 25, 1952, they argued a very familiar defense of poor facilities for African-American children: to each according to the taxes that they pay. The poverty of African-Americans meant a low tax base among them and thus a generous white subsidy of their schools.

Robinson and Hill presented a now-familiar cast of witnesses who discussed the psychological impact of segregation. Moore rebutted one witness for the plaintiffs specifically for his Jewish background and the others for their unfamiliarity with the mores of the South. Moore ridiculed educator and psychologist Kenneth B. Clark for his research methods and overreaching conclusions. During Moore's cross-examination of Clark, Moore and Hill clashed vehemently – and just short of physically – over Moore's contention that the NAACP and Hill himself stirred up and fomented critical situations. The passions of this exchange portended events to come.

The court found unanimously for the school board. The students and their parents were disappointed, given their honest, albeit idealistic, belief that they would win because their cause was just. Robinson and Hill were neither surprised nor disappointed; they were now prepared to appeal to higher courts. *Davis v. School Board* reached the Supreme Court in July and joined with other school desegregation cases for argument on December 8, 1952.

The drama of a local school strike reaching the US Supreme Court was not over, although many of the original actors in the school strike had exited the stage. Barbara Rose Johns left Farmville soon after the strike. Her family, concerned for her safety, sent her to Montgomery, Alabama, to live with her uncle Rev. Vernon Johns, minister of the Dexter Avenue Baptist Church. The education board fired Boyd Jones, and he and his new wife, Moton High School teacher Inez Davenport, also moved to Montgomery so he could attend graduate school. Ironically, the couple became members of the Dexter Avenue Baptist Church.

The arguments of December left the Court with the task of deciding the legality of school desegregation and possibly the constitutionality of *Plessy v. Ferguson*, the 1896 decision that found separate-but-equal to be constitutional. A divided Court, with at least two dissenting votes, was ready to overturn *Plessy* but sought a stronger majority. Justice Felix Frankfurter bought some time for the Court by developing a set of remaining questions, and the Court asked that the case be re-argued on October 12, 1953. In the interval Chief Justice Fred Vinson died and Earl Warren, former governor of California, replaced him as the new chief justice. Warren worked to gain a consensus among his fellow justices, who had become deeply divided during Vinson's tenure regarding civil liberties in the McCarthy era. Firmly opposed to the constitutionality of *Plessy v. Ferguson*, Warren relied on diplomacy and compromise in language to make it possible for the Court, including a hospitalized member, to render a unanimous decision on May 17, 1954. The Court ruled that school segregation was unconstitutional and that separate-but-equal could not be applied to schools.

Local authorities and their reactions

The Court's decision engendered a severe backlash in the South, particularly in Prince Edward County and other parts of Virginia. As long as the courts did not set a remedy for segregation, one of Warren's compromises, segregation remained the de facto practice in Prince Edward County and other parts of the South. In 1956 the courts finally ordered desegregation but still did not set a timetable for it. Prominent Virginia politicians and editors invoked the theory of interposition – the right of state government to position itself between the federal government and those otherwise bound by its laws. They called for 'massive resistance' in much the same way that Johns had, certain that they could avoid punishment for noncompliance with the new federal law by presenting a united front. Extremists promised to put an end to public schools rather than integrate them.

Reprisals and resistance hit Prince Edward County particularly hard. On the personal side John Lancaster lost his job as Negro county farm agent and Rev. Griffin, besieged by every creditor, was left penniless. His wife suffered a nervous breakdown as a result of the stress. On the policy side the Prince Edward County Board of Supervisors had been providing funding for the public schools one month at a time as long as the schools remained segregated. But in 1959 the federal appeals court ordered Prince Edward County and the rest of Virginia to desegregate its schools in September. In response, the board of supervisors did not allocate any funds for public schools. Instead it provided tuition assistance to students desiring to attend all-white private schools that had been established in the county in the event of court-ordered integration. The county's public schools remained closed until 1964, perhaps offering the most radical example of massive resistance on the local level in the nation.

For the five years the public schools were closed, the NAACP litigated for public funding of integrated schools. African-American residents established learning centers for their children. A few families were able to send their children to live with relatives outside the county where they could attend public schools.

New tensions arose in the African-American community. Attorneys for the NAACP sought a legal remedy rather than a local remedy that they feared might undermine their case. Intent on having the courts decide the controversy, the NAACP did not want the learning centers to approximate the quality of school instruction and steadfastly avoided a compromise with officials that would lead to the reopening of the public schools. African-Americans heeded the NAACP's advice and began to register to vote in an effort to vote local authorities out of office rather than submit to them.

By 1960 Prince Edward County had gained notoriety and came to represent what needed to be changed in the South. It attracted organizations other than the NAACP and more direct action protest: Black Muslims supported separate and better schools; the Sit-In Movement inspired direct action; and the Student Non-Violent Coordinating Committee sent in organizers to plan boycotts as well as to tutor the children locked out of their schools. Griffin managed to bridge the gap between the increasingly 'old' efforts of NAACP litigation and the 'new' methods of movement organizing. He supported the latter in the county even as he became president of the NAACP statewide. Ironically, the 'new' movement tactics of direct action had an exemplar: a school boycott organized in 1951 by high school junior Barbara Rose Johns.

ANALYTICAL ELEMENTS

What elements contributed to change in this case? Are these elements present in organizational, community, political, and other social contexts? In this section we explore these questions by proposing several analytical elements that may be useful for understanding this case and others.

Causality

Accounts of leadership often reduce causality to a limited set of factors. This enables us to portray leadership as links in a chain of cause and effect, such as when we credit Clinton's fiscal policies with the prosperity of the 1990s or a CEO with the turnaround of a company, without considering the many other factors that played a part in these outcomes. In the case of Prince Edward

County, Barbara Johns's leadership undeniably influenced school desegregation. But an exclusive focus on her role reflects an oversimplification of the chain of events and seriously underestimates the nature of leadership. Leadership is infinitely more complex than the efforts of any one individual; rather, it is the impact of efforts to influence the actions of leaders and followers opposed to and supportive of the same or related changes. This perspective on leadership requires attention to a network of actors and the sea of other changes in which a leader's influence efforts take place. Four analytical frames help us to attend to this network of influence rather than to a specific leader: Kurt Lewin's field theory; Gunnar Myrdal's principle of cumulative effect; Stephen Jay Gould and Niles Eldredge's theory of punctuated equilibrium; and Margaret Wheatley's work on systems.

Kurt Lewin, field theory

Kurt Lewin's field theory espouses that effective change requires understanding 'the totality of coexisting facts which are conceived as mutually interdependent' (Lewin 1951, p. 240). Lewin, a psychologist with training in physics and mathematics, concerned himself with individual and group behavior, including change. He contributed 'action research' to the field of problem-centered scholarship. Problem solving, just like effective change, requires placing a problem within a system or field with as many relevant and interdependent elements as possible. Within this field each individual also becomes a dynamic field with interdependent parts, including 'life spaces' of family, work, church, and other groups. People take positive and negative influences from their experiences that shape their identity and help explain their behavior. Lewin advocated assembling all the relevant, mutually independent factors to explain social phenomena such as leadership and change. For example, Johns may or may not have been aware that before she met school superintendent McIlwaine he had tangled with her uncle Vernon Johns over black students' access to county school bus transportation and with Oliver Hill over black teachers' pay a dozen years before. Nonetheless, McIlwaine remained aware of those experiences, and they undoubtedly influenced his assessment of Barbara Johns's efforts to lead and his judgment about the nature of the student strike. Because of their influence on McIlwaine, these prior conflicts became part of the field of the controversy. Their hidden nature suggests the difficulties of gathering and assessing all the facts relevant to an event.

Gunnar Myrdal, the principle of cumulative effect

Gunnar Myrdal and his colleagues completed their epic study, *An American Dilemma: The Negro Problem and Modern Democracy*, before the appearance of Lewin's field theory. They offered a theoretical framework for the condition of African-Americans very much like Lewin and extrapolated it to a method of social research (Myrdal 1944, p. 1066). Myrdal's study begins with the notion of a system in stable equilibrium and rejects it as inadequate to provide a 'dynamic analysis of the process of change in social relations' (Myrdal 1944, p. 1065). The static equilibrium of a system is merely a starting point of the balance of opposing forces. In the simplest of systems, with only two opposing elements, a change in one brings about a change in the other, which in turn brings on more change. The changes may be subtle enough to appear stable but only because of the constant state of adjustment. Any system is far more complex with many interrelated elements; even the simplest system with two opposing elements becomes complex when we examine the composites of each element.

Myrdal proposed a principle of cumulation to explain change within a system of dynamic social causation. Change accumulates as one change brings on another change, and the elements of a system and their composites or subsystems represent a second form of cumulation. The principle states, assuming an initial static state of balanced forces:

> [A]ny change in any one of [its] factors, independent of the way in which it is brought about, will, by the aggregate weight of the cumulative effects running back and forth between them all, start the whole system moving in one direction or the other as the case may be, with a speed depending upon the original push and the functions of causal interrelation within the system. (Myrdal 1944, p. 1067, italics in the original)

Myrdal elaborated that the final effects of the cumulative process may be out of proportion to the magnitude of the original push. More to the point of our case, although the initial push may be withdrawn – the school strike ended – 'the process of change will continue without a new balance in sight' (Myrdal 1944, p. 1066). This happens largely because the system in which any change occurs is far more complicated than it appears. Every element of the system interrelates with every other element, and every element has its peculiarities and irregularities (Myrdal 1944, p. 1068).

Myrdal concluded in terms central to our concern about causality: 'This conception of a great number of interdependent factors, mutually cumulative in their effects, disposes of the idea that there is one predominant factor, a "basic factor"' (Myrdal 1944, p. 1069). This includes leadership.

Indeed, the notion of leadership may be a construct of our attempts to understand causality within a system of change. This radically alters the enduring debate: Does change create leaders or do leaders create change? The cumulative principle would suggest that the actions of leaders may influence others to take action that in turn influences others in a continuing chain – thus the answer to the question is neither and both. Change does not create leaders nor do leaders create change *and* change creates leaders and leaders create change. Observers apply the construct of leadership to people's actions – actions that are intended to influence the actions of other people – within a system of change. The construct of leadership may be used retroactively to suggest causality. The accuracy of that assessment depends upon the boundaries of the system; the broader the boundaries, the less likely any set of actions has a primary causal relationship to systemic change. Leadership is more easily applied to actions in a system of static equilibrium and a circumscribed set of cumulative factors.

Both Myrdal and Lewin borrowed heavily from quantum mechanics in particular for concepts of field and the steady state of disequilibrium. Both men emulated physics in their hope that human behavior and systems of change, however complicated, could be expressed mathematically.

Stephen J. Gould and Niles Eldredge, punctuated equilibrium
Concepts of equilibrium and change also feature prominently in the work of scientists Stephen Gould and Niles Eldredge (1972). Their theory of punctuated equilibrium explains major changes in nature after long periods of stasis that cause divergence or branching of a new animal or plant species (Gould 1991). Real change occurs if this divergence establishes a trend wherein the new species succeeds more frequently than the previous one.

Like field and systems theories, social scientists extrapolated the concept of punctuated equilibrium to explain changes in social systems that occur after long periods of incremental change punctuated by brief periods of major change (Schlager 1999). This phenomenon helps to explain how Johns and the other student leaders could launch a successful trend of mass resistance to racial inequality after decades of incremental change facilitated by previous generations stretching back to the era of slavery. Brief periods of punctuated equilibrium, such as the creation of a community of free blacks in 1810 (Ely 2004), established a trend of sustained resistance to an unjust racial system in Prince Edward County and other black communities, even in the face of retribution from white power holders.

Margaret Wheatley, the new science and leadership
Margaret Wheatley's work (1992) permits us to bridge the concepts of punctuated equilibrium in paleobiology and the physics of quantum mechanics to leadership in a manner that builds upon the field theory of Lewin and the cumulative principle of Myrdal. Wheatley explains that physics had introduced field theory to explain gravity, electromagnetism and relativity. The common element of fields in each of these is that they are 'unseen structures, occupying space and becoming known to us through their effects.' The space of fields and, we may add, their time, is not empty but 'a cornucopia of invisible but powerful effective structure' (Wheatley 1992, p. 49). Both Lewin and Myrdal also suggested that to understand human behavior and social change we need to

recognize that time and space are not empty and begin to fill in their invisible but effective structure.

Wheatley also explains the relevance of field theory in the life sciences in a manner analogous to Myrdal's principle of cumulation. Morphogenic fields develop through the accumulated behaviors of a species' members. Successive members find it easier to acquire a skill, such as bicycle riding, in a setting where many others have accumulated it. Contrary to Newtonian concepts of causation, it is the energy of the receiver that takes up the form of a morphogenic field (Wheatley 1992, p. 51). In leadership terms the efficacy of leaders comes from shaping a field in which others, by their own actions, may participate in the energy and forms of the field. Barbara Johns certainly did this for students, their parents and many others. But she was also within the fields that others – including Rev. Griffin, Superintendent McIlwaine, Principal Jones and teacher Inez Davenport, and the other teachers at Moton High School – had shaped.

Wheatley elaborates on the consequence of this conception of field for leadership. The idea that leaders have vision, set goals and then marshal their own energy and that of others to achieve these goals is a Newtonian view of change focused on a prime mover and a mechanistic concept of change. Although partially true – some elements of old science still hold in the new science – this focus overlooks the complex fields of cumulative interactions across time and space in which all of this takes place. We might conceive of change as a destination sought through the leader as engine – a linear and railroad track analog. This would ignore the fact that even railroads function within fields – including elements from appropriations to weather – that influence when and where trains arrive or if they run at all. Better, Wheatley argues, to think about organizational culture and the deliberate and intentional formation of fields that reinforce the values and goals of an organization and fill its spaces and history with coherent messages (Wheatley 1992, pp. 52–7). Of course, this view is limited to those fields within an organization – such as the Moton High School PTA – and does not take into account the field in which these organizations interact with other actors with opposing values and goals – such as the Prince Edward County School Board.

Dynamic Systems of Interdependent Parts, Change and Causality

Wheatley's work invites us to view the field of leadership as a dynamic system in which change is a constant. Myrdal describes it as rolling equilibrium and alerts social scientists that they have to study '*processes of systems actually rolling* in the one direction or the other, systems which are constantly subjected to all sorts of pushes from outside through all the variables, and which are moving because of the cumulative effect of all these pushes and the interaction between the variables' (Myrdal 1944, p. 1067). Peter Vaill describes this system as 'permanent white water' (1996, p. 2) and 'chaotic change' (1989) but attributes these conditions to recent changes rather than newly discovered enduring attributes of systems as Wheatley does.

Regardless of these important differences, many leadership scholars acknowledge that in the context of a dynamic, interdependent system, leaders play a far different role than the one often ascribed to them. For example, Adam Yarmolinsky takes issue with James MacGregor Burns about leaders initiating change. Yarmolinsky (2007) points out that leaders join a system in the midst of change and simply do their best to mediate and direct change in a shifting environment. Ronald Heifetz similarly, if implicitly, acknowledges that leaders, especially those without authority, modulate the distress within dynamic systems (Heifetz 1994, p. 207).

Likewise many leadership scholars acknowledge the complexity of such systems of fields and recognize that these fields undergo constant change. Vaill writes of organizations as universes with galaxies of knowledge and information (Vaill 1989, p. xii). Heifetz (Heifetz and Linsky 2002) and Vaill also place importance on the personal attributes of the leader, thus opening up a whole other dimension that can affect and further complicate the fields of organization and change, much as Lewin predicted.

The organizational and personal complexities of this constant change were fully evident in the Prince Edward County case. For example, the series of events that played such a pivotal role in the Supreme Court's unanimous decision on this case were at least as complicated as the events comprising the racial history of Prince Edward County. To offer only one example, the death of Chief Justice Vinson made possible a strong majority opinion in *Brown v. Board of Education*. Earl Warren, who assumed the role of chief justice, was determined to have a unanimous decision. His determination was no doubt influenced by the guilt he felt for the role he had played in the internment of West Coast Japanese Americans when he was governor of California during the Second World War. *Brown v. Board of Education* gave him the opportunity to repent his own transgressions and to end those of the nation (Kluger 1975, pp. 661–2).

Warren began his penance before *Brown*. In 1946 a federal district court declared the segregation of Mexican-American school children in California unconstitutional in *Mendez v. Westminster*. The case anticipated the issues of *Brown*, although the grounds of segregation were national origin rather than race. After the federal circuit court upheld the lower court, Governor Warren lobbied the legislature in 1947 to pass bills that ended legal segregation for all groups in California. Even a scholar as conscientious as Richard Kluger overlooked how influential this experience would prove to be for Warren. The California case, like the *Brown* case, was a complex field that developed its own twists and ironies. Gonzalo Mendez, the lead plaintiff in the case, was able to pursue his grievance because of the income he derived farming land that he had leased from the Munemitsus after the Japanese-American family had been 're-located' to an internment camp. Warren's most egregious public policy indirectly provided him the opportunity to pursue one of his most progressive official acts (Teachers Domain n.d. 2001).

Wheatley offers another element of fields that Lewin and Myrdal did not foresee, namely, the manifestation of the entire system in each of its parts. Fractals best express this property of systems of dynamic change. Zoom in on any part of a chaotic system and one finds recurring patterns. Every part of a field of change may manifest the transformative change of the entire field, but a focus on a minute part of the field may obscure the perception of the pattern that comes from examining subsets in relation to large sets. The pattern of the entire system may be found in each of its elements, but without some sense of the whole, the pattern may go unrecognized. Needless to say, without a sense of that pattern the nature of each part of the system may be misunderstood. When considering each part of the system of change in the Prince Edward County case, for example, elements of other systems of change are readily apparent. The school strike had precursors in other forms of resistance within the slave and freed black community of the county and in the repressive measures of the white community. The fullest meaning of those preceding resistance acts and the school strike emerges from the pattern they share with each other. An exclusive focus on one or the other or on any other factor apart from its relationship to the system of change limits its meaning and our perception of the recurring pattern among them.

The principle of uncertainty, which Wheatley mentions and which makes up part of the new science, provides particularly rich insight into causality. Physicist Werner Heisenberg helped to usher in the new science of quantum mechanics. Heisenberg resolved many of the controversies of quantum mechanics by explaining that one cannot know the position and momentum of a subatomic particle at the same time. The more one knows about its position, the less one knows about its momentum and vice versa. The properties of the observed depend upon the instruments used to observe them. The leadership of Barbara Johns depends then upon what other factors we take into account in the system of change in racial segregation. When considering the Moton High School strike factor, her leadership plays a pre-eminent role. At the level of federal decisions for school desegregation, her leadership fades into a fractal subsystem of a larger system. Moreover, a fair evaluation of Johns's leadership depends upon examining this system of change from her perspective. Her leadership would be less prominent if we examined the system through the efforts and actions of Rev. Griffin, Oliver Hill or Superintendent McIlwaine. In terms of the uncertainty principle, the more we focus on the leadership of Johns, the less discernible other leadership becomes.

This has profound implications for causality. If our certainty about one actor comes at the cost of uncertainty regarding other parts of a dynamic system, how can we be sure that the actions of one influenced the intended change? Although the case is quite clear that Johns's leadership spurred the student strike, we might also consider the other factors that influenced people's action and argue that Johns's exhortations would not have had any effect had it not been for the interaction with other elements of the system – the lack of success and frustration of the Moton High School PTA; the World War II service of Rev. Griffin, Principal Jones and Johns's father; the support of the initial small band of student strike leaders; etc. This uncertainty seems to demand that we examine every inexhaustible subset to the greatest microscopic level of scrutiny and then relate them. In truth, we could never examine every relevant fact and interrelated event in sufficient detail to explain with certainty what caused what. According to Heisenberg, 'In the sharp formulation of the law of causality – "if we know the present exactly, we can calculate the future" – it is not the conclusion that is wrong but the premise' (American Institute of Physics and David Cassidy 2005). The academic implications of these matters are that we can understand the leadership of this case only by the patterns that we look for and, once we find them, we may be surprised to learn that constituent elements of the case may vary from what we would expect. In this case, for example, it is possible that some white residents of the county wanted integration more than some African-American residents. The practical implications are that such micro-variations do not affect our understanding of the leadership of Johns and others. However, our understanding will be insufficient without incorporating enough elements of the system into our analysis to make clear the patterns of behaviors and the probability of their interrelatedness. This is precisely the caution that authors such as Wheatley and Vaill offer: a focus on leaders and their actions distorts our understanding of leadership in systems of change.

Mindfulness

Underlying this investigation into the theories and observations of Lewin, Myrdal, Gould and Eldredge and Wheatley is the common emphasis on mindfulness – a central tenet of Buddhism. In order to understand and practice leadership, it is necessary to engage in critical reflection on the acts of leaders, the context in which those acts take place and their likely consequences. The tenets of this critical reflection include conceptualizing acts within a field of interactive and interrelated parts rather than in a straight line from acts to results. In this manner both leaders and those who study leadership are more likely to anticipate unintended and unwanted consequences. Our perception of these consequences increases with our knowledge of the boundaries of the system of change or field in which someone attempts to lead.

In the *I-Ching* Chinese scholars posit a universe composed of a single unifying element with two complementary and opposing parts – a *yin* and a *yang*.

The complexity of the universe is contained in its basic element and in all the derivative elements that flow from the original *Tao*. These elements combine in systems of equilibrium based on complementarity and in a dynamic flow of energy, *Feng Shui*, founded on their oppositional characteristics (Couto and Fu 2004). The premises of this realm – fields of energy, change and stability, complementarity and opposition – provided Neils Bohr and other pioneering physicists a metaphysical context for discovering quantum mechanics and expanding scientific thought beyond theories of Newton and even Einstein. Physicist Werner Heisenberg and his colleague Erwin Schroedinger found their inspiration in the metaphysics of Hinduism. These systems of thought provide a very different metaphor for causality than the mechanics of a machine, to which Scottish philosopher David Hume subscribed. Instead causality is rooted in dynamic, interactive systems of interrelated parts that resemble and differ from each other (Capra 1982, pp. 79–89).

Lest it appear that we have strayed too far from causality, change and leadership, let us not forget the numerous references, albeit cursory and oblique, to Lao-Tsu, Taoism and Confucius in leadership scholarship. Peter Vaill deals somewhat more substantially with Taoism, after first confessing to the elusiveness of its elliptical thinking. Vaill dwells on the concept of *wu-wei*, or nonaction, and its place in leadership. *Wu-wei* was evident in the Johns case when the teachers and principal left the assembly hall at the students' request during the organization of the strike. Vaill also hints at the significance of examining this and other epistemological and ontological systems for the understanding of change. He envisions the possibility of organizations benefiting from the Eastern realization that the meaning of organizational capabilities, including leadership and change, 'can emerge only through the most careful and continuous contemplation' (Vaill 1989, p. 190).

Social Tensions

In our conversations about the links of causality and mindfulness to actions that result in change, Fred Jablin suggested that the impetus for change might emerge from social tensions. This idea resonated as a meaningful way to understand the dynamic and socially constructed nature of change in human systems.

Social tensions arise among groups from conflicts about identity, resources, power and ethics. These tensions are embedded in interactions within and between groups as they form and continually reform the structures and systems that comprise society. Table 7.1 identifies several social factors and ensuing tensions that underlie change. In the Johns case, conflict arising from these tensions created pervasive conditions for change in Prince Edward County.

Table 7.1 Social tensions

Factors	Social Tensions
Identity and Meaning	Assigning identity – Asserting identity
	Rendering insignificant – Establishing value
Resource Availability and Distribution	Restricted resources – Accessible resources
	Individual resources – Collective resources
Power	Disenfranchised power – Authorized power
Ethics	Inequitable actions/conditions – Equitable actions/ conditions

Identity and meaning

Individuals and groups create meaning in society by naming, defining and assigning value to themselves and others in their environment. Social tensions concerning meaning commonly develop as strains between assigned identity (naming) and asserted identity (self-claimed) and upon rendering identities insignificant (worthless). When one group assigns a name and lower social worth to another group, the resulting tensions can evolve or erupt into social change. Rosenblum and Travis (2003) assert, 'Because naming may involve a redefinition of self, an assertion of power, and a rejection of others' ability to impose an identity, social change movements often lay claim to a new name, and opponents may express opposition by continuing to use the old name' (p. 6).

In 1951 whites identified African-American citizens of Prince Edward County as 'coloreds' in the most polite terms and as dehumanizing epithets in the worst terms. There was no doubt that African Americans were deemed inferior and unequal, while white citizens were valued highly and deemed superior. These name and value distinctions shaped disparities in other aspects of society including the rights of blacks to resources, power and ethical treatment.

Resource availability and distribution

Tensions concerning resources emerge from the availability and distribution of goods, services, wealth, property and other benefits or needs that groups in society value or require. Accessibility and restriction of resources are more often determined by social mores (the haves and have-nots) than natural abundance or limitations. Tensions for change emerge from struggles over who has the right to possess resources – the individual, the collective or some combination of both.

US citizens established the right to universal public education as a valued collective resource long before Barbara Rose Johns entered Moton High School. In 1951 resources for educating black children in Prince Edward County were sorely lacking, even under the separate-but-equal standards of *Plessy v. Ferguson*. Moton High School's PTA, principal and community members continuously appealed to the all-white school board to upgrade buildings and supplies only to be placated or summarily ignored. Even when funds for buildings and supplies were available, white school board members had no intention of supporting equal public education and facilities for African-American children.

Power

Participants in the change process create, leverage or challenge power constructs to bring about major change. In our session at Mount Hope, members of the Gold Team agreed that 'power is not fundamentally a thing that individuals possess in some greater or lesser quantity but is more than anything an aspect of social relationships' (Couto, Faier, Hicks and Hickman 2002, p. 3). The capacity to impact social relations is affected by a group's attainment of or restriction from various forms of social power and the group's ability to use power to influence others. Tensions develop among groups that have attained various forms of power (authorized or legitimate, reward, coercive, expert, informational or referent [French and Raven 1959]) and groups that are restricted, disenfranchised or negatively impacted by the exercise of these forms of power.

The exercise of legitimate power contributes to stability and organization in social interactions; however, misuse or exploitation of power bases results in inequality and loss of rights or freedoms for selected groups. In 1896 with the landmark case *Plessy v. Ferguson*, white Southerners succeeded in reversing and suppressing any gains African Americans had made in terms of civil rights and human dignity. The US Supreme Court used its power in this case to establish a legal basis for separate-but-equal conditions for blacks and whites in the South. The result of this decision gave tacit permission to white power holders to create separate but decidedly unequal conditions for black citizens.

Ethics

Joanne Ciulla (2004, p. 4) maintains that ethics is 'the heart of leadership'; likewise, inequity, inequality and excessive self-interest are at the heart of social tensions and conflict. Ethics in social interactions compel members of society to take into account the impact of their actions on others and consider what 'ought to be' done in situations with other human beings. Al Gini explains that 'ethics, then, tries to find a way to protect one person's individual rights and needs against and alongside the rights and needs of others' (Gini 2004, p. 29). Social tensions emerge when groups experience or perceive inequitable treatment at the hands of power holders and dominant groups.

Inequities in the treatment of black and white citizens in the Jim Crow South were intentional and inhumane. In 1939 the Prince Edward County School Board built its first public high school for African-American students with no cafeteria, auditorium, locker rooms, infirmary or gymnasium – features that were standard in white schools in the county. Moton High School was built to hold 180 students, but in 1947 it served more that 360 students.

The county school board responded by building temporary facilities made of wood and covered with tar paper behind the school. These 'shacks,' as they were called by local citizens, leaked when it rained and were poorly heated. Barbara Johns and other Moton High School students were well aware of the superior quality of facilities and equipment at the white high school. These inequities coupled with long-term neglect and disregard by school board officials increased frustration and tensions among students.

From an ethical perspective, change in its most humane and enlightened form intentionally uplifts the human condition of some without harming the welfare of others, while change in its most detrimental form fosters the aims of egocentric or amoral individuals and groups at the expense or demise of others. Leadership studies research examines both elevating and harmful forms of change. Scholars James McGregor Burns (1978, 2003) and Bernard Bass (1985; & Avolio 1994) examine the uplifting effect of transforming and transformational leadership, just as scholars Jean Lipman-Blumen (2005), Barbara Kellerman (2004) and others research the causes and consequences of toxic or bad leadership.

Illustrations of both harmful and elevating forms of change permeate the story of Barbara Rose Johns and school desegregation in Prince Edward County. Leadership by Southern whites created and sustained social arrangements that legitimated their own amoral needs and wants by denying the civil rights and well-being of black citizens. In contrast, strike organizers at Moton High School used their moral agency to advocate for improved educational conditions for black students without harming the rights of white citizens.

Conditions for Change: Climate, Timing and Threshold Points

Though social tensions underlie change, tensions alone do not initiate change. The elements in Table 7.2, climate, timing and threshold points, are essential factors in prompting change. Climate encompasses the totality of environmental cues, feelings and experiences of groups in social contexts. Conditions for change emerge over time as social climates affecting the well-being of specific groups become more threatening or uncertain.

Threatening conditions were present in the situation surrounding events in Prince Edward County. Moton High School's PTA, principal and community members advocated for improved resources and facilities for their children on

Table 7.2   Conditions for change

Factors	Conditions		
	From		To:
Climate	Passive	→	Threatening
Timing	Premature	→	Opportune
Threshold Points	Lacking	→	Prevalent

a continuous basis. In the existing separate and unequal environment it was evident that postponements and rejections of their requests were not isolated incidents. As a result, each obstacle contributed to the black community's cumulative experience of discrimination and mistreatment.

Timing is also a central factor in change. Cumulative acts, that when taken together are larger than any singular or specific moment in history, create opportune openings where concerted action is capable of sparking change – a punctuation in social equilibrium. The previous actions of many African Americans to defy segregation – including the actions of Johns's uncle, Rev. Vernon Johns, that resulted in better school bus services for African-American children in the county in 1939 – paved the way for Moton High School students to stage a sustainable strike. The actions of Vernon Johns formed part of a complex web of change leading to desegregation.

The concept of thresholds provides further insight into conditions that trigger change. Mark Granovetter (1978) describes threshold as 'that point where the perceived benefits to an individual of doing the thing in question ... exceed the perceived costs' (p. 1422). By extending the idea of threshold to groups, we conclude that significant social change is set in motion when a group collectively reaches a threshold point.

It is conceivable that thresholds are also points where courage transcends fear. Legalized racism and accepted acts of violence toward African Americans reinforced fear and uncertainty in people who dared to assert their objections to an unethical structure. At the same time these acts served to build cumulative experience, conviction and collective courage.

There were several major threshold points in the Moton High School case. One threshold point occurred when Barbara Johns recruited a small group of trusted friends to meet secretly and plan a student strike in the foreseeable event that efforts by the school principal and PTA would not result in a decision to build a new high school. When the school board failed to announce plans for a new school, Johns's strike group put their plan into action.

The group arranged for the school principal to be away from campus, then notified each classroom that there would be a brief assembly in the auditorium.

Johns and her compatriots then called on the 450 students gathered at the assembly to unite in collective purpose and stage an orderly strike on the school grounds. On April 23, 1951, Johns and the entire student body marched out of Moton High School determined to change the abysmal conditions in their school.

Another crucial threshold point occurred on the fourth day of the strike. NAACP lawyer Spottswood Robinson asked students to bring their parents to a meeting where he would determine whether they supported their children's willingness to proceed with a lawsuit to end segregation in public schools. Rev. Francis Griffin held the mass meeting at his church and urged black solidarity in the fight to end segregation. Barbara Johns spoke passionately on behalf of the students. The desegregation plan received a rousing endorsement from the majority of those present, though there were some dissenters. At the close of the meeting, Rev. Griffin summarized the sentiments of the group: 'Anyone who would not back these children after they stepped out on a limb is not a man' (Kluger 1975, p. 478).

Leadership as Intended Change

This detailed account permits us to address questions of change and causality. In what way did Barbara Rose Johns provide leadership to end school desegregation? Did her actions pass the litmus test that James MacGregor Burns set for leadership – 'the achievement of purpose in the form of real and intended social change' (Burns 1978, p. 251)? Clearly, there is a succession of related events from the school strike to *Brown v. Board of Education*. There is also, clearly, a succession of related events, albeit less direct, from the school strike to the campaign of massive resistance. Figure 7.1 outlines some of the sequential relationships of events and actors from the school strike to *Brown v. Board of Education*. It includes subsequent events such as massive resistance on both the state and county level and occurrences on both the national and local level in the civil rights movement.

If Johns was a leader in school desegregation because her actions tied into the Supreme Court's *Brown v. Board of Education* ruling, was she also a leader in the campaign of massive resistance for the same reason? Did her leadership cause the closing of the schools in Prince Edward County as well as their eventual reopening and integration? Clearly she intended improved school facilities and not school closings. Was she then only responsible for the changes she intended? If so this might suggest a very low ethical standard, namely, that leaders are responsible only for their intended outcomes and not for the consequences of their actions. As a leader did she bear any responsibility for the poverty that Rev. Griffin was reduced to or for Lancaster's loss of his job as Negro county farm agent?

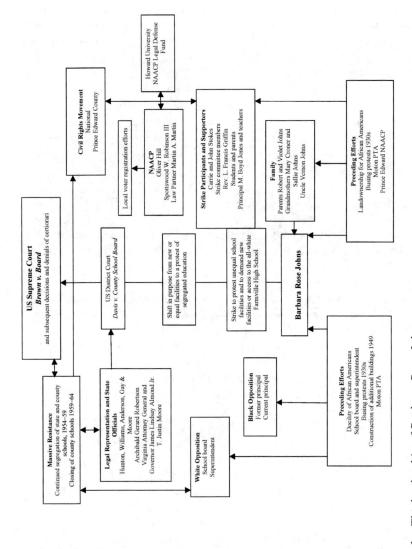

Figure 7.1 The leadership of Barbara Rose Johns

Perhaps we can absolve Johns of these negative outcomes to the extent that we cannot hold her responsible for the expected and unexpected actions that others took in reaction to her leadership. Max Weber, however, made acceptance of the intended and unintended outcomes of our efforts to influence public events a mark of the calling to political leadership. Johns was in a system of change and, according to Weber, it would be irresponsible for her not to acknowledge the interdependence of contending factors in these fields. Johns and the school board had their own separate but interdependent systems of power. Each bears responsibility in the dual sense of causality and moral accountability for their system's actions, actions which they intended to influence. But, again citing Weber, responsibility in the sense of moral accountability also requires that we use judgment to anticipate negative reactions and outcomes and attempt to avoid them. An ethic of responsibility requires that we pursue values with proportionality (Weber 1946, pp. 115–16). Weber helps us understand that Johns and the school board operated in separate but interrelated dynamic fields. Johns can only be held responsible for the negative outcomes of massive resistance and school desegregation in Prince Edward County if those outcomes can be traced to her intentions or to an excess in her actions. Clearly, they cannot.

Just as clearly we have identified a sobering caveat of leadership. Burns's litmus test of the achievement of real and intended social change comes with Weber's measured melancholic observation: 'The final [and intermediate] result of political action often, no, even regularly, stands in completely inadequate and often even paradoxical relation to its original meaning' (Weber 1946, p. 117).

Questions remain about the role of intended change in Johns's leadership. Initially she did not intend to desegregate the schools but only to improve the facilities of Moton High School. She supported and championed the NAACP's shift to desegregation as a means to gain improved facilities. Do we test her leadership by the achievement of desegregation or the improvement of facilities? The state immediately took steps to improve facilities as a means to avoid desegregation, but by that time the NAACP's position had hardened to the point of preferring closed schools to improved ones. In this sense, the NAACP bears more responsibility than Johns for the lost educational opportunities from 1959 to 1964.

Just as the overall *Brown* decision had some unintended consequences (Sullivan 2004), Johns's actions brought about some changes she intended and some she did not. While her initial goal was one of equalization, the NAACP viewed equalization as a very limited form of change because racial subordination could and often did continue even after students of all races obtained equal facilities. When the county ultimately desegregated its public schools, Johns achieved her intended purpose – equal facilities for black and white students – albeit in an unforeseen, unintended way. In this sense did equalization and desegregation symbolize a deeper form of change: the recognition of the value and intelligence of all the county's students and the end of all forms of racial discrimination within the school system? How do Johns's leadership and the NAACP's leadership rate against these intended outcomes? The difference the efforts of Johns and the NAACP made in improved educational opportunities, processes and outcomes provides the best measure of their effectiveness.

Although she played a part in the formative stages of the lawsuit, Johns did not play a part in subsequent events in the county after her parents, fearing for her safety, sent her to live with her uncle Vernon in Montgomery, Alabama, shortly after the student strike. Johns married on New Year's Eve 1953 and subsequently moved to Philadelphia, far removed from the consequences of the strike and its ensuing controversy. Did her leadership stop after she launched the strike or did it continue because of the consequences of her initial action? Regardless of intention then, did her role as leader end when she no longer influenced events in the present? Or did her leadership remain to influence later events, again regardless of her intentions? Can we distinguish her role as leader from her leadership – the former being the actions that she took to influence the actions of others, and the latter being the consequences of those actions? If we are to accept the time and space of a field as relevant to the actions of influence within it, then Johns's leadership remains a factor in the field of civil rights movement in Prince Edward County and beyond.

Leadership as the Cause of Change

Johns did not operate in a leadership vacuum; rather, she interacted with other leaders in this narrative of change. It is instructive to examine the influences on each of the other leaders involved in the Prince Edward County case: the Howard University Law School education of Oliver Hill and Spottswood Robinson; the conflict that Superintendent McIlwaine had with Vernon Johns over transportation for African-American children twelve years prior to meeting his niece; the impact that fighting a war of liberation in a segregated army in World War II had on Rev. Griffin, Principal Jones and Barbara Johns's father as well as the effect of the subsequent desegregation of the armed forces by President Truman in 1948. This examination suggests that a set of interdependent actors each with their own set of influences comprised a system of change in the Prince Edward County case, a system limited only by our ability to ferret out all of its conditions. In this type of immense and interactive system, Johns's actions might be considered analogous to a butterfly flapping its wings in the Amazon basin, thereby setting off a string of events that ultimately causes rain in Des Moines, Iowa. Or Johns's actions might have had much more of a direct impact, causing us to analyze the specific circumstances of the case, such as the conversations in the Johns's family store; Inez Davenport's reasons for encouraging Johns to take a lead in improving the school facility; and Principal Jones's determination to run a democratic school and support student-led initiatives, a determination that extended to his momentous decision to leave the assembly hall at Johns's request at a time when he could have squelched the strike before it got started.

Events did not unfold in a straight line from Johns to the US Supreme Court. Johns dealt directly with students, students' parents, other residents in the county and the Richmond office of the NAACP. She aligned herself with the elected student leaders of Moton High School who should possibly also be considered leaders in the school desegregation effort. Johns received advice and assistance first from Inez Davenport and Rev. Griffin and later from the NAACP. Did the boundaries of her leadership diminish when the NAACP entered or did they broaden under the influence of all the people who interacted with her? If it was the latter, should we then examine the influences on those people who influenced Barbara Rose Johns – not only those mentioned in this account but also her family members and the community of property-owning African-American farmers served by her family store?

Some of these influences were small and personal – a spoken word. Some were momentous and public – the inability of the Moton PTA to make progress. Some influences were specific to that time and place, while others had historical roots, which although long forgotten, were compelling nonetheless. For example, historically large numbers of free blacks lived in Prince Edward County during a time of legalized slavery. In the years preceding the desegregation case, an economically independent group of African-American farmers and landowners had grown and flourished in Prince Edward County, of whom Vernon Johns was just one example, albeit the most dramatic. In time Johns's efforts in the Prince Edward County school desegregation case may fade from the collective memory just as memories of some of these earlier historical events had faded by 1951.

Burns's litmus test of leadership as the achievement of real and intended change sets a high standard. Clearly Johns achieved her purpose of conducting a school strike and, as a consequence, she influenced the actions of others. It is relatively easy, as we have seen, to detail the action that leaders take to influence others. It is much more difficult to judge the influence of those actions on other leaders. Whereas leading is replete with intentions, leadership concerns the assessment of the consequences of leaders' actions. And how do we deal with and assess the changes that ensued because of a leader's action? Joseph Rost's critique of Burns only compounds the problem. His definition of leadership as 'an influence relationship among leaders and followers who intend real changes that reflect their mutual purposes' (Rost 1991, p. 103) obfuscates the possibility that some influence relationships may make real changes, although unintended, and may stimulate some to act for contrary purposes. In order to move beyond the dilemma of unintended changes and contrary purposes, we may have to distinguish between leading and leadership.

Leading is an attempt to influence others in the present moment. The story of the strike offers numerous examples of efforts to lead, including the students' letter to the NAACP lawyers, the massive resistance tactics employed by some of Virginia's politicians and newspaper editors and Earl Warren's determination to win a unanimous opinion in the US Supreme Court. We can define these attempts at leading as *leadership* only after assessing their full impact. Even then, what is and is not leadership depends upon what is and is not included in the system of change.

By limiting the influence relationship to leaders and followers and insisting on intention, Rost and many, many others confuse the nature of leadership. The actions of a person may influence a leader to take action even though it was not intended. Barbara Johns's paternal uncle and grandmother both instilled a great deal of confidence in her and served as role models of resistance to racial subordination in personal and public matters. Their actions would not be considered leadership in an ordinary interpretation of Rost's definition, but an extraordinary interpretation – which focuses on influence relationships primarily – would incorporate their actions into the leadership that brought about school desegregation. Although they did not directly affect the change effort in the way that Rev. Griffin and the NAACP lawyers did, Johns's uncle and grandmother nurtured Johns's self-esteem, making it possible for her to assert herself in the school desegregation case. The omission of significant influential relationships is but the first shortcoming in any theory of change that limits its focus to leaders and followers.

The second shortcoming of Rost's conception of leadership is that it tends to concentrate on the efforts of one set of leaders and followers. In truth and in practice, leaders – those who take action to influence others – set off reactions in other leaders for conflicting purposes. Obviously, Johns's plans for the school strike had severe critics who took action to prevent the strike and desegregation. There were African-American leaders opposed to the strike and efforts to integrate who vied with Johns for influence in the African-American community. Principal Jones, for example, wrote a letter to parents asking them to send their children back to school. In sum, a system of change does not have only one set of leaders and followers; rather, it has many interdependent and interactive sets of leaders and followers.

These two factors of change, namely, myriad influences and many sets of leaders and followers, came into play most dramatically on the morning of April 23 when Principal Jones left the assembly at the request of Johns and the other strike leaders. He could have refused to leave and ordered the students to return to their classrooms, protesting that their strike plans would only harm his own change efforts. Certainly his boss, the superintendent of schools, thought this is exactly what he should have done. And had he done so, it is very unlikely that events in Prince Edward County would have unfolded as they did. Here was a leader, a person in authority, who did not use his influence to coerce compliance.

Several factors might have influenced his action: he might have withdrawn his opposition because he tacitly supported the students' actions; he might have been making a concession to Inez Davenport, Johns's favorite teacher and Jones's fiancée, who had encouraged Johns to take some action to address the poor facilities; he might have wanted to show support for the orderly and democratic manner in which the students conducted themselves regardless of whether he agreed with their plans. He sought to instill initiative and organization in his students and may have been reluctant to squelch their efforts for this reason. Richard Kluger describes Jones as a man trapped between his convictions as a black leader and his obligations to his white employees (Kluger 1975, p.469). His convictions won out at the moment he was asked to leave. The assembly was itself the result of his influential encouragement of student initiative and his own example of striving to acquire better resources for the school. Ironically, Jones was a leader in terms of the influence he had on an action he could not ultimately support. His leadership, his influence on the school strike, came from his decision not to use his authority, or to act by inaction.

When we examine change through one particular leader, we can see how seemingly unrelated events become a network of influence because of their effect on that one person. When we analyze a change event from the perspective of different leaders, we must add and subtract elements of influence and think about how the consequences of the events affected different leaders differently. For example, if we choose to examine the whole system of change in Prince Edward County through T. Justin Moore, lead attorney for the school board, we would have to consider very different influences and consequences than we would if we were considering the same system of change from the perspective of Johns or Jones.

Leadership as Action for Change

Action to bring about change entails more than a single leader or initiator, as the Prince Edward County school desegregation case illustrates. Individuals can achieve a common purpose only when they join together in an act of generativity – forming a group to accomplish goals that an individual could not achieve alone (Forsyth 1999, p.67). During our Mount Hope discussions, the concept of generativity was especially important in the Gold Team's conceptions of leadership. The scholars at Mount Hope grappled with the question: What processes or conditions characterize the emergence, maintenance and transformation of leadership and followership? The Gold Team responded, 'Leadership is a creative and generative act – literally bringing new realities into being through collaboration with others' (Couto et al., 2002, p.2).

Members of the Moton High School student body assumed active roles as leaders or followers in an effort to attain their common goal. Robert Kelley

(1995) explains that leadership and followership are *equal* but different roles often played by the same people at different times. Individuals who assume leadership roles have the desire and willingness to lead as well as a clear vision and interpersonal, communication and organizational skills and abilities. Effective followers (or participants) form the other equally important component of the equation and are distinguished by their capacity for self-management, strong commitment and courage. Individuals involved in leading change are willing to bring their respective abilities to the change effort in whatever roles they choose or accept.

Leaders and participants achieve momentum or movement through their coordinated actions (co-acting) for change. Paradoxically, individuals who assume leadership roles rely on their imagination – an invisible thought process – before attempting to implement a plan of action. Groups seeking change must be able to imagine or envision alternative social arrangements and define problems or issues in new ways (Couto et al., 2002, p. 2). A pivotal role of leaders in the change process involves communicating imagined futures and creating new meanings that inspire action. During our discussions at Mount Hope, the Gold Team proposed the following:

> Leading change frequently entails competing narratives about the necessity, sufficiency, and possibility of change. Narratives fulfill various purposes; they motivate, define group identity, make limits, provide the building blocks for imagination and creativity, teach lessons, and legitimate or undermine forms of power, authority, and coercion. One way in which humans convey these social constructions of knowledge is through storytelling, a uniquely social discourse of human life.
>
> Telling a story offers an account of reality that seeks either to affirm or contest an existing meaning, which expresses the nature and origins of a particular set of social relations that can have economic, political, and/or cultural dimensions. The need for change results in contested or negotiated interpretations, definitions and values. (Couto et al., 2002, p. 2)

Barbara Rose Johns and the group of student leaders envisioned a high school for black students that provided them with facilities and resources to receive the quality education to which they were entitled. They developed a plan for Moton High School students to challenge an existing power structure and gain parity with white schools in Virginia. The climate, timing and threshold points converged to form a prime opportunity for movement – a point of punctuated equilibrium (Gould and Eldredge 1972) where significant and sustained change became possible for black children. The strike committee put their plan into action by calling together the entire student body, communicating a collective vision for change and proposing a strike plan. The strike plan gave form, meaning and power to a common purpose that seemed attainable through collective action by the students. Certainly this cadre of leaders met the criteria for the role of leaders described by Kelley (1995): they had the desire and willingness to lead as well as a clear vision and interpersonal communication and organizational skills.

The role of the student body represented an equally important component of this equation. A successful strike was fully dependent on the willingness of the students to assume roles as effective participants or followers. These roles would require an equally strong commitment to the goal and plan of action, a capacity for self-discipline and self-management and tremendous courage in the face of danger. No one knew what would actually happen once the strike committee revealed its plan and put it into action. The risks of punishment, expulsion, violence and other repercussions loomed ominously. What the students did know was that the conditions in their school were totally unacceptable. They had waited long enough and were determined to remain steadfast until their situation changed.

The school principal, teachers, parents and community members comprise a second group of effective participants or followers in the school desegregation case. The decision of the principal and teachers to leave the auditorium when asked by student leaders required commitment to the students' common purpose (or at least commitment not to interfere), self-control to refrain from using their positional power and courage in the face of imminent sanctions from the school board. The parents and community members exhibited a similar commitment and a willingness to embrace the actions of their children. They, too, refrained from using positional authority to stop the strike and exhibited exceptional courage despite inevitable repercussions from white power holders.

The Prince Edward County school desegregation case also illustrates Kelley's (1995) assertion that the same people often play different roles of leadership and followership at different times. The school principal, teachers, parents and community activists functioned in leadership roles and advocated tirelessly for better conditions in black schools. Yet on April 23, 1951, the adult leaders assumed roles as followers and let the students take on leadership roles.

CONCLUSION

This discussion of leadership, change and causality grounded in the leadership of Barbara Rose Johns and the Moton student body offers an opportunity to provide several generalizations about leadership across contexts. Figure 2 summarizes the analytical factors discussed throughout this chapter. These factors will likely take distinct forms and occur at varying stages or degrees based on contextual elements at macro and micro levels. Our challenge as a community of leadership scholars, educators, practitioners and students is to identify the broadest range of contributing factors, understand their impact, generate new

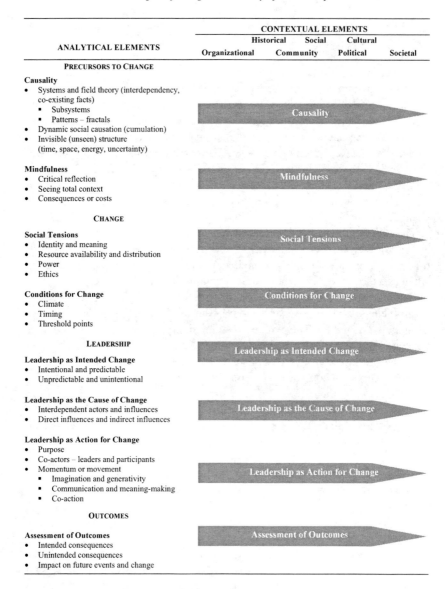

ANALYTICAL ELEMENTS	CONTEXTUAL ELEMENTS			
		Historical Social	Cultural	
	Organizational	Community	Political	Societal

PRECURSORS TO CHANGE

Causality
- Systems and field theory (interdependency, co-existing facts)
    - Subsystems
    - Patterns – fractals
- Dynamic social causation (cumulation)
- Invisible (unseen) structure (time, space, energy, uncertainty)

Mindfulness
- Critical reflection
- Seeing total context
- Consequences or costs

CHANGE

Social Tensions
- Identity and meaning
- Resource availability and distribution
- Power
- Ethics

Conditions for Change
- Climate
- Timing
- Threshold points

LEADERSHIP

Leadership as Intended Change
- Intentional and predictable
- Unpredictable and unintentional

Leadership as the Cause of Change
- Interdependent actors and influences
- Direct influences and indirect influences

Leadership as Action for Change
- Purpose
- Co-actors – leaders and participants
- Momentum or movement
    - Imagination and generativity
    - Communication and meaning-making
    - Co-action

OUTCOMES

Assessment of Outcomes
- Intended consequences
- Unintended consequences
- Impact on future events and change

Figure 7.2   Analytical and contextual elements

factors that contribute to the leadership of change in human systems and use them ethically.

Barbara Rose Johns and the Moton High School students proceeded with intention, purpose and collective action to gain facilities and conditions equal to their white counterparts. Yet they had no idea when they met with attorneys Oliver Hill and Spottswood Robinson that their actions would ultimately lead to the overthrow of legally segregated schools in the United States. The student strikers achieved more than separate-but-equal schools; they achieved legal desegregation of schools throughout the country. Major unintended consequences also accompanied this major change – the closure of Prince Edward County schools, job losses and the unanticipated relocation of many teachers, families and students, including Barbara Rose Johns.

How can leadership groups in any context anticipate and prepare for the intended and unintended consequences of their actions and thus be responsible in Weber's sense of intention and proportion? In truth, there is no absolute way to foresee and plan for the various outcomes that change may bring. However the Native American wisdom of the Iroquois advises us to consider the impact of the decisions we make today on the seventh generation of humans (Lyons 1992).

Peter Schwartz advocates a process of scenario development that helps decision-makers take a long view in a world of uncertainty (1996, p. 3). He contends that scenarios are not predictions but mechanisms to help people learn. Scenario building involves more than guessing. It requires a process that uses factual information and indicators of early trends to project alternative futures. The process entails eight sequential factors:

1. Identifying a central issue or question
2. Listing key factors in the micro-environment that may directly affect the central question
3. Identifying forces in the macro-environment that may affect the central issue
4. Assigning rank and weight to the micro- and macro-environmental factors based on their impact on the original issue or question
5. Identifying the forces that are most significant and most uncertain, clustering and plotting each force along an axis from uncertainty to certainty or the reverse and choosing the two most significant axes to form a grid with four distinct quadrants
6. Amplifying details of each quadrant to form four different plots (or scenarios)
7. Considering the implications of each scenario
8. Taking action based on early indicators of movement toward or away from a desirable scenario. (Schwartz 1996, pp. 241–7)

A final factor, 'acting with feedback' (Harman 1998, pp. 193–4), fosters ongoing learning and flexibility as leaders and participants move toward a desired common goal. Although scenario building is a method used most often in business or organizational settings, it provides a useful means for developing informed action in other settings, including community, social and political environments.

We offer several concluding observations for further reflection based on our use of four analytical factors – field theory, cumulative effect, punctuated equilibrium and systems thinking – to examine the Prince Edward County school desegregation case. We hope these analytical factors and the observations they provide are useful across contexts.

- We can assess leadership only after some change has occurred. We can observe leaders acting to influence outcomes in the present.
- The nature of leadership in any change effort corresponds to the historical and social context in which we place it and the leader(s) through which we examine a network of change.
- The less we consider historical and cultural context, the fewer influential events and factors we take into account.
- The interaction of a leader's effort with the efforts of other leaders and participants shapes the outcome and hence the significance and nature of leadership.
- Every change effort takes place within a system of change that provides opposition and modification of other leadership.
- The more credit a particular leader is given for change, the less we recognize the impact of systems in which events take place and the contributions of co-actors to the outcome.

Our Mount Hope colleagues asked members of the Gold Team how we could ever know or conclude anything or sustain order and stability if we believe that reality, including leadership and change, is socially constructed. If we extrapolate lessons from the natural sciences to social systems, we conclude that the 'long view' provides perspective on human capability to imagine and change social systems. While social construction of human systems can result in restricted or inequitable systems of power, privilege and access, our hope for social relationships is in leadership that helps people imagine and effect humane futures for themselves and the seventh generation. In the words of the Gold Team, 'Imagination enables self-reflection and social criticism, as well as socialization, and thus makes possible a form of leadership that proposes alternative social arrangements and new forms of legitimate human needs and wants' (Couto et al., 2002, p. 2).

NOTE

1. The framework and concepts for this chapter emerged over various sessions with scholars in the General Theory of Leadership (GTOL) project. We also incorporated considerable portions of the Gold Team's concept paper, written by Richard Couto, Elizabeth Faier, Douglas Hicks and Gill Hickman during the GTOL project.

REFERENCES

American Institute of Physics and David Cassidy (2005), 'Heisenberg – Quantum Mechanics, Implications of Uncertainty, 1925–1927'. Retrieved July 14, 2005 from http://www.aip.org/history/heisenberg/p08c.htm.

Bass, Bernard M. (1985), *Leadership and Performance Beyond Expectations*, New York: Free Press.

Bass, Bernard M. and Bruce J. Avolio (1994), *Improving Organizational Effectiveness Through Transformational Leadership*, Thousand Oaks, CA: Sage.

Brown v. Board of Education, 344 U.S. 1 (1952).

Burns, James MacGregor (1978), *Leadership*, New York: Harper Torchbooks.

Burns, James MacGregor (2003), *Transforming Leadership: A New Pursuit of Happiness*, New York: Atlantic Monthly Press.

Capra, Fritjof (1982), *The Turning Point: Science, Society, and the Rising Culture*, New York: Bantam Books.

Ciulla, Joanne B. (ed.) (2004), *Ethics, the Heart of Leadership*, 2nd edn, Westport, CT: Praeger.

Couto, Richard A. and Caroline Fu (2004), 'The Authentic Leadership of the Sacred Texts'. Paper presented at the Summit on Authentic Leadership University of Nebraska-Lincoln and Gallup Center Lincoln, NE, June 10–12.

Couto, Richard A., Elizabeth A. Faier, Douglas A. Hicks and Gill Robinson Hickman (2002), 'The Integrating Leadership Project: Gold Team Report', unpublished paper.

Davis v. County School Board, 103 F.Supp. 337, 340 (E.D. Va. 1952).

Ely, Melvin P. (2004), *Israel on the Appomattox: A Southern Experiment in Black Freedom from the 1790s Through the Civil War*, New York: Knopf.

Forsyth, Donelson R. (1999), *Group Dynamics*, Belmont, CA: Wadsworth.

French, John R.P., Jr., and Bertram Raven (1959), 'The Bases of Social Power', in Dorwin Cartwright (ed.), *Studies in Social Power*, Ann Arbor, MI: Institute for Social Research, pp. 150–67.

Gini, Al (2004), 'Moral Leadership and Business Ethics', in Joanne B. Cuilla (ed.), *Ethics, the Heart of Leadership* (2nd edn), Westport, CT: Praeger, pp. 25–43.

Gould, Stephen Jay (1991), 'Opus 200', *Natural History*, 100 (8), 12–18. Retrieved March 14, 2005 from http://stephenjaygould.org/library.html.

Gould, Stephen Jay and Niles Eldredge (1972), 'Punctuated Equilibria: An Alternative to Phyletic Gradualism', in Thomas J.M. Schopf (ed.), *Models in Paleobiology*, San Francisco: Freeman, Cooper & Company, pp. 82–115. Retrieved March 14, 2005 from http://www.blackwellpublishing.com/ridley/classictexts/eldredge.asp.

Granovetter, Mark (1978), 'Threshold models of collective behavior', *American Journal of Sociology*, 83 (6), 1420–43.

Harman, Willis W. (1998), *Global Mind Change: The Promise of the 21st Century* (2nd edn), New York: Warner Books.

Heifetz, Ronald A. (1994), *Leadership Without Easy Answers*, Cambridge, MA: Belknap Press of Harvard University Press.

Heifetz, Ronald A. and Martin Linsky (2002), *Leadership on the Line: Staying Alive through the Dangers of Leading*, Boston: Harvard Business School Press.

Hume, David (1748), 'Of the Idea of Necessary Connexion', Part I and Part II, in *An Enquiry Concerning Human Understanding*, Vol. XXXVII, Part 3, The Harvard Classics, New York: P.F. Collier & Son, 1909–14; Bartleby.com, 2001. Retrieved March 10, 2005 from www.bartleby.com/37/3/.

Kellerman, Barbara (2004), *Bad Leadership: What It Is, How It Happens, Why It Matters*, Cambridge, MA: Harvard Business School Press.

Kelley, Robert (1995), 'In Praise of Followers', in J.T. Wren (ed.), *The Leader's Companion: Insight on Leadership Through the Ages*, New York: Free Press, pp. 193–204.

Kluger, Richard (1975), *Simple Justice: The History of Brown v. Board of Education and Black America's Struggle for Equality*, New York: Alfred A. Knopf.

Lewin, Kurt (1951), *Field Theory in Social Science: Selected Theoretical Papers*, New York: Harper.

Lipman-Blumen, Jean (2005), *The Allure of Toxic Leaders: Why We Follow Destructive Bosses and Corrupt Politicians – and How We Can Survive Them*, Oxford, UK and New York, US: Oxford University Press.

Lyons, Oren (December 10, 1992), *The Year of the Indigenous Peoples (1993)*, speech to the United Nations delegates. Retrieved July 13, 2005 from http://www.ratical. org/many_worlds/6Nations/OLatUNin92.html.

Marx, Karl (1869), *Eighteenth Brumaire*, Chapter 1, p. 1. Retrieved August 17, 2005 from http://www.marxists.org/archive/marx/works/1852/18th-brumaire/.

Myrdal, Gunnar with the assistance of Richard Sterner and Arnold Kose (1944), *An American Dilemma: The Negro Problem and Modern Democracy*, New York: Harper & Row.

Plessy v. Ferguson, 163 U.S. 537 (1896).

Rosenblum, Karen Elaine and Toni-Michelle C. Travis (2003), *The Meaning of Difference: American Constructions of Race, Sex and Gender, Social Class, and Sexual Orientation* (3rd edn), New York: McGraw-Hill Higher Education.

Rost, Joseph C. (1991), *Leadership for the Twenty-First Century*, Westport, CT: Praeger.

Ruiz, Vicki L. (2001), 'South by Southwest: Mexican Americans and Segregated Schooling, 1900–1950', reprinted from the *OAH Magazine of History*, 15 (Winter 2001). Retrieved August 18, 2005 from http://www.oah.org/pubs/magazine/deseg/ruiz. html.

Schlager, Edella (1999), 'A Comparison of Frameworks, Theories, and Models of Policy Processes', in Paul A. Sabatier (ed.), *Theories of the Policy Process: Theoretical Lenses on Public Policy*, Boulder, CO: Westview Press, pp. 233–57.

Schwartz, Peter (1996), *The Art of the Long View: Planning for the Future in an Uncertain World*, New York: Doubleday.

Smith, Robert Collins (1965), *They Closed Their Schools: Prince Edward County, Virginia, 1951–1964*, reprinted (1996), Farmville, VA: Council of Women.

Sullivan, Kathleen M. (September 23, 2004), 'What Happened to "Brown"?' *New York Review of Books*, 51 (14), 47–52.

Teacher's Domain (n.d.), *Mendez v. Westminster: Desegregating California's Schools.* Retrieved August 18, 2005 from http://www.teachersdomain.org/6-8/soc/ush/civil/mendez/.

Vaill, Peter B. (1989), *Managing as a Performing Art: New Ideas for a World of Chaotic Change*, San Francisco: Jossey-Bass.

Vaill, Peter B. (1996), *Learning as a Way of Being: Strategies for Survival in a World of Permanent White Water*, San Francisco: Jossey-Bass.

Weber, Max (1946), *From Max Weber: Essays in Sociology*, in Hans Gerth and C.W. Mills (eds and trans.), New York: Oxford University Press.

Wheatley, Margaret J. (1992), *Leadership and the New Science: Learning about Organization from an Orderly Universe*, San Francisco: Berrett-Koehler.

Yarmolinsky, Adam (2007), 'The Challenge of Change in Leadership', in Richard A. Couto (ed.), *Reflections on Leadership*, in press.

8. A constructionist lens on leadership: charting new territory

Sonia Ospina and Georgia L.J. Sorenson[1]

The April, 2003 meeting of the general theory scholars included invitations to scholars utilizing action-research methodologies as well as to practitioners on the frontline of leadership development in communities. Scholars like John L. Johnson, Professor Emeritus, University of the District of Columbia; Deborah Meehan, Executive Director of the Leadership Learning Community; and Sonia Ospina, faculty of NYU's Wagner School, joined the group for a robust discussion.

Ospina discussed the participant-centered research she and her colleagues are undertaking for the Ford Foundation's Leadership for a Changing World program and shared with the other scholars some findings emerging from this approach.[2] Using a constructionist lens, Ospina and her colleagues are working with social change leaders to understand how leadership emerges and develops in community-based organizations engaged in social change agendas.

A constructionist lens suggests that leadership happens when a community develops and uses, over time, shared agreements to create results that have collective value. Grounded in culture and embedded in social structures such as power and stratification, these agreements influence and give meaning to members' actions, interactions and relationships, and help people mobilize to make change happen. Among the agreements that help to illuminate the nature of social change leadership in the studied communities, Ospina and her colleagues have identified a worldview composed of implicit assumptions about the nature of knowledge, change, humans and the world; articulated formulations of the expected outcomes of change, mediated through levers of personal and organizational power; and a set of ethical references or core values of social justice that help anchor decisions and actions. From these agreements, in turn, emerge authentic practices that coincide with the group's worldview, visions of the future and values (Ospina et al., 2005).

This chapter addresses the constructionist view in leadership studies and touches on some promising interpretative approaches, notably narrative inquiry and cooperative inquiry. All of these approaches rest on the assumption that leadership is intrinsically relational and social in nature, is the result of shared meaning-making, and is rooted in context or place. Leadership from this perspective is not only necessary and possible, to re-state the Mount Hope challenge put to the scholars, but ubiquitous and emergent.

CONSTRUCTIONISM, REALITY AND KNOWLEDGE

As Gill Hickman and Dick Couto discuss in Chapter 7, there are two existential stances taken in leadership research. Essentialists maintain that reality (social and natural) exists apart from our perceptions of that reality and that individuals *perceive* the world rather than construct it (Rosenblum and Travis, 2003, p. 33). Conversely, constructionists believe that humans *construct* reality and give it meaning through their social, political, legal and other interactions (Crotty, 1998).

The emergence of constructionism was rooted in the early work of 19th-century scholars as distinct as Karl Mannheim, George Herbert Mead, and Karl Marx. It is embedded in important intellectual movements of the 19th and 20th centuries, such as pragmatism, existential phenomenology, critical theory, and later the postmodernist movement, especially in the works of Michel Foucault, Jacques Derrida, and Kenneth Gergen. Empirical work has been undertaken in the fields of sociology of knowledge (Berger and Luckman, 1966), sociology of science and technology (Grint, 2004), and the history of science (Sorenson, 1992).

Constructionism 'is the view that all knowledge, and therefore all meaningful reality as such, is contingent upon human practices being constructed in and out of interaction between human beings and their world, and developed and transmitted within an essentially social context' (Crotty, 1998, p. 42).[3] A constructionist lens suggests that meaning is not discovered in the world, but constructed from it. Furthermore, meaning is not created in the mind, but it is constructed from the world and its objects. In other words, meaning results when human beings engage in the world that they experience and interpret (a world that also includes other human beings).

Constructionists bring together the ideas of an 'objective' reality and a 'subjective' interpretation of it into a single perspective. It suggests that meaning (and therefore understanding, knowledge and truth) results from the interplay of object and subject, that is, of humans engaging with the world. Crotty illustrates this defining feature of a constructionist lens as follows: 'The chair may exist as a phenomenal object regardless of whether any consciousness is aware of its existence. It exists *as a chair*, however, only if conscious beings construe it as a chair. As a chair, it too is constructed, sustained and reproduced through social life' (Crotty, 1998, p. 55). The generation of meaning is always a social, rather than an individual process, because to engage in meaning-making human beings draw from existing previous meanings in their culture, and the latter, in turn, is embedded in historically grounded social structures.

A CONSTRUCTIONIST VIEW OF LEADERSHIP

A constructionist view presumes that our understanding of leadership is socially constructed over time, as individuals interact with one another, rather than being something embodied in individuals or possessed by them. It is relatively recently that leadership scholars have employed various constructionist ideas in their search for leadership constructs which transcend individual leader qualities or traits. Yet the idea that leadership is relational – or as Sorenson says 'emerging in the space between' people rather than 'in' a person – has been percolating over the last 30 years in the leadership and organizational literatures. This perspective has gained currency over the years as trait-based, leader-focused research has given way to more group-oriented perspectives such as described in the preceding chapter.

Organizational scholars like Pfeffer (1977), Smircich and Morgan (1982), Smircich (1983), Tierney (1987) and Tierney and Lincoln (1997) pursued the idea that leadership emerges from the constructions and actions of people in organizations. More than two decades ago, Smircich and Morgan posed an invitation to look deeper into the leadership phenomenon and to 'focus on the way meaning in organized settings is created, sustained, and changed [to] provide a powerful means of understanding the fundamental nature of leadership as a social process' (Smirchich and Morgan, 1982, p. 261). Only recently have scholars started to take this invitation seriously in developing an explicit constructionist perspective of leadership.

According to a constructionist view, leadership becomes a reality when one or more individuals in a social system succeed in framing and defining how the demands of the group will be taken up and who will address the need for direction in collective action. Through a process of attribution, people agree to assign each other different roles and functions, including the role of leader, to help move the work forward, or to satisfy other social needs (Hunt, 1984; Meindl et al., 1985; Meindl, 1995; Drath, 2001).

Recent approaches move the study of leadership away from person-centered leadership into a more complex role analysis. While this shift has moved the literature closer to a more subtle understanding of leadership, constructionists would claim that the leadership of a group is more nuanced and interpenetrating. They pose that 'the leader', while relevant to action, represents a different phenomenon than that of 'leadership', and that each demands to be treated distinctly. This shifts the attention from individual persons to communities of practice

(Drath and Palus, 1994; Drath, 2001). Ospina and Schall (2001, p. 4) writing in an earlier article describe this challenge:

> It [constructionism] will help us explore the ways people understand and attribute leadership and allow us to distinguish between the emergence of the collective practices that constitute the work of leadership and the individuals involved in those practices. By highlighting these dimensions, we hope to contribute to the development of the body of literature that views leadership as a collective achievement, or the property of a group, rather than something that belongs to an individual.

Thus scholars using a constructionist lens see leadership as a group-wide process and despite only rudimentary tools at their disposable to discern it, they are clear on their objectives: to allow exploration in 'the ways people understand and attribute leadership and also ... [to] distinguish between the emergence of leadership as a collective process and the practices designated leaders engage in' (Ospina and Schall, 2000, p. 1). Constructionism examines leadership as a *process* of meaning-making: it investigates the unfolding of leadership over time, rather than a snapshot of a particular moment, such as ones utilized in critical incidents or case studies. In short, constructionism views leadership as a dynamic and on-going undertaking. The following sections develop a constructionist view of leadership by exploring its relational, systemic, emergent and contextual dimensions.

The Relational and Systemic Dimensions of Leadership

First and foremost, constructionists claim that leadership is relational. This, of course, is not a new thought. The relational view of leadership is present, implicitly or explicitly, in some of the most insightful contemporary work on leadership. For example, Burns's seminal work starts with the premise that leadership, like power, is 'relational, collective and purposeful' (Burns, 1978, p. 18). Burns's view is that leaders convert followers to leaders and in some cases followers convert leaders to moral leaders. In his later work, *Transforming Leadership: The Pursuit of Happiness* (Burns, 2003) Burns explores how people, rather than leaders and followers per se, create environments conducive to social change.

Other contemporary work on leadership calls attention to the shared and distributed nature of leadership, as evidenced by the increasing importance given in the leadership literature to concepts like dialogue, collaboration, and collective, shared and dispersed leadership (Crosby, 1999; Gronn, 1999; Goldman and Kahnweiler, 2000; Hesselbein et al., 1999; and Lipman-Blumen, 1996). For example, by focusing on leadership as activities that stem from a collective challenge, Heifetz's work (1994) directs attention away from an exclusive focus on the 'leader' to consider the acts of leadership, leadership in process, and the public aspects of leadership work, all elements that point to the importance of relationship.

Others have explored particular forms of leadership that are based on the sharing of authority relations. For example, Bennis and Biederman (1997) and their associates document cases of shared leadership and co-leadership as types that differ considerably from the individual model. Chrislip and Larson (1994) as well as Huxham and Vangen (2000) describe a different type of leadership in the collaborative processes they study. They suggest that collaborative leadership creates the conditions and mechanisms for people themselves to do the work they need to do to address their collective problems.

To some degree, however, even the most sophisticated thinking about leadership still vests the 'power' in individuals. Constructionists are attempting to change the lens. Lambert et al. (1995) define leadership as 'the reciprocal process that enables participants in [a] community to construct meanings that lead toward a common purpose' (Lambert et al., 1995, p. 32). They continue, '[s]ince leadership represents a possible set of actions for everyone in the community, anyone can choose to lead' (Lambert et al., 1995, p. 50). In this definition, the leader *qua* leader is replaced by a community whose individual members have the potential to engage in leadership acts (not roles). While not empirically based, Lambert's approach to leadership highlights the importance of community, reciprocity and purpose for understanding leadership, making more explicit its social and relational aspects, while eliminating almost entirely the figure of the leader.

Juan-Carlos Pastor takes these ideas a step further in suggesting that leadership is 'a collective social consciousness that emerges in the organization' as individuals interact with one another (Pastor, 1998, p. 5). As this process of social construction goes on, as people develop a shared understanding of the work and the roles assigned to members in pursuing it, leadership takes on an independent life that continues to be enacted over time. In this sense, as it emerges, leadership becomes the property of the social system, rather than being just a shared idea in people's minds, or a quality located in a single individual, 'the leader'.

Sorenson and Hickman's work on invisible leadership (Sorenson and Hickman, 2002) fits nicely within these novel discussions. They argue that much leadership is invisible because it transpires in the 'space between' people. They compare this form of leadership to Thelonious Monk's masterly use of 'blue notes' in music. Blue notes comprise the music that takes place in the 'space' between notes. Jazz critics attribute the genius of Monk's remarkable music to the nuance, phrasing and rhythm of the spaces between the formal notes. That space of course, is completely invisible. But it is the relationship between notes that makes them powerful, not the notes themselves. If we extend this analogy to leadership, invisible leadership takes place in the space between people, in everyday life and in extraordinary circumstances.

Applications of other theoretical perspectives such as critical interpretivism, critical theory and feminism link more explicitly this relational, systemic view – and its cognitive orientation – to an outside material world, by connecting the systems of interdependency to historically grounded structures of power (Ospina et al., 2005). This more grounded constructionist approach emphasizes culturally derived and historically situated interpretations of leadership in context, in contrast to universal traits, fixed contingent styles, or disembodied cognitive structures. This approach also challenges the dynamics of exclusion that have incorporated very few voices in the mainstream narratives of leadership, and uses conceptual tools to understand the structural dynamics of exclusion that characterize social relationships. Finally, this approach tries to 'fill the gaps' (Crotty, 1998) in traditional narratives of leadership because of the dominance of a masculine, and thus partial, perspective in the construction of earlier leadership theories.

To sum up, from a constructionist view, leadership is relational and systemic. It emerges and manifests itself through relations and in relationships, and it cannot exist outside of these relations. These relationships, in turn, are grounded in wider systems of interdependence and constrained by social structure.

The Emergent Dimension of Leadership: Meaning-Making in Communities of Practice

A second important dimension of constructionism is the notion that reality is a shared construction and that the process of making sense and ascribing meaning to events is central to human life. Constructionists recognize that people collectively construct our world and give it meaning. They would argue that even the most basic human concepts such as 'death' (Grint, 2004), 'love' and 'work' are culturally and historically bound. So, too, is 'leadership'. Constructionism asserts that leadership is essentially about making-meaning in communities of practice (Drath, 2001; Drath and Palus, 2004), and is thus an emergent reality.

But all meaning-making does not produce leadership. Leadership is a unique type of meaning-making process compared with more general cognitive processes that are part of human life. This is so because the shared agreements that produce leadership are articulated and generated within a community of practice, that is, a group working to achieve results. These agreements are purposive and 'other regarding'. They connect wills and help transform wills into action.

The potential for leadership exists when there is a collective need to accomplish something, that is, a need for purposive action that involves change. Any group who shares that need faces a set of demands to attain it. Parsons et al. (1953) described the four functional prerequisites of organizing that all groups coping with any material problem face: setting direction, actualizing the goals of the enterprise, sustaining the commitment of the group, and creating adaptive mechanisms to re-create the process as needed. If a group does not respond to these demands, it will not survive to serve its purpose. When the individuals in the group are willing and are able to address these demands, leadership happens.

As Wilfred Drath (2001) puts it in *The Deep Blue Sea: Rethinking the Source of Leadership*, these demands call for leadership and thus leadership can be viewed as the result of the group's efforts to address them successfully.[4] He states that leadership happens when members of a community create a shared understanding of the moral obligations each has with the others to make sure that these demands are taken care of, so that the common cause is realized. The work of leadership is the work the community achieves together in setting direction, creating and maintaining commitment and facing adaptive challenges. In this sense, 'leadership is people making sense of events and circumstances within a community, as the community invents and pursues its activities' (Palus and Horth, 1996, p. 54). Rather than a fixed phenomenon or a set of qualities that belong to an individual, as meaning-making, leadership is an emergent phenomenon that develops in community, over time.[5]

An example illustrates this view. Even in our own GTOL group, most of the members would agree that the leadership of the GTOL group was an emerging phenomenon, rather than a person-centered activity. While three of us initially presented the idea of a quest for a general theory, others emerged who took on critical aspects of the functioning and production of the group's efforts. Certain aspects of the intellectual work of the group were managed by various theorists at different times.

The GTOL-group-as-a-whole examined theories but also processes to some degree: seniority, discipline, voice, and place were all taken up, often more than once. Sometimes the work was in the context of the group-as-a-whole, and other times it was taken up between individuals. While a core group of people stuck with the process over three years (and there was substantial debate about the use of 'core'), the group tolerated a few newcomers and visitors as well as venturing out into the International Leadership Association and the Leadership Learning Community gatherings, with varying degrees of comfort.

In the end the group settled on two complementary approaches addressed by Wren at the start of the book: We would tell the narrative of our quest rather than attempt to come to a conclusion about our search for a general theory and we would allow leadership in our own group to emerge in our 'as if' group. For a group of independent leadership scholars intent on finding a general theory as well as retaining our intellectual independence, that in itself was an accomplishment.

The Importance of Context

The meaning-making processes that help construct leadership and the attributions of leadership made in particular settings do not just occur in people's minds, nor are they disembodied from material environments. These processes are always social, rooted in social interaction, and therefore sensitive to identifiable contingencies associated with the material aspects of these settings. How communities agree to undertake the demands of direction, commitment and adaptation to realize their common cause, is context specific.

For example, the degree of complexity of the system affects how a community agrees to address the tasks that call forth leadership. Over time, as happens with all collective sense-making, some taken-for-granted sets of ideas and rules about how to best deal with these demands have become articulated as leadership formulas, or shared understandings of leadership; what Drath (2001) calls 'knowledge principles'. These core sets of ideas become 'short-cuts' that other people use to address the demands of collective work. With increased complexity, simpler tools of sense-making for action have hit a limit of usefulness, and new formulas have become more acceptable. Even though people are not born with these principles in their minds, they can easily absorb them through culture and use them as needed in their particular contexts. One way to understand leadership in a community is to uncover the underlying dominant knowledge principle that its members are using to make sense of their work.

Drath argues that Western society has favored three knowledge principles of leadership which have emerged over time, as social systems have become increasingly more complex: personal dominance, interpersonal influence and relational dialogue. Sometimes these are combined, because the formulas that help solve more complex challenges incorporate elements of those used to address simpler ones.

Leadership as personal dominance is a knowledge principle in which a dominant figure – the person of a leader – is the source of leadership. This formula has worked best in simple systems. More complex systems may rely on the knowledge principle of interpersonal influence, a formula where the source of leadership shifts from a single individual to the roles of actors in negotiation and competition to influence each other. Finally, in the knowledge principle of leadership as relational dialogue, the source of leadership is not a person or a role, but a system, as leadership emerges by way of dialogue and collaborative learning to achieve a shared sense of the demands of collective work.

An effective way to understand how these principles work and how leadership happens is 'by entering into the community and inquiring into the shared meaning-making languages and processes of the community' (Drath, 2001, p. 49). In other words, leadership can only be understood in context and by way of understanding how people make sense of it as they tackle the challenges of collective work.

Finally, the claims that leadership is relational and systemic, emergent and contextual, and that it is socially constructed, do not necessarily lead to the conclusion that it always takes a collective form; nor does it mean that it is by nature democratic. Formal and informal leadership takes many forms, depending on the attributions those in relation make about each other in concrete historical and organizational contexts. Emerging from collective processes that support it, visible leadership can manifest in strong charismatic individuals; or in dyads, as in the case of co-directorships; or in groups as in the case of committees with authority to make decisions; or in organizations with very flat and democratic structures where leadership is collective. Similarly, the tasks that call forth leadership can be, in fact, distributed so that different individuals take up different roles and leadership emerges in many places within a given system or is rotated over time. Furthermore, while all individuals in a given system have the capacity to exercise leadership, and not all do, those that do may choose to enact their choice in ways that evidence any style from democratic to autocratic. What form leadership takes, and how individuals exercise leadership are, in fact, questions that must be answered empirically, by looking at leadership and its manifestations in the real world.

IMPLICATIONS FOR RESEARCH

To explore, with a constructionist lens, the nature of leadership and how it happens in a community, requires a new approach to research, with implications for how the research agenda is conceptualized, designed and implemented (Ospina, 2003). A constructionist approach sensitizes researchers to the dangers of confusing leadership with the person who is identified as the leader (Rost, 1993; Vanderslice, 1988). It also challenges the assumption that leadership must be embodied in the leader–follower relationship, an assumption that greatly reduces the scope of what constitutes the work of leadership.

A new approach is grounded in at least four premises. First, viewing leadership as a social construct and as something that is relational, emergent and contextual suggests a research agenda that shifts attention away from the individual leader and toward the work of leadership; from leadership qualities to collective agreements and the actions that embody them; and from behaviors to practices and experiences. Second, a constructionist view poses that a participatory approach (involving those engaged in the work of leadership as co-inquirers rather than subjects) will yield deeper understanding of the experience of leadership as meaning-making for action. Third, because context is central, this perspective suggests that a participatory approach must be grounded in community. Fourth, from this view, understanding the way leadership emerges in a particular community requires eliciting a range of perspectives within the community. Hence a multi-modal approach to research, one that engages diverse methodologies, is best suited to this task.

Researchers using a constructionist lens will pay attention to the nature of the challenges and questions that the community faces as its members try to achieve change, and the ways people make sense of these challenges. Research embedded in context – in community – would explore questions such as: How does a community clarify what matters most? What stakeholders participate in this clarification process? What difficulties do they experience when facing the demands of organizing and collective work? These questions may require identifying the extent to which the roles of leadership concentrate on a single person, but this is not a given, and must be answered in context. In fact, a critical empirical question is: If one person becomes responsible for clarifying the community strategy, how and why does this happen?

Appropriate methodologies for implementing a participatory multi-modal approach that is grounded in community include, among many possibilities, narrative inquiry, participatory ethnography and cooperative inquiry. Narrative inquiry is a promising methodology for understanding experience and the sense people make of it because of the power of stories as a sense-making tool (Dodge, Ospina, and Foldy, 2005). Ethnography, done with a participatory approach, offers an excellent opportunity for an in-depth look at leadership in a community over time. Cooperative inquiry is an action-oriented approach in which all involved act as both co-researchers and co-subjects that inquire together into burning issues of their practice, thus exploring the experience of leadership from the inside out.

The process of a cooperative inquiry (CI) offers great potential to explore leadership as a relational, emergent and contextual reality. CI itself as a methodology is also relational, emergent and grounded in the context of its participants' practice (Heron and Reason, 2001), as illustrated by the four stages that characterize it:

Stage I.   Examining areas for inquiry, identifying initial research questions and propositions to test through action

Stage II.   Initiating the agreed actions and observing and recording the outcomes of their own and each other's behavior

Stage III.   Bracketing off prior beliefs and preconceptions and intending to see experience in a fresh way

Stage IV.   Returning to consider original theories in light of experience, modifying, reformulating, and rejecting them, or adopting new propositions to be tested again in the next cycle of action

Lastly, a constructionist approach to research demands a broadening of the scope when determining *where* to study leadership. Scholars have too often looked for leadership only in the expected places, often in hierarchical organizations or systems. Indeed, we may be 'looking for leadership in all the wrong places' (Allen, 1990, p. 8). Kathy Allen (1990) identifies three assumptions underlying the most typical sampling techniques in leadership research: sampling by position, by individual reputation or by organizational success. The first assumption is that leadership happens at the top of the hierarchy, in formal positions, and can be enacted only with organizational authority or power resources. The second assumption is that there is a shared cultural definition of leadership. The third assumption is that there is a direct cause–effect relationship between the leadership of a single individual and success.

Reliance on these assumptions and the consequent choice of sampling criteria, argues Allen, decreases our ability to find leadership because it reduces the pool from which to sample. Allen argues for the need to 'look where we have not looked before' (Allen, 1990, p. 8) to better understand leadership and to expand our present knowledge of it. We would add that as scholars we should not only look at different kinds of people, but most importantly, look at different kinds of contexts, as well as pay greater attention to the nature and content of work in these contexts.

IMPLICATIONS FOR PRACTICE

The currency gained by the application of constructionist ideas to leadership has implications for practice, as has been documented by action-oriented scholars. Indeed, with the shift in understanding of organizations as rational machines to one of organizations as living organisms, new ideas of leadership effectiveness have started to shift from the mental model of the heroic leader to that of post-heroic leadership, characterized by 'leadership practices embedded within a network of interdependencies at different levels within the organization' (Fletcher, 2002).

This perspective emphasizes relational processes that depend on social networks of influence, so that leadership is enacted at all levels of the network. The 'visible' leaders represent only the tip of an iceberg (McIntosh, 1989, cited in Fletcher, 2002), or the white caps in the ocean (Drath, 2001), but they are supported by many other people, practices and processes that make things happen. These underlying leadership dynamics support visible leaders in the same way that the underlying piece of the iceberg supports and balances its tip, or in the same way that the deep blue sea produces its sea caps (Fletcher, 2002, p. 3).

Action-oriented leadership scholars propose to translate these ideas into leadership practices that are more in accordance with the demands of contemporary organizations. This proposal approximates Drath's notion of relational dialogue as the most appropriate knowledge principle or leadership formula to cope with the challenges of complex systems. For example, in their work on public leadership, Terry (1993), Bryson and Crosby (1992), Crosby (1999) and Luke (1998) suggest that the interconnectedness of contemporary society demands a different kind of leadership to address public problems, one that is more collective than individual, so that the interdependencies of the environment are addressed. While these scholars do not consider themselves constructionists, their work is premised on assumptions such as the relational, emergent and contextual nature of leadership.

Some scholars propose fully developed programs that are directly consistent with a constructionist lens on leadership. For example, focusing on the agenda of social change for global transformation, Kaczmarski and Cooperrider (1997) argue that the cooperative work required today demands a type of leadership that helps bridge diverse knowledge systems, that is, cultures of inquiry, which are typical of the global commons. The authors define leadership as the 'art of creating contexts of appreciative interchange whereby people from different traditions of knowing come together to create a new culture of valuing in which differences are embraced rather than being a source of dominance and conformity pressures' (Kaczmarski and Cooperrider, 1997, p.251). This type of leadership, they argue, is required in contexts where diverse perspectives and truths co-exist and where the complexities of organizing are extreme.

In the context of the USA, Raelin (2003) proposes a new type of leadership practice for contemporary organizations, where the collective demands for direction, actualization, commitment and adaptation are distributed across all organizational members. The result, he says, would be a system full of leadership, or a *leaderful organization*. Leaderful practices, Raelin argues, are based on an understanding of leadership that shifts from the traditional notions that leadership is serial (one leader at a time), individual, controlling and dispassionate, to the notions of leadership as concurrent, collective, collaborative and compassionate.

To make the shift toward a leaderful organization, Raelin argues, one must believe that more than one person can offer their leadership to a community at the same time, from their position, without taking away the leadership of others (concurrent). From this it follows that mobilization of action or decision-making emerges from multiple members as needed (collective). The shift also requires believing that all group members represent the community and control it by way of dialogue around differences (collaborative). Finally, the shift is based on the value of respect for the worth of each member (compassionate). Leadership practices derived from these ideas provide normative guidance to develop more democratic and participatory approaches to organizing.

CONCLUDING REFLECTIONS

As scholars and practioners involved in understanding leadership, we carry assumptions about the concept and practice of leadership that are consistent with
the underlying assumptions of the culture within which it is embedded. Peter
Senge refers to these assumptions as 'mental models' – similar to Sorenson's
'cognitive structures' – described as 'deeply ingrained assumptions, generalizations or even pictures or images that influence how we understand the world
and how we take action' (Senge, 1990, p. 8).

Contemporary dominant mental models of leadership are shifting gradually,
but most people still carry (and use in practice) a perspective of leadership as
personal dominance and interpersonal influence, to use Drath's knowledge
principles as reference. These mental models of leadership offer only a narrow
understanding of how leadership works. Therefore, these models keep us from
recognizing the multiple sources of leadership, the multiple forms leadership
may take, and the multiple places where it can be found. Sorenson (1992) and
Ospina and Schall (2000, p. 2) describe what they see as a dominant leadership
model in the USA, as shaped by narratives about individuals, generally men,
and all too often white men. They 'offer incomplete understandings of how
leadership works because they rely on a "heroic" version compiled from a narrow set of voices' (Ospina and Schall, 2000, p. 2). They further claim that the
dominant mental model has 'kept the public from recognizing alternative models
of leadership and the extent to which they are developing in communities' (Ospina and Schall, 2000, p. 2). Sorenson writes of the personal cost of the heroic
myth, 'involving tremendous personal sacrifice and struggle' (Sorenson, 1992,
p. 328).

The use of mental models both facilitates and inhibits our understanding of
leadership. Telling the leadership story (or naming it) as dominance or influence
may serve a social function in our collective minds by allowing people to attribute actions with personal qualities a critical role in explaining existential
dilemmas and anxieties of the times. In this sense 'leadership', as Hunt suggests
(Hunt, 1984, pp. 159–78), could be thought of as a cognitive tool that helps
people make sense of events that otherwise would be linked to social forces too
intangible and removed to be controlled. Heroic leadership may be a collective
way to constructively cope with uncertainty. At the same time, there is also a
danger that scholars and practitioners may be inhibited by these agreed-upon
mental models of leadership.

The constructionist approach to understanding leadership invites us to look
anew at the focus and insights of existing empirical research and normative
approaches to leadership. Attention to traits, behaviors, styles, processes, relationships and activities, for example, can add to our understanding of how
things happen when a group with a purpose tries to achieve it. The construc-

tionist approach views the gestalt of the social relationships, the meaning constructed in the process, and the context within which leadership happens. This approach invites questions such as how people working together make leadership happen, what role individuals and groups play in bringing leadership into being, and how contexts affect the actual work of leadership in communities.

Narrativist Wallace Martin suggests that 'by changing the definition of what is being studied, we change what we see; and when different definitions are used to chart the same territory, the results will differ, as do topographical, political and demographic maps, each revealing one aspect of reality by virtue of disregarding all others' (cited by Barry and Elmers, 1997). A constructionist lens on leadership offers precisely this: An opportunity to look at the same territory of leadership that we all share by virtue of our membership in contemporary society, in a way that will help reveal aspects of leadership that we have missed before.

NOTES

1. The authors want to acknowledge the earlier work Ospina coauthored with Ellen Schall (2000, 2001) where several ideas developed in this chapter were first proposed and refined.
2. See the 'Research' link on the program's website: www.leadershipforchange.org.
3. Crotty's important distinction between *constructivism*, which focuses on the meaning-making process of individuals and *constructionism*, which focuses on the collective generation and transmission of meaning has implications for understanding leadership through a constructionist lens, because it renders meaning-making as collective rather than individual.
4. Drath summarizes the demands that trigger a call for leadership in a group in three rather than four tasks: direction, commitment and adaptation – and defines the latter in Heifetz's terms.
5. This perspective is consistent with the new understandings of complexity theory, a branch of chaos theory that gives primacy to the idea of emergent, fluid social orders developing out of chaos (Marion, 1999).

REFERENCES

Allen, Kathleen (1990). *Diverse Voices of Leadership: Different Rhythms and Emerging Harmonies*, Ann Arbor, MI: UMI.

Barry, David and Michael Elmers (1997). 'Strategy Retold: Toward a Narrative View of Strategic Discourse'. *Academy of Management Review*, **2**, 429–52.

Bennis, Warren, and P. Biederman (1997). *Organizing Genius: The Secrets of Creative Collaboration*, Reading, MA: Addison Wesley.

Berger, Peter and Thomas Luckman (1966). *The Social Construction of Reality: A Treatise in the Sociology of Knowledge*, Garden City, NY: Doubleday.

Bryson, John M. and Barbara Crosby (1992). *Leadership for the Common Good: Tackling Public Problems in a Shared-Power World*, San Francisco: Jossey-Bass.

Burns, James M. (1978). *Leadership*, New York, NY: Harper & Row.

Burns, James M. (2003). *Transforming Leadership: The Pursuit of Happiness*, New York: Atlantic Monthly Press.

Chrislip, David D. and Carl E. Larson (1994). *Collaborative Leadership: How Citizens and Civic Leaders Can Make a Difference*, San Francisco, CA: Jossey-Bass.

Crosby, Barbara (1999). *Leadership for Global Citizenship*, Thousand Oaks, CA: Sage.

Crotty, Michael (1998). *The Foundations of Social Research: Meaning and Perspective in the Research Process*, London, Thousand Oaks, New Delhi: SAGE Publications.

Dodge, Jennifer, Sonia Ospina and Erica Foldy (2005). 'Integrating Rigor and Relevance in Public Administration Scholarship: The Contribution of Narrative Inquiry', *Public Administration Review*, May/June, **65** (3), 286–300.

Drath, Wilfred (2001). *The Deep Blue Sea: Rethinking the Source of Leadership*, San Francisco, CA: Jossey-Bass Inc.

Drath, Wilfred and Charles Palus (1994). *Making Common Sense: Leadership as Meaning Making in a Community of Practice*, Greensboro, NC: Center for Creative Leadership.

Fletcher, Joyce (2002). 'The Paradox of Post Heroic Leadership: Gender, Power and the "New" Organization'. Paper presented at the 2002 Academy of Management Research Conference.

Evans, Sara M. and Harry C. Boyte (1986). *Free Spaces: The Sources of Democratic Change in America*, New York: Harper & Row.

Gergen, Keneth (1994). *Realities and Relationships: Soundings in Social Construction*, Cambridge, MA: Harvard University Press.

Goldman, Samuel and William M. Kahnweiler (2000). 'A Collaborator Profile for Executives of Nonprofit Organizations,' *Nonprofit Management & Leadership*, **10** (4), 435–50.

Grint, Keith (2004). 'Constructionism', in George Goethals, Georgia Sorenson, and James Burns (eds), *Encyclopedia of Leadership*, SAGE.

Gronn, Peter (1999). 'Substituting for Leadership: The Neglected Role of the Leadership Couple', *Leadership Quarterly*, **10** (1).

Heifetz, Ronald (1994). *Leadership without Easy Answers*, Cambridge, MA: Harvard University Press.

Heron, John and Peter Reason. (2001). 'The Practice of Co-operative Inquiry: Research "with" rather than "on" People'. In *The Handbook of Action Research*, pp. 179–88

Hesselbein, Frances, Marshall Goldsmith and Iain Somerville, (1999). *Leading Beyond the Walls*. San Francisco: Jossey-Bass.

Hunt, Sonja (1984). 'The Role of Leadership in the Construction of Reality', in B. Kellerman (ed.), *Leadership: Multidisciplinary Perspectives*, Englewood Cliffs, NJ: Prentice-Hall.

Huxham, Chris and Siv Vangen (2000). 'Leadership in the Shaping and Implementation of Collaboration Agendas: How Things Happen in a (Not Quite) Joined-Up World', *Academy of Management Journal*, **43** (6), 1159–75.

Kaczmarski, K. and David Cooperrider (1997). 'Constructing Leadership in the Global Relational Age', *Organization & Environment*, **10** (3), 235–58

Ladner, Joyce (2001). *The New Urban Leaders*, Washington, DC: Brookings Institution Press.

Lambert, Linda Deborah Walker, Diane P. Zimmerman and Joanne E. Cooper (1995). *The Constructivist Leader*, New York, NY: Teachers College Press.

Lipman-Blumen, Jean (1996). *The Connective Edge*, New Jersey, Jossey-Bass

Luke, Jeffrey (1998). *Catalytic Leadership: Strategies for an Interconnected World*, San Francisco, CA: Jossey-Bass.

McIntosh, Peggy (1989). 'Feeling like a Fraud, Part 2'. Working Paper No. 37, Center for Women, Wellesley College, Wellesley: MA.

Marion, Russ (1999). *The Edge of Organization: Chaos and Complexity Theories of Formal Social Systems*, Thousand Oaks, CA: Sage.

Meindl, James (1995). 'The Romance of Leadership as a Follower-centric Theory: A Social Constructionist Approach', *Leadership Quarterly*, **6** (3), 329–41.

Meindl, James R., S.B. Ehrlich and J.M. Dukerich (1985), 'The Romance of Leadership', *Administrative Science Quarterly*, **30**, 78–102.

Ospina, Sonia (2003). 'Qualitative Methods', In George Goethals, Georgia Sorenson and James MacGregor (eds). *Encyclopedia of Leadership*, London: Sage Publications, 2004, 1279–84

Ospina, Sonia and Ellen Schall (2000). *Perspectives on Leadership: Our Approach to Research and Documentation for the LCW Program,* http://leadershipforchange.org/insights/conversation/files/perspectives.php3.

Ospina, S. and E. Schall (2001). *Leadership (re)constructed: How Lens Matters.* Paper presented at the 23rd Annual Research Conference of the Association for Public Policy and Management (APPAM), Washington DC.

Ospina, Sonia, Jennifer Dodge, Erica Foldy, Amparo Hofman and Marian Krauskopf (2005). 'A Framework for Social Change Leadership'. Working Paper, Research Center for Leadership in Action, NYU/Wagner. New York City.

Palus, Charles J. and David M. Horth (1996). 'Leading creatively: The art of making sense', *Journal of Aesthetic Education*, **30** (4) 53–68.

Parsons, Talcott, R.F. Bales and E.A. Shills (1953). *Working Papers in the Theory of Action*, Glencoe, IL: Free Press.

Pastor, Juan-Carlos (1998). *The Social Construction of Leadership: A Semantic and Social Network Analysis of Social Representations of Leadership*, Ann Arbor, MI: UMI Dissertation Services.

Pfeffer, James (1977). 'The Ambiguity of Leadership', *Academy of Management Review.* **2**, 104–12.

Raelin, Joseph (2003). *Creating Leaderful Organizations: How to Bring out Leadership in Everyone*, San Francisco, Berret Koeler.

Rosenblum, Karen E. and Toni-Michelle C. Travis (2003). *The meaning of difference* (3rd edition), Boston: McGraw Hill.

Rost, Joseph (1993). *Leadership for the Twenty-first Century*, Westport, CN: Praeger.

Senge, Peter (1990). *The Fifth Discipline: The Art and Practice of the Learning Organization*, New York: Currency Doubleday.

Smircich, Linda (1983). 'Leadership as shared meaning', in L. Pundy, G. Morgan and T. Dandridge (eds), *Organizational Symbolism*, Greenwich, CT: JAI Press

Smircich, Linda and Garret Morgan (1982). 'Leadership: The Management of Meaning', *Journal of Applied Behavioral Science.* **18**, 257–73.

Sorenson, Georgia (1992). 'Emergent Leadership: A Phenomenological Study of Ten Transformational Political Leaders', Ann Arbor, MI: UMI Dissertation Services.

Sorenson, Georgia and Gill Hickman (2002). 'Invisible Leadership: Acting on Behalf of a Common Purpose', in Cynthia Cherrey and Larraine R. Matusak (eds), *Proceedings of the International Leadership Association*, James MacGregor Burns Academy of Leadership.

Terry, Robert W. (1993). *Authentic Leadership: Courage in Action*, San Francisco: Jossey-Bass.

Tierney, William (1987), 'The Semiotic Aspects of Leadership: An Ethnographic Perspective', *American Journal of Semiotics*, **5**, 223–50.

Tierney, William and Yvonna Lincoln (eds) (1997). *Representation and the Text: Reframing the Narrative Voice*, Albany, NY: State University of New York Press.

Vanderslice, Virginia (1988). 'Separating Leadership from Leaders: An Assessment of the Effect of Leader and Follower Roles in Organizations', *Human Relations*, **41** (9), 677–96.

9. Contemplating context

J. Thomas Wren and Elizabeth Faier

In the following dialogue, historian J. Thomas Wren and anthropologist Elizabeth Faier, both original members of the General Theory of Leadership group convened in 2001, embark on a journey to 'contemplate context' within a general theory of leadership. As discussed in Chapter 1 of this volume, initial discussions within the general theory group exposed rather deep rifts concerning the importance and role of context in the leadership relation. These early debates inspired Wren and Faier to sit down and reflect more thoroughly on the troubling issue of the role of context. As the ensuing exchange makes clear, the two have some basic disagreements. It is evident that the more traditionalist Wren and the more constructivist Faier diverge in their approaches with regard to the role of context. Wren perceives context as an environment in which leadership takes place while Faier considers context more abstractly, as a space constructed by participants through performance. Despite the disparate starting points, Wren and Faier approach some middle ground through the creative exploration of metaphors and applications. The ensuing dialogue is a conceptual piece, designed not to establish authoritative answers but to lay bare essential questions regarding the ways in which context might inform theoretical thinking about leadership.

*   *   *

T.   OK, Liz. We have decided that the best way to approach our topic of the role of context in leadership theory, given our different perspectives, is by having a dialogue. The working title is 'Contemplating Context.' We've come up with our title, so let's contemplate.

L.   I was thinking – even though I've been trying not to think about this – I was thinking this morning about one of the problems we face in beginning this discussion is the same problem you face in considering context itself, which is that it is very hard to jump into something. I think such a discussion will treat context as a container, and you're either *in* it or you're *out* of it. And so in some ways, you know, if you're in the discussion or out of the discussion it is like the false reality of context being bounded, because obviously you have to start somewhere and through the starting you create something, but of course something exists already.

T.   I find it ironic that our constructivist has been thinking about this conversation ahead of time, while I have not. But let's start with the boundedness.

L.   But I'm an empiricist; don't forget that.

T.   OK. Let's start with the boundedness that we were talking about. You say that the context boundedness is like a vessel. I'm always the historian. I've perceived the context of a surrounding situation as a vessel if you will, within which things happen – although I think we are going to come to some middle ground where players interact with that surrounding vessel. I believe that there are these long-term political, social, economic and intellectual forces that create opportunities and constraints for people who operate within them. Knowing something about these long-term forces helps one to perceive what the leadership possibilities are between leaders and followers. I'm not sure that I would call that some vessel or container like you perceive it, but I certainly perceive a more traditional way of viewing context than you do, so that might be a starting point for our discussion. Ultimately, of course, we have to think about how we would fit our conceptions into a theory of leadership.

L.   Let me back up. I'm not sure that a vessel is quite fair. I tend to think of context as a membrane, and there's movement in and out. For example, when I think about doing research on leadership as an anthropologist, I think about going to another context. So context is often some kind of conflation of geography and people. But at the same time it is very hard not to recognize my own participation in the creation of context because it is an artificial construct that I make, in saying that this is my community. But it's also hard to not recognize that lots of things are going in and out of this membrane. I move in and out of the context and my subjects move in and out of the context. It seems to me that one of the problems with me thinking about context and culture is that it suggests or it puts the brakes on those types of flows. So context at the same time becomes something *out* there but also something produced. I think the same thing, for me, when I think about history. I don't know if you've read Michel-Rolph Trouillot. He is either a cultural historian or an anthropologist of history, I'm not sure, but he is very critical of both the positivist approach and the constructivist approach. He tries to chart a happy medium by saying that in history we are both actors and narrators, and so the historical object is somewhat elusive. You have the narration, but every time you retell the story we recreate, you know, the context, but in a slightly different way. I guess my final thought is after reading Trouillot and after hearing you talk about what does it mean to do history and think about leadership; I'm as unclear when history begins as when cultural difference begins. I'm unclear when we move from one context to another and I'm unclear, for example, how perspective affects that. So obviously if you did history of Jefferson and Jefferson's time period it might look different, right? Than today, or not?

T.   I'm not exactly sure what you mean. Jefferson's time period is certainly different from our time period.

L.   I mean if you were a historian, how does the historical object or the way we think about context change depending on who is looking at them?

T.   I think that historians long have acknowledged that every generation rewrites history, as they sometimes say, because you're looking at issues. You choose issues that are important to you and you interpret them in light of things that seem important to you. So it depends on what is going on in your own age. Historians choose differing topics and things of that nature, so that I don't think there's any doubt that it is acknowledged widely that when historians look at things it is not an *objective* pursuit, it is in many ways a *subjective* pursuit. But I guess the goal is to move toward some kind of objectivity or something along those lines if that's possible to do.

L.   That's what we anthropologists do, by the way, too. You're dealing with archives and people and we're dealing with people and observations of people. It would be nice if it isn't simply our own story.

T.   Right, right, that's why historians amass all the detailed sources and the citations and things, so that theoretically people could go back and retrace the same track. Nobody ever does because there's too much to do but ...

L.   That's why we don't call ourselves postmodernists. I believe in the empirical trail of something.

T.   Well, we may be getting somewhere then. We may have more in common than we first believed. I don't think any historian would have any problems suggesting that the kinds of trends that I mentioned before, when traced forward, become the building blocks of what you call culture; indeed, become the culture. If one defines 'Culture' as that which is learned, shared and transmitted, the things that are learned and shared and transmitted certainly, to historians, link back to the types of things that have gone on in the past. So in some ways we're probably talking about two related facets of the same phenomenon. But it seems to me that one issue that we should be talking about before we get done, is the issue of human agency and the interactions between humans and their surrounding context. As a historian I'm comfortable saying that we have this sort of context that surrounds us, although it is an immensely complex type of thing. But we also need to understand how each individual has to interact within that context, and there is where the agency is. Now I would say I do think that the historical context does make some actions or reactions less likely to occur because it just doesn't fit the possibilities in that context. But it doesn't deny that any individual *could* react in any certain way. So I guess my point is that any human agent can do anything he or she wishes, but that the context makes some actions more likely or, perhaps, more 'rational' than others.

L.   I think much to our horror we are going to find out that we are much closer than we ever thought at some levels. Are you suggesting then that context is not deterministic but creates a framework in which agency occurs and perhaps even agency structures?

T.   Yes, I think that's exactly right; I think we do agree on that. Where we may differ more is in our emphasis. I might think that the surrounding context probably may do more in the way of structuring than you do. That may be where we have some difference of perspective on things. But both interpretations may be important as we think about how we work this into a theory, ultimately.

L.   Can I jump in? Do you mind if I interrupt for a second?

T.   No.

L.   Are you sure? One of the reasons I'm so hot under the collar about context is because when people talk about culture, it doesn't account for movement, doesn't account for agency. To me it's just a reductionistic, deterministic approach to context and it is important for me in thinking in terms of humans actively engaging with and shaping their context.

T.   Well that may be a good starting point to go on further down the path. Maybe we can ultimately determine, be thinking about what that ultimately means, in theoretical terms. We need to see if we can consider the implications for a human relation like leadership.

L.   One thing that might be interesting to think about – and we've already started talking about it – is the relationship between the individual actors within specific – can we say spaces, or contexts?

T.   Yeah, spaces is, again, not something we historians talk about. Context is something historians are comfortable with.

L.   OK. So we can think about how different people in contexts construct their inner vessel, so to speak, and how it relates to the outer.

T.   And your inner vessel is?

L.   Well I'm using your terms.

T.   I don't think I said that.

L.   No, we have proof, Tom.

T.   I'll be drummed out of the historical profession if I said inner vessel.

L.   When I do interviews I'm essentially tapping into people's perspectives. [Authors' subsequent annotation: According to Liz, 'inner vessel' and 'outer vessel' refer to the relation between different frameworks. For example, gender might be an inner vessel context while nongovernmental organization might be the outer vessel context. 'Inner' refers to a more personalized yet still socialized construction of context.] For anthropologists the inner vessel is not a psychological inner vessel and I think probably for you, too, it is not a psychological inner vessel, is it?

T.   I'm suspicious of historians who try to get into the psychology of people because there's not enough proof for it.

L.   So let's get down to basics: Do we think that context is socially constructed or socially produced?

T.   It might be a semantic problem that we struggle with when you say socially constructed or socially produced. To me, not knowing what either of those terms really mean, 'socially produced' sounds more logical to me than 'socially constructed.' My sense of context is that the world happens around you and it shapes you. One of the jobs of a historian is to look at that world to see what has happened and why it has happened and who has been involved in creating what. And ultimately we get to the point where it has some impact on somebody in real time.

Let me suggest one thing – and I'm gonna play to your strength and away from mine because you'll know more about this. As a demonstration, let's think in leadership terms about what is occurring in Iraq. Let's compare how a historian and an anthropologist might study leadership there. Maybe we'll come up with something that will be useful that we can translate into theoretical terms.

As a historian, if I were to go to study Iraq, I would look at long-term things like their religious beliefs, their cultural beliefs, how men and women interact with one another, the roles of families, how they look at leaders and how they perceive the role of followers and things, but I'd also be looking at the long-term economic factors, and all these things that go in to make modern-day Iraq. And then I would say OK, now the leadership challenge for these Iraqis is that they are encountering, or having imposed upon them, the opportunity for democracy of some sort. So, the historian's analysis of this context would go like this: As a historian I would essentially say, OK, these people are dealing with democracy but they are constrained by their long history of belief in a certain religious order and their economic situation, and so on and so on and they also have, perhaps, some possibilities. What I would do is look at the long-term situation that brought them to this point. Then, I would assess the likely impact of the surrounding circumstances, to ascertain how they shape possible responses to the challenge facing a leader or a follower, or some participant in this situation. So to me it is, I think it is – not dangerous, that's too strong – but it is not wise, when we are thinking of theorizing, or thinking about predicting leadership, or thinking about integrating ideas about leadership, to ignore those longer-term things that create the circumstances within which our actors participate. If that makes any sense at all.

L.   Yeah. I'm gonna disappoint you in a second.

T.   It will be the first time you ever disappointed me, Liz.

L.   I also have *that* on tape. I agree with just about everything you say. If I were to go and address leadership in Iraq, I would do it in a similar fashion. I'm not fond of people who use context in a predictive or a deterministic manner. I am much more comfortable when they use it in a suggestive manner, as you do. Does that make any sense? I would do probably the exact same thing that you would do. I would talk to people, I would take note of the changes in political structure, social structure, I'd look at specific events, I would look at specific discourses and how they've changed over time. I would look at the role individuals have played. I would give agency a pretty strong role there. And I would do much of what you were discussing in terms of trying to address whether democratic procedure or democracy is what is in store for Iraq given its turbulent history. At the same time, though, I would try to address or I would try to compare and contrast Iraq with other cultural contexts that might be appropriate. Normally when people say cultural contexts they mean other geographic areas where there are similar peoples. When talking about Middle Eastern culture, I may actually be talking about Iranian dissidents in France, I may be talking about other Middle Eastern spaces or communities. I would look at how they also dealt with some of these issues and then I would look at the ways in which people negotiate meaning.

I constantly battle the question of context. It is very clear to me that context matters but what is unclear to me is how do you get a handle on it? I don't believe in context being only the here and now, but at the same time I think that context constantly shifts. I think it matters, but I think it is constantly being shaped and I'm back to the old discussions of agency and structure.

T.   OK. Can I.... Whenever I hear things I'm always synthesizing them in my head, so let me say what I've been hearing and thinking as we've been talking here and where I think we might be.

L.   We're doing great.

T.   It seems like there are lots of areas of agreement here. I think we both see context as suggested rather than predicted, [L. Yeah.] which is good. Neither one of us is deterministic about it. We both, I think, see a role for human agency within the context – we're all on board there. But there's a couple of differences that are important, that I see, and that we might want to have to play out a little bit more.

One is the extent to which our views of context are capable of being generalized; in other words, whether our approaches to context are so idiosyncratic to each particular study that it is impossible to make any grand statements about the role of context (which, of course, is our ultimate goal here). Historians, for example, are quite skeptical about their ability to make generalizations. They're just interested in their particular chain of events and causation of things and so they wouldn't worry about taking the next step. In fact that's one reason that historians tend not to like leadership studies because leadership studies tends to try to make this kind of connection to things. But if you're going to look at context in leadership terms then I think you have to go beyond the pure historian and think about using some generalization you can make or else again you run into problems. The issue is: Can we generalize in a theoretical way? And this is where you hit your anthropological stumbling block, you know.

L.   Sure.

T.   If context is purely only localistic, then the theoretical possibilities I think are limited. We might be able to come up, at the most, with some structured way to think about context. That may be as far as we can go, however, if it is truly localistic, and if it is impossible to make any generalizations from the study of a particular context.

In terms of making a theoretical statement, I don't know if we can get there. The pure historian also tends to be, in your terms, localistic, saying: 'All I can say is what I have found through the study of these documents. I am not comfortable making any further claims.' But, if we both acknowledge that context is important as part of the leadership relationship, we need to get beyond such narrow thinking. It seems to me that somehow it would be nice if we can come up with a way that people can think productively about context as they look at interactions that could be deemed leadership interactions. Otherwise we marginalize ourselves into this corner and say, well, if you want to know about this particular thing, hire me for 12 months for several thousand dollars and I will give you a study on that, and you would do the same thing – you'd probably charge more.

L.   Less … we're cheap.

T.   But anyhow, you see my point. And so I guess we're at the stage of our conversation where we can begin thinking about whether we can make a contribution to this project [i.e., creating a General Theory of Leadership] in those terms. Now, let me just shut up and let you talk.

L.   OK. A couple of things came to mind. I think it's one thing to talk about context as being locally specific. The question is, I'm going to use slightly different language.

T.   You may have to define your terms.

L.   I'm going to start speaking to you in Arabic.

T.   I wouldn't know the difference.

L.   I know, exactly! Let's see if we can proceed in this way: It seems to me that context is not completely constructed. That is, it is not completely the creation of the participants.

T.   Right.

L.   Here is one way to think about it. Look at this pretty egg yolk diagram.

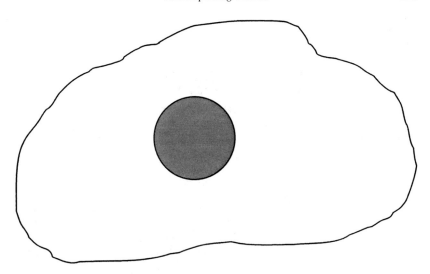

Figure 9.1   Egg yolk drawing

We have the subject here [pointing at the center of the yolk], and it has some kind of personal immediate context [the remainder of the yolk], and we have some sort of larger structural context that has porous boundaries [indicating the white of the egg]. This larger context, it seems to me, could be the values of a time period, could be political events, whatever.

T.   Those are all defined as structural for you?

L.   Yeah.

T.   OK.

L.   Or at least structural in that they provide a parameter in which our little subject guy [the center of the yolk] can bounce around in the bigger picture [the remainder of the yolk and the egg white]. Our theoretical problem, it seems to me, is: How do we convey the importance of context as a 'thing,' yet still enable people to engage it in a dynamic way? That is the crux of things from both our perspectives.

T.   OK, let me build on that a little bit because you're right, and I like your idea of the egg with the yolk in the middle. One time my students and I came up with what we called the leadership amoeba, which is a similar type of thing to what you're talking about.

L.   Yeah.

T.   But instead of having yolk in the middle we called them 'L-cells,' meaning 'leadership cells' – I know, I know, amoebas don't have cells, they were really vacuoles or something – but the point was that the amoeba was being pushed into different shapes by the surrounding fluid [context], and the L-cells were being re-arranged accordingly. This image, I know, is too passive for you, and it needs more active engagement, but it was in some ways the same type of metaphor. But let's stay with your egg and yolk things.

L.   I like the amoeba.

T.   Well maybe we can end up with the amoeba, but let's just talk now. Your yolk is the…. Well let's start with the white. The white is the structural, political and social context that we talked about. The yolk is the individual or group that exists within that context. What happens within the yolk is what I understand as personal agency. That is to say, the individual has free will to interact with his or her surrounding context in an infinite number of ways [in theory], but the reality is that the surrounding context makes some actions more 'rational' and more likely than others. That is represented by the shape of the boundary between the egg white [context] and the yolk [personal agency within that context]. What I'm saying is that although we cannot predict with precision how any specific individual will act within a given context, we can nevertheless construct a rigorous way in which we can analyze the context and can thereby identify the parameters within which each actor in the leadership relation operates. This doesn't get us to the level of a theoretical statement, but it does give us some organized way to think about context and its effect.

L.   Yeah, and I'll explain it to you more in a second. I just realized what I actually meant. Go on.

T.   OK. But if that's so, we're thinking in theoretical terms about what we can say that's beyond somebody's personal case study [which is a step in the right direction]. One way that you could think about it is, well, is there a set of standard questions that we could devise that participants in the leadership relation [or, for that matter, observers] could ask. This would get to the structure part. It might not get to our agency part. You might ask, for example: 'What is it about the economic and social and intellectual context that seems to be important?' This gets us to the constructivist aspect of context, and should satisfy your constructivist genes. Because I do agree that much of what we are talking about is perception, and not some sort of fixed 'reality.' If something doesn't seem to be important to an individual, s/he is unlikely to respond to it or take it into account. Of course, the traditional historian in me insists that there are some objective things, I guess. You are in Iraq, not in Iowa. You know what I mean; there are some things like that. But what I suggest is that we ask some questions about people involved in the leadership relation, to try to articulate what it is out there and how they perceive its impact upon them and things.

L.   Mm hm, right.

T.   But anyhow, there may be some potential here. It is nowhere near the point of theory, maybe, but at least it may suggest useful ways of going forward, of using and drawing upon our insights about the importance of the context.

   Now I'm a little less clear about how we can generalize about agency, because by definition it is so individual. But even here there might be some theoretical potential. Everybody engages in it, I think we've both agreed on that. That is to say, we both agree that everybody acts, and that their actions are not determined; that is, it's not a deterministic type of thing. There might be a way we can get at that too in a way that's productive.

L.   Two thoughts. I like the question idea. As academics, we begin with questions. But we need to take care that we devise the appropriate questions. What's unclear to me is, how do we structure questions so that they're not so broad, that you don't have to take on everything. In other words, how do we begin to question? We need to determine what part of the context or the structure is influential either on the actual agent or in making certain things more important.

   So let's think more deeply about the 'agency' part; that is, how we can better understand an individual's response to the surrounding context. There's a theorist named Pierre Bourdieu, who wrote a book called *The Outline of a Theory of Practice* in the 1970s. He was trying to play with the structure and agency thing, and what he basically said was that the structure is out there; it is all the different things that influence human agency but every individual has what is called a mini-structural habitus – it is a nontranslatable French word – but it basically suggests that all of these points of influence created by the larger context create a kind of a microstructure that is unique to each individual. Within that we all engage in what's produced by our own experiences that are reflective of larger structural pieces out there.

T.   You sounded like a psychologist – be careful.

L.   No, it's experiential. So for example let's say that in a larger structure [context] we have racism, and then the ways in which our subject experiences racism begins to create a microstructure that's much more immediate in his or her actions. So one's actions are reflective of his or her experiences; this is the stuff that really shapes the agency of the subject. I'm not so comfortable with Bourdieu because his outside structure is fixed. What happens is that his inside structure is constantly in flux in response to this subject's interaction with the larger structure. I would argue that the larger context is also in a state of flux, but I do like his idea that we constantly learn context.

T.   There is still, I fear, a disagreement between us. I thought we were moving toward some kind of consensus, but now I hear you suggesting that one's interaction with the surrounding context is so individualistic as to defy any valid generalizations. Our disagreement may come regarding how much agency a person has within that surrounding context. Can a person invent their own reality? I'm not sure. I don't want to take that too far. My thinking is that, as a general rule, context kind of constrains how they respond. I acknowledge that anybody can do anything they want, although it may not be rational in terms of the context, but, like I said, as a general rule context *does* structure the possibilities.

L.   But it seems to me that you are missing something here. Even if context can be constraining, you ignore the possibility that individuals can be spurred by the context to rise above it, and even change it. If you think about leadership, one way of talking about leadership is people as change agents. And then we have to think about the ways in which agency breaks open structures and reconfigures them.
    Let me give an example. I'll use one of my activists (in my study of Palestinians who are citizens of Israel). She told me that she'd bought her daughter a double bed. Not a big deal in our society, but in that society it implies that someone else is going to be sleeping in that bed, and that becomes an issue, a public concern if it's a daughter.

T.   We're trying to sell books, huh? Let's get some sex in here.

L.   Yyyeah. It's actually in my book that came out in October. So ... but for her it was a natural way of changing the larger structure of her community. So. Let me back up again. Let me shift.

T.   Before you leave that example, I want to ask a question. By buying that double bed, she was acknowledging what she was doing but she was accepting the meaning of what it meant to have a double bed. She was constrained by her cultural beliefs and expectations. By buying that double bed she was acknowledging that that double bed had a specific meaning within her culture and her world, and so in a way the structure was imposing itself upon her. I mean she was being the agent but she was accepting or acknowledging...

L.   I think I see your point. On the one hand change agents recognize that there is a surrounding context and generally accepted structures. They reaffirm the meaning of certain structures while at the same time trying to challenge it as part of the change.

T.   I'm OK with that. I think we can agree on that one.

L.   Let's talk about agency and its relationship to the surrounding context, to see how much we disagree.

T.   Good. That gets us back to the theoretical plane.

L.   You go first.

T.   Let me just say that in my work I build up an elaborate historical context within which people operate. All I'm saying is I cannot predict what any one individual will do in response to that, to their perception of that context, which is their agency. They can choose to be totally conformist, or they can choose to be change agents, or any other level of response to the contextual cues and constraints. That to me is their agency. As a historian I can look back to choices already made and try to explain what people did, and, hopefully, why they did it. But as a leadership scholar all I can do is to suggest the contextual constraints and opportunities in which individuals operate. That's the best I can do; I can't predict what any individual will do, given agency as I have described it.

L.   OK. But we're both interested in how we convey the importance of context. So we are both suggesting that context is not simply background. It is influential, but at the same time it is not foreground; it is not the main story, but it is important in – I don't know – something. I guess another way of putting it, and I'm not comfortable saying that context is deterministic, but I think it's influential.

T.   I will agree with that.

[In a separate session sometime after the preceding dialogue, the authors reconvened and agreed upon the following as an appropriate conclusion]

L. & T.   So, it is time we came up with something that might help those who think about leadership with some way of integrating the construct of context into 'theoretical' discussions of leadership. Permit us to propose some tentative conclusions, and to suggest a way that contextual aspects can be addressed in a prospective manner.

First, let us summarize (which we trust draws faithfully from our discussions):

1. The surrounding context does create both opportunities for and constraints upon the actions of individuals.
2. The influence of context upon actors is not, however, a one-way street, with the context impinging upon passive individuals. In dealing with the surrounding context, individuals are more-or-less (within reason) free agents to respond to its cues as they will. As suggested in (1), above, however, the context will make it more likely or less likely that any leadership action will succeed.
3. Nor do individuals just react to contextual realities. They can also be proactive. Our conception of context does not obviate the possibility of change agents. Even here, one can view the surrounding context as being the instigator or catalyst for such change. But it also suggests that actors can shape the context just as much as vice versa. However, this implies that those who seek to confront an existing or hegemonic context will face formidable challenges.
4. We are rejecting a purely constructivist interpretation of context. Although we acknowledge the centrality of an individual's interpretation of the surrounding contextual cues, we are at the same time suggesting that there are sufficient observable features of the context that an outside observer – say, a theorist – can use to suggest or understand behavior.

This brings us to our suggestions for ways in which contextual factors in any leadership situation can be taken into account – which is as close as we can come to a theoretical statement about context. As we suggested above, this can be accomplished by positing a set of questions about any leadership situation:

a. *What are the interests or aspirations of the respective actors in the leadership situation?* Only by knowing (or deducing) these do we gain a baseline from which to gauge the impact of the surrounding context.
b. *What aspects of the surrounding context stand to enhance or impinge upon such interests and aspirations?* This requires the insights that can be provided by the analysis of historians, sociologists, and the like.
c. *How does the actor in question perceive these contextual attributes?* This portion of the assessment looks to the 'interior rationality' of the actor. That is, it seeks to view the surrounding context from the perspective of the actor, irrespective of whether that view appears 'rational' to the observer. For example, even terrorists respond to their contexts in ways they think are rational. This helps us to uncover the individual perceptions that are so important.

These queries lead us to a consideration of context in a theoretical sense, and bring us to the final question of our protocol:

d.   *How does or can our knowledge of these matters help explain/predict the impact that context might have on a particular leadership relation?* This question simply calls upon the observer to pull the above observations together into a conclusion that advances our understanding of the role of context.

Upon reflection, we think this is about as far as we can go in addressing the role of context in leadership. It is not theoretical in any pure sense. But if you think about it, what we have accomplished is not too shabby. We have created an interesting dynamic of agency and constraint, of context and constructivism. It seems as if we are thinking about context with more clarity than prior to our debate here.

*   *   *

As the preceding dialogue makes clear, Wren and Faier differ in their approach to the role of context in the leadership relation, yet find much common ground. As their exchange illustrates, historians and anthropologists tend to pursue different objectives in their examination of context: the former uses context to create a web of surrounding institutions and influences within which to place actions and events, while the latter sees context as an inherent element in the construction of meaning. Despite this fundamental disparity in perspective, both scholars acknowledge surprising similarities in the dynamics of their respective models. Neither views context as deterministic, but instead elaborates a vision of individuals with agency interacting with (and to some extent creating) the context that shapes the leadership relation. Both acknowledge that the context can be constraining, yet also offers opportunities for conduct and, for some change agents, catalyzes action. These similarities ultimately allow them to agree upon a protocol of questions that can help bring understanding to the role context plays in leadership.

In the process of achieving this result, Wren and Faier confronted several challenges that have significance for developing a theory of leadership, which in turn generated corresponding lessons for anyone who aspires to theorize about the role context plays in leadership. It is worthwhile to briefly summarize these here.

First – and again, partly due to their disciplinary differences – language posed a problem for the two scholars. As the dialogue proceeded, Wren and Faier had to grapple with how to speak about context. They had to negotiate a shared understanding of such constructs as agency and structure, objectivity and subjectivity, and the role of rationality. For those hoping to incorporate context when thinking theoretically about the leadership relation, this suggests the importance of articulating with specificity the understanding and use of such constructs.

A second challenge that follows from Wren and Faier's discussion relates to the extent to which one can generalize theoretically about the role of context. It is almost a truism that all contexts are distinct, and that individual agents will interact with such contexts in unpredictable ways. Yet Wren and Faier recognize that an inability to generalize at some level beyond the idiosyncratic and the localistic dooms any pretence to a theoretical statement about the role of context in leadership. The two scholars eventually agreed that grand deterministic statements about the role of context are not possible. They must content themselves, ultimately, with that protocol of structuring questions that help the analyst perceive the dynamic interaction between the individual and her/his context. While falling far short of a theoretical statement in any traditional sense of the term, this nonetheless does provide a technique for understanding the role of context more thoroughly.

This dialogue between Elizabeth Faier the anthropologist and J. Thomas Wren the historian, spurred by the difficulties the idea of context posed for a theory of leadership, becomes one more thread in the complex tapestry that is the quest for a general theory of leadership.

REFERENCES

Michel-Rolph Trouillot, *Silencing the Past: Power and the Production of History* (Boston: Beacon Press, 1997).

Pierre Bourdieu, *Outline of a Theory of Practice* (Cambridge: Cambridge University Press, 1977).

10. What we learned along the way: a commentary

Joanne B. Ciulla

If the only purpose of our quest was to arrive at a general theory of leadership, then it was a terrific failure. We sometimes disagreed on which way to go, we got irritable and lost, and we did not even visit all of the areas of leadership studies. Nevertheless, like all great quests, ours was never really about finding the Holy Grail of leadership studies; it was about the journey. It took us away from the constraints of our disciplines and homes in academia. When we got lost, we found ourselves in surprising new places, some of which are described in this book. This chapter is a commentary on the journey and what we learned along the way.

SOME GENERAL OBSERVATIONS

The chapters in this book are eclectic in style and content. For example, we have Tom Wren's dialogue with Liz Faier on context, and Michael Harvey's account of our Mount Hope papers, framed as a story about the beginnings of leadership in some primordial state of nature. Not only are the styles of writing in the chapters different, the essays themselves are idiosyncratic. Each chapter reflects the research interests, and academic background, of the authors. Mark Walker compares theories of leadership to theories of international relations. Gill Hickman and Dick Couto anchor their discussion around a case study from the civil rights movement. Terry Price and Doug Hicks use the concept of equality to write about ethics. Like the rest of the chapters, this commentary reflects my own discipline and research lens – other members of the group would have written it differently. As mentioned in Chapter 1, I take the view that ethics is about all human relationships and that leadership is simply a specific variety of human relationship. Hence, I see the study of leadership as the study of a distinct type of moral relationship and my commentary reflects that assumption.

The chapters also differ in tone. When Crystal Hoyt, Al Goethals, and Ron Riggio write about group dynamics, influence, and social perception in Chapter 5, they do so with a crisp confidence. I would not call them positivists, but their chapter does sound more positive than the rest and it covers familiar terrain in leadership studies. Contrast the Hoyt, Goethals, and Riggio chapter with Sonia Ospina and Georgia Sorenson's somewhat angst-ridden constructionist view of leadership in Chapter 8 or Liz Faier and Tom Wrens' struggle to understand each other in Chapter 9. The difference in tone reflects a difference in epistemology. How we know about leadership is inseparable from what we know about leadership.

I originally suggested that by the end of the project, we would be able to map leadership studies. There are already plenty of maps in Chapter 3. The tables in Mark Walker's chapter on theory are conceptual maps, drawn from the perspectives of both the content of the study of leadership and various epistemological approaches to it. In retrospect, the last thing that we needed was another map of leadership studies. The group clearly had a general idea of what is there. For example, after over two years of discussion, it was relatively easy to decide what chapters to put in this book. Maybe this is because, as leadership scholars, we have known all along that there are clearly certain things one takes into account when one studies leadership. Leadership is part of the human condition and, as such, is about wants, needs, power, conflict, equality, liberty, change, causality, group dynamics, cooperation, coordination, leader–follower relationships, ethics, meaning, context, culture, etc. There are also certain things one talks about in regard to the epistemology of leadership. They include methods of research, theory, and meta-theory. The problem that became clear to our group was that we knew what the pieces of leadership studies are, but we did not know how to put them together. In short, we did not need to find a map, we needed to find a navigator.

Early on in the project, Jim Burns said it would be nice if the GTOL project could simply come up with some basic principles that could be taught in a leadership course. This sounds like a modest request, but it reminded me of how difficult it is to decide what one teaches in a leadership course. In 1991, Richard Couto and I, along with four colleagues, designed the curriculum for the Jepson School of Leadership Studies. Despite the fact that, at that time, none of us considered ourselves leadership scholars, it was fairly easy to draw up the curriculum. The curriculum took us a day to write. The introductory course took us a whole semester, and the resulting course was a nightmare. Our curriculum encompassed two very broad aspects of leadership literature – traits and context; or to put it another way – the leader and everything else. The actual relationship of leaders to followers seemed to fall in between traits and context. Even today, most contingency theories only scratch the surface of how these two areas intersect. The same tension between leaders and context was a reoccurring theme in our discussions.

The context of leadership heavily influences the way that a scholar thinks and writes about it. Most of the authors in this collection were not thinking about business leadership when they wrote their chapters. All of the chapters, except for the one on groups, assume leadership in politics, communities, and social movements. Most of the leadership literature comes from business schools and researchers with backgrounds in organizational behavior and social and industrial psychology. When we study leadership as a phenomenon, we look for features of it that span across different contexts. Nonetheless, there exists one major difference between the relationship of leaders and followers in business and in politics – business leaders are not democratic. Moreover, I think that assumptions about democracy make a bigger difference in how scholars theorize about leadership than we generally acknowledge. The work of this group was theory-laden with Enlightenment ideas and democratic assumptions. It would be very interesting to see what a group of scholars from different disciplines or from a non-Western culture would do if they were asked to come up with a general theory of leadership. Sadly, this is the kind of literature that is missing in leadership studies.

Another curious outcome of our project was the emergence of Thomas Hobbes as a key player in our discussions. There were no Hobbes aficionados in the group, but the questions that concerned Hobbes about human nature and leadership kept popping up. While Niccolò Machiavelli's work is a staple in leadership studies, his near contemporary Hobbes is not. So why does Hobbes's spirit or Hobbes himself show up in Chapter 2 on the Mount Hope papers, Chapter 5 on power and conflict, Chapter 6 on ethics and equality, and Chapter 7 on causality and change? First, because we started the Mount Hope project with a state-of-nature question: 'What is it about the human condition that makes leadership possible?' Hobbes offers a theory of human nature based on common wants, needs, dispositions, conflict, power, liberty, equality, and justice – many of the same elements of leadership discussed by the GTOL group. Hobbes gives us a baseline account of why we need leaders. We need them to give us order and security so that we can be free to pursue our wants and needs. This idea of leadership applies to the sovereign of a state or to the volunteer who stepped into the street to direct traffic during the 1965 blackout in New York. The second reason why Hobbes kept coming up in our discussions is because of the way that he links equality to questions about morality and power. These are specific themes that run throughout these chapters even though the authors do not necessarily embrace the same conclusions as Hobbes. So, let us begin by looking at equality.

EQUALITY

Hobbes talks about equality in a descriptive and prescriptive sense. He says people are equal in the sense of having the same needs and they are morally equal as human beings. Price and Hicks's Chapter 6, while perhaps not by intent, is a Hobbesian project of sorts. The important underlying question is: Are leaders equal to followers? They answer that if leaders are unequal to followers, then this has to be justified under some larger claim of equality (p. 124). Their use of equality here is normative, meaning *should* leaders get different treatment?

Another way to ask this question is: 'Are leaders different from followers?', which is actually a rendition of 'What is a leader?' Most leadership scholars answer the first question with a resounding 'Yes' and go on to explain how leaders are different, based on research into influence tactics, social perception, personality traits and a number of other psychological factors discussed in the chapter on groups. Psychologists regard leadership as a cocktail of behaviors and types of relationships. The leader plays a different role in relationships or exhibits different behaviors. Historians and biographers chronicle the deeds and lives of people who made great contributions to the world, whereas constructivists argue that leaders are not different as individuals with special traits or personalities, but differentiated by the way that society constructs the idea of leaders or by the context. Research on social perception and implicit leadership theories seems to imply the same thing as the constructivists, but they do so using different terms (Chapter 8, p. 200). If we take the theories discussed in the chapter on groups as a whole, they say leaders are not the same as followers *and* followers construct ideas about leaders and their relationship to leaders. These may be different routes to the same conclusion.

Some leadership scholars and members of the GTOL group seem to have a discomfort with leaders. We see this in Price and Hicks's chapter, but also in Chapters 4, 7, and 9. This is a strong democratic, egalitarian and perhaps libertarian unease with the idea that anyone is better than the rest or that anyone has the right to tell us what to do. So one aspect of the equality question as started by our man Hobbes and continued in Price and Hicks, is part of the dialectic between traits and context. Their concern is that we should not give leaders special rights and privileges even if they possess superior traits, skills, and intelligence like Plato's guardians in the *Republic*. Price and Hicks criticize Plato because he proposed picking out the best and the brightest and most fit to rule, and then giving leaders special treatment.

In the *Republic*, Plato says leaders are not at all equal to followers in the descriptive sense of 'same' but he believes they are morally equal and equal under the law. I think is it even more interesting to notice that Plato changed his mind on this point later in life. He lost faith in his conviction that leadership was about 'the Great man.' In *Epistle VII* he wrote, 'the older I grew, the more I realized how difficult it is to manage a city's affairs rightly. For I saw that it was impossible to do anything without friends and loyal followers' (Plato, 'Epistle VII' [1971]). Plato also concedes that leaders are like their followers. In the *Republic*, he portrays the leader as a shepherd to his flock. But in a later work, *The States-*

man, he says that a leader is not at all like a shepherd because shepherds are quite different from their flocks, whereas human leaders are not very different from their followers (Plato, 'Statesman [1971]). Furthermore, Plato argues, people are not sheep; some are cooperative and some are very stubborn. Hence, Plato's revised view was that leaders are like weavers. Their main task is to weave together different kinds of people such as the meek and self-controlled and the brave and impetuous into the fabric of a society (ibid., 310e). Notice the difference between the idea of a leader as a philosopher king and the leader who facilitates group processes.

Leaders may not be equal in the sense of being the same as others, but Price and Hicks argue that leaders should be morally the same as others. So in some respects, leaders are born and in some respects leaders are in the eyes of the beholders. One reason why leadership scholars may feel like they were spinning their wheels is because they rarely go any farther than this in their analysis. Here is where the ethics and history fill out the picture and the second meaning of equality comes into play.

The normative sense of equality is fundamental to almost all ethical systems. It is the idea that all people are deserving of equal respect and consideration as human beings. Followers and leaders are moral equals. Immanuel Kant offers a nice way to think about the moral equality of people. He says we all live in a 'Kingdom of Ends' in which all people legislate morality and are subject to it (Kant 1993). This idea is a refinement of the Golden Rule, which Hobbes cites as essential for society – 'do unto others as you would have others do unto you' or 'do not do unto others as you would not have them do unto you.' The 'others' in the rule are the same as you and me. They are human beings whom you must assume are rational and hence, capable of being able to reciprocate. Even if they do not look or act like you, you assume that you share enough of the same capacities for reason and imagination. Kant alters this rule by removing the idea of reciprocity. He tells us to act as you would want everyone to act. This implies that you cannot make yourself an exception to the moral rules that you would want everyone else to live by. John Rawls's theory of justice draws from these basic concepts.

Yet, when we read history or the daily newspaper, we see that the issue of moral equality is the source of problems with leaders and their relationship to followers. Some leaders believe that they are not subject to the same moral rules as everyone else. Other leaders do not regard other individuals and groups worthy of the same moral consideration as everyone else. We read about leaders who do not think that they have to pay taxes, or of leaders who persecute or kill minority groups in their own countries or exploit their workers. The first kind of problem stems from what Price and Hicks call the privileges of being leader, or as comedian Mel Brooks once said, 'It's good to be the King!' Kings or unelected leaders think they are unequal by birthright or by their position.

Institutions and organizations socially construct the role of a leader and implicitly or explicitly give extra advantages to leaders. In the case of democracy, Price and Hicks say that when followers are the source of unequal treatment, they get the leaders they deserve (Chapter 6, p. 130). But this is not the complete story either. Context matters, but it also depends on who the leader is. Psychologists have written extensively on the problems with narcissistic leaders, leaders who have a weak internal locus of control and socialized and non-socialized uses of power (Maccoby 2000). People in a democracy do not always know what they are getting when they vote for a leader. They can sometimes be fooled, but usually not for long.

A leader's job description is inherently utilitarian. It is interesting to note how John Stuart Mill's replies to critics of utilitarianism help us understand the moral responsibilities of leadership (Mill 1987). One objection is that most people cannot or do not know what the greatest good is for the greatest number of people. Mill points out that, usually, we do not make utilitarian judgments that concern everyone in the world. We know from our own experiences what other people want and we make choices based on what is good for a specific group of people, not the whole world. Yet, it is the case that some leaders actually do make choices that have an impact on large numbers of people, many of whom they never know about or meet. Another objection to Mill's theory is that the utilitarian calculation concerning how to determine what will bring about the greatest happiness or serve the common good is too cold and calculating and does not consider individual relationships. Mill replies that morality *is* about the application of principles such as the greatest good and the minute you start molding your idea of the good to the relationship you have with particular individuals, you lose the principle.

Utilitarianism emphasizes moral equality and consistency that does not allow for exceptions for family and friends. While Mill is talking about morality that applies to everyone, if you think about it, this is an explicit part of a leader's job. Consider, for example, the absurdity of this job description: 'Wanted: leaders who will make exceptions to laws, policies, and procedures for themselves, friends, family, ethnic and religious groups, and people that they like better than their other constituents.' While there are leaders who behave this way (it is descriptively true), we would not consider this part of what it means to lead (so in this sense it is descriptively false). This is one reason why I think certain basic moral principles are embedded in the concept of what it means to be a leader.

POWER

All leadership scholars recognize that one of the factors that differentiates leaders from followers is power and influence. Power is both a cause and an effect of inequality. There are many good reasons to want strong leaders, but there are just as many reasons to fear them. As Harvey points out, we find stories about the violent abuse of power in history, the newspaper, and the even in the jungle. This kind of power is crude and some leadership scholars would not even want to call people who used fear and intimidation leaders (the ancient Greeks called these people tyrants not rulers). Such leaders also do not pass any test of legitimacy. In the business literature on leadership, there is an implicit desire for what Max Dupree called the illusion of 'leading without power' (Chapter 4, p. 75). Notice in the first part of the chapter on groups, Hoyt, Goethals, and Riggio explain how leaders can intervene to make work groups more productive. Does understanding group dynamics allow one to lead without power? Academics who are skeptical about leadership programs argue that such programs teach students how to psychologically manipulate people. That might be the case if you only taught the psychology of leadership without teaching students anything else about literature, art, history, ethics, society, etc. The dark side of understanding the psychological aspects of leadership is manipulation; the bright side of it is that it enables leaders to help groups lead themselves.

What kind of power sustains leadership over time? Harvey tells us it is the power that followers are willing to give the leader. In his example from Shakespeare's play *Coriolanus*, a commoner says, 'We have power in ourselves' and then says 'a power that we have no power to do' (Chapter 4, p. 74). Followers make the leader, but sometimes only so long as the leader does what they cannot do. Leadership is a constant power transaction. Sometimes it is an open conflict and struggle and at other times it is a silent accounting process. Followers sometimes get the upper hand, as in Orwell's story of 'Shooting an Elephant,' where the social influence of the crowd forces the leader to do something that he does not want to do – namely, shoot the elephant. As Le Bon observed, sometimes crowds act but do not think. Nonetheless, there are also instances when the morals of a crowd are higher than those of the individuals in it (Chapter 5, p. 97).

Machiavelli tells us power is about the emotions of love and fear, but I would argue these emotions often run parallel to the morality and immorality of leaders' vision, values, behaviors, and relationships to followers. Morally good leaders are more likely to evoke love, and bad ones are more likely to evoke fear. By morality, I mean the basic rightness or wrongness of how leaders and followers treat each other, starting with respect for persons, which has been discussed as moral equality by Price and Hicks. We morally assess leaders and followers in three areas that can be summed up this way: Do they do the right thing, the right way, and for the right reason?

We may need leaders for order and control, but we will always face the problem of controlling the controllers. Democracy and the law offer ways to do this in public life. The structure of organizations is supposed to do this in business.

Trust is a combination of faith and security. When people do not trust their leaders, they feel insecure because they cannot tell whether a leader will keep promises, tell the truth, etc. In this way, morality negotiates the distribution of power. Leaders who do not have the trust of their followers have less power and need more power to lead. Leaders who trust and have the trust of their followers have more power and need less power to lead. Tyler and Lind's experiments with leader–follower relations in organizations found that people regarded leaders who practiced procedural justice fairer than those who practiced distributive justice (Chapter 5, p. 115). This is not surprising because procedural justice establishes a structure for trust that is somewhat separate from the leader. The process is public and hence outside of the leader. Leaders who use procedural justice make part of their notion of fairness visible. It is easier to trust things that you can see. Distributive justice requires more faith in leaders when followers cannot see the process that is used to make decisions. There is always the chance that these leaders will not distribute the rewards fairly in the future.

Aung San Suu Kyi offers an interesting illustration of how morality negotiates power. Harvey describes her power as 'the power of charisma.' He cites Weber's definition of charisma: 'a certain quality of an individual personality by virtue of which he is considered extraordinary and treated as endowed with supernatural, superhuman, or at least specifically exceptional powers or qualities' (Chapter 4, p. 82). The scene that Harvey describes of Suu Kyi leading people past soldiers with guns, is at least as much about the moral rightness of what she represents as it is about her personality. Some people become leaders because they represent things that people recognize or come to recognize as fundamentally morally right or just. The word charisma has come to mean so many things these days that it is difficult to tell if it is the source of a leader's power and success or the result of a leader's power and success.

The source of Suu Kyi's power, like the power of Mahatma Gandhi, Nelson Mandela, and Martin Luther King, Jr. rests on a solid moral foundation. Even today we recognize these three leaders as great because they tried to do the right thing, the right way, and for the right reason. In some cases, charisma may be the cause of such leaders' success, but in other cases charisma is the effect of their success or their efforts. People can have moral power without charisma and they can have charisma without being moral. The distinction is important because charismatic leadership based on the feelings that a personality evokes may not be as sustainable a force as the moral principles that a leader represents. This is what Kelman calls internalization of influence (Chapter 5, p. 108). Leaders who behave morally or represent important ideals of justice, fairness, equality, liberty, etc. are more likely to have lasting influence on people, regardless of their personalities or their proximity to or contact with followers.

CHANGE

It is useful to look at how morality negotiates power in the case of Barbara Rose Johns, the 11th grader who contributed to the end of school segregation in 1951 (Chapter 7). Hickman and Couto never mention anything about her charisma. It seems unnecessary when describing someone who is doing something that he or she feels is morally right. One might assume from the description in their chapter that Barbara Rose is tenacious, brave, and talented at influencing and mobilizing people. Another reason why the authors of Chapter 7 do not dwell on her personality is because their essay addresses the question: Do leaders create change or does change create leaders? Their interest is in the social conditions of change. Most conditions of social change rest on questions of justice, fairness, equality, or some kind of harm to people. These are all moral problems as well as social problems. In the Johns story, the ethical issue is inequality in the education system. As Hickman and Couto analyze the social conditions of the case, the causal connection between Johns's leadership of the school strike and the Supreme Court decision of *Brown vs. Board of Education* is not at all a straight one. They conclude that action to bring about social change requires more than one leader. It requires a web of committed followers and groups.

Clearly leaders cannot do things alone; as a matter of fact, by definition they do things with followers. This raises a number of questions about the agency of leaders. First, history frequently gives credit to leaders as initiators of change. Second, researchers such as Jim Meindl and his colleagues found that people tend to attribute events and control to individual senior leaders. They call this 'The Romance of Leadership' (Meindl et al. 1985) and note that it is irrelevant whether leaders actually have control over events. People want to believe that the heroic single leader changes the world. Leaders may not have agency if we analyze the entire system or context of a social change in history or if we try to draw a linear path of causation from the leader to the intended change, but maybe this is not important. Perhaps what is important is that people think that they do. Going back to Hobbes, if the primordial function of a leader is to create order or have someone in control, wouldn't we also want someone who could be held responsible? Those who are reluctant to give leaders too much credit for a positive social change, are often not reluctant to blame leaders for problems. For example, if the police killed some of the students in Johns' student demonstration, would not there be a sense in which she was responsible, even though the actual events were out of her hands?

Herein lies one of the moral peculiarities of people who take on leadership. Leaders, like everyone else, are responsible for the things that they do but they are also held responsible for things that they do not do either because of the position that they hold or because 'they started it.' Leaders are praised or blamed for their own actions, the actions of their followers, and for a variety of factors that go wrong in the environment. For instance, politicians have won and lost elections because of economic conditions that are beyond their ability to control. In short, when it comes to the context of leadership, some leaders experience good or bad moral luck. They try to do the right thing, but are defeated by external factors that are outside of their control, or they do something careless, stupid, or risky and things turn out all right (Ciulla 2004).

The question of agency takes us back to the tension between the leader and the context. Another way that the GTOL group differed from traditional leadership scholars is that several of its members held the view that the context of leadership was more important than the leader. As Ospina and Sorenson point out in their essay, the popular literature and the literature of social psychologists has focused on the influence process and the heroic notion of leadership. Hickman and Couto also frame the relationship between the leader and the context as a debate between the essentialists and constructivists. Essentialists are those who believe 'that reality (social and natural) exist apart from our perceptions of that reality and that individuals *perceive* the world rather than construct it.' They tell us, 'constructionists believe that … reality cannot be separated from the way people perceive it' (Chapter 7, p. 152). There is an inherent contradiction in the constructivist position. If reality is what people perceive it to be and if society believes that leaders cause social change, then does it not follow that in that society leaders cause change? (This may be a little like Meindl's Romance of Leadership.) A constructivist would have a difficult time refuting this point without assuming certain objective ideas about causation.

AGENCY AND CONTEXT

Questions about agency lurk in the corners of every chapter in this book. They are fundamental to understanding what a leader is and what a leader does in relation to others. Wren and Faier's dialogue on context specifically addresses the question of human agency but in a slightly different way than Hickman and Couto's chapter on change. They frame the question of agency in terms of how people interact with their context. Through dialogue, Wren and Faier discover to their surprise, that they agree – 'context is not deterministic but creates a framework in which agency occurs and perhaps even structures' (Chapter 9, p. 208). The issue then shifts to whether context structures what is possible or whether it produces what is possible. How one responds to this question determines how much agency a leader has.

Underlying the agency/context question is a larger question about free will and determinism, which is the mother of all philosophic questions. Are human actions free or are they determined by a variety of outside forces? Different people ask this question in different ways. A historian might wonder, did a leader or an event cause change or did things just fall into place? Free will lurks in the shadows of theories and research in psychology. No matter how sound the research is about causes and patterns of behavior and human interactions, people can still decide to behave differently. The psychologist's question of free will and determinism is bound up with the moral and theological questions. If human behavior is determined by a variety of individual and group factors or, in the case of religion, by God, then how can we hold individuals morally responsible for their actions? For example, does the fact that the mass murderer was an abused child morally excuse him? Would we treat him differently if he had a happy well-adjusted childhood? For the theologian who believes that God is good, all-powerful, and omniscient, there is the question: 'Why do we have so much evil in the world?' As you can see, these huge questions still point back to old Hobbes. They are questions about how much control we have over our lives, the lives of others, and the world around us. As such, they are also questions about power, influence, and responsibility for our actions. It is in the context of these fundamental questions that leaders have played a distinctive role or, if you like, have been perceived as playing a distinctive role.

I have never been happy with the idea that leaders create meanings. It sounds a little too much like demagoguery. This probably reflects my discomfort with charisma as well. I think that meaning is something that, by its very nature, has to be found, not spoon fed. Most would agree with Ospina and Sorenson that meaning is socially constructed. As we see in the chapter on groups, there is clear empirical evidence that people are influenced by the meanings in a group, but I still think that the individual intervenes in the process. Meaning is a normative concept that is intimately intertwined with what is important to people, what they value. Sometimes leaders help people to realize what is important. As Ospina and Sorenson note, leaders play a role in helping communities clarify what matters most (Chapter 8, p. 193). Harvey's description of Suu Kyi and the case of Johns are both about leaders who believed in justice enough to do something about injustice. Those who chose to follow them may have always believed in the same thing, but were never motivated to do anything about it.

Leaders may bring about change or groups may bring about change, but as human beings, the connection between human agency and context is important because causation is an essential part of responsibility. We need responsibility for order and for justice. Like answers to all great questions, the best answer to the free will/determinism question is that we have some of each – our choices are free *and* they are determined. Philosophers, historians, theologians, psychologists, and others, continue to debate it, because few agree on exactly how much of each we have. I would frame the discussions of context and the agency of leaders by asking the transcendental question: What is it that makes it possible for this particular person to be a leader in this particular context? In doing so, it forces us to consider leaders and context, but it also opens up the possibility for a variety of answers. For example, sometimes leadership does come, as Thomas Carlyle said, from great men and women. Other times it comes from a group or a complex web of individuals, as in the case of Johns and school desegregation. There are also times when leadership is thrust upon a person by circumstance. As William Shakespeare observed, 'some are born great, some achieve greatness, and some have greatness thrust upon them' (Shakespeare [1994]). No matter what the genesis of a leader is, he or she only leads as long as people follow.

AT THE END OF THE ROAD

Throughout the years that the GTOL group met, I wondered if Burns was being coy about his real goals for this project. In the beginning, he said that leadership studies needed a 'grand' or generalized theory of leaders and subordinates. He suggested that such a theory would 'legitimize a field that some skeptics still dismiss as lightweight and ill-defined … . We are intent,' said Burns, 'on making [leadership studies] an intellectually responsible discipline' (Managan 2002). These are different agendas that are tied together by the assumption that you have to have a theory to have legitimacy. But maybe the idea of finding a theory was just a ruse to get people talking.

I think this project demonstrated, first, that you do not have to have a theory to be legitimate; second, a grand theory would not be helpful. The academic world, like today's social and political world, has become increasingly polarized. Scholars live behind the closed walls of their departments, sometimes divided into theoretical camps that talk only to other true believers. While there is nothing wrong with having a theory or holding a strong philosophical position, such approaches rarely get us closer to the truth, unless we engage in dialogue with people who hold different views and come from other academic and cultural backgrounds. Psychologists and organizational theorists have been working in leadership studies the longest, but even they complain that they do not seem to be getting anywhere. They have discovered many things about human behavior, but without the rich context of the humanities to put it in, their work on leadership appears fragmented and incomplete. Humanists look at leadership against an enormous social, cultural, and philosophic landscape. Without the empirical work of psychologists and other social scientists to either verify or falsify their impressions of human behavior, the humanists' observations on leadership appear speculative or anecdotal.

When we step back and look at the ruminations about leadership in this book, we see that the study of leadership provides another way to ask very big questions about who we are, how we live together, and how we shape the course of history. It reinforces my belief that leadership is ultimately a moral endeavor.

When it is done right, leaders help to create the conditions for people to flourish physically, mentally, and as human beings, and they do so without harming others or the world around them. At the end of the road, the GTOL met one of Burns's goals. These chapters are not perfect or all encompassing expositions but, taken as a whole, they demonstrate that the real problem with leadership studies is not that it is too lightweight, but that it is too heavy. It takes more than one scholar, discipline, or theoretical approach to understand leadership. The study of leadership forces us to tackle the universal questions about human nature and destiny. For those questions, there will probably never be a general theory.

REFERENCES

Ciulla, Joanne B. 'Ethics and Leadership Effectiveness,' in John Antoniakis, Anna T. Cianciolo, and Robert J. Sternberg (Eds.), *The Nature of Leadership*. Thousand Oaks: Sage Publications, 2004, pp. 302–27.

Kant, Immanuel. J.W. Ellington (Tr.), *Foundations of the Metaphysics of Morals*, Indianapolis, IN: Hackett Publishing Company, Inc., 1993.

Maccoby, Michael. 'Narcissistic Leaders,' *The Harvard Business Review*, 78, 1.1 (2000): 69–75.

Managan, Katherine, 'Leading the Way in Leadership: The Unending Quest of the Discipline's Founding Father, James MacGregor Burns,' *The Chronicle of Higher Education*, 31 May 2002, p. 1.

Meindl, J.R., S.B. Ehrlich and J.M. Dukerich. 'The Romance of Leadership,' *Administrative Science Quarterly*, 1985, 30: 521–51.

Mill, J.S. Alan Ryan (Ed.), *Utilitarianism and Other Essays*, New York: Penguin Books, 1987, pp. 276–97.

Plato, 'Epistle VII.' L.A. Post (Tr.), ed. Edith Hamilton and Huntington Cairns *The Collected Dialogues of Plato*, Princeton: Princeton University Press, 1971, 325c–326.

Plato, 'Statesman.' J.B. Skemp (Tr.), in Edith Hamilton and Huntington Cairns, 1971, 275b–c.

Shakespeare, William. 'The Twelfth Night or, What You Will,' *William Shakespeare: The Complete Works*, New York: Barnes & Noble Books, 1994, p. 654.

Afterword

James MacGregor Burns

Like other members of the GTOL group, I expect, I turned years ago to the study of leadership because I wanted to broaden my range of thought beyond my traditional disciplines. I had been teaching and writing for many years in my professional field of political science and in American history. Both of these fields had become so all-embracing and hence fragmented – as evidenced by their annual professional meetings – that I sought a rewarding field of study that had more intellectual unity, or at least coherence. As I began work in this new field, however, I found that I needed to educate myself further in psychology, because motivation is a central force in leadership, and in philosophy, because it posed the moral and ethical tests of leadership.

All this raised a further difficulty. Was I moving beyond political science and history because of their extreme specialization only to encounter even more fragmentation in the study of leadership? This depended on the state of leadership studies. History and political science were old and established, with little intellectual discipline in their disciplines. No one expected more from them. But the study of leadership in the late 1900s was still developing. There still might be an opportunity to develop a general theory or take a major step toward it. Thus I challenged my colleagues to attempt to develop the general theory.

By the time the General Theory of Leadership Project held its long meeting at Mount Hope Farm in Williamstown in June 2002, the doughty participants were fully aware of the daunting intellectual endeavor that lay ahead. We came from different disciplines, as we had planned, but our work would be both enriched and complicated by the diverse fields and backgrounds of the participants. Still, we had some advantages. We had long worked together, at the Academy of Leadership at the University of Maryland, at Williams College, and especially at the Jepson School of Leadership Studies at the University of Richmond. Some had 'team-taught' leadership classes across different disciplines. And we knew how to disagree agreeably.

Why, specifically, were we there? To try to work out a general – even a grand – theory of leadership, or at least an 'integrated' one, or failing even that, to lay the intellectual foundations for others to build on. We knew, with Joanne Ciulla, that we could not make progress unless we engaged 'in dialogue with people who hold different views and come from other academic backgrounds.' At Mount Hope we had hope but no illusions.

And what, specifically, did I want when I envisaged a general theory of leadership? I wanted an intellectual frame within which I at least could organize my own thinking. I wanted a strenuous effort to prevent the study of leadership from becoming as morselized as other fields of study, or even worse, trivialized. I wanted to use leadership as a better way of understanding the crucial factors in historic causation and social change – factors that can be prioritized such as ideas, motivation, political structures (such as parties), and historic openings and closures within which these variables operate. Above all, I wanted a discipline that tested action by a clear set of moral values and ethical norms.

My own understanding of the relevant crucial variables begins with the human conditions of wants and needs among masses of people experiencing hunger and happiness, order and disorder, tension and mystery. People in want thoroughly know only one thing – their wants, whether food, a good school, a road to that school, medical aid, literacy, sanitation, shoes, etc., etc. What they lack is knowledge as how to gain these things – they lack also the self-confidence, self-efficiency, self-respect, and the skills necessary to gain what they wish. Rather they feel powerless, hopeless, clueless, perhaps also angry and violence-prone. It is the job of leadership to legitimate certain of their wants, just as a mother legitimates milk rather than soda to her thirsty child or a doctor prescribes one kind of drug and not another. Complicating this process is the likelihood that the wants are not only simple deprivations but varieties within every want of poor nourishment, lack of transportation, medical condition, education, etc., which again the impoverished can feel but cannot solve on their own.

It is the job of leadership not only to legitimate certain wants or collections of 'sub-wants' but to educate and instruct and guide followers toward solutions. This creates a leader–follower relationship. Can we generalize about this relationship? We agree that all people are interdependent, that they know the necessity of coordinated action, that coordination does not just happen but has to be constructed, that people have different roles and capacities, that people have different goals (which for the moment we can generalize and simplify as 'happiness'), and that leadership is necessary to articulate these goals as well, of course, as to the means of realizing them.

In the emerging leader–follower relationship the first – but by no means the only – task of leadership is interaction with followership in meeting the priority of order. But order in itself is hopelessly inadequate unless it is employed to meet a second challenge; that of protecting core values, such as freedom, justice, opportunity, equality of opportunity or of condition, or ultimately happiness

What might serve as examples of the leader–follower relationship? A seemingly simple example might be that of a politician walking down a city street, spotting a person walking up the opposite sidewalk, and approaching her. He would like her support, especially since she is a women's rights activist, and she of course wants his support in the legislature or city hall. Perhaps they do a deal, or disagree and part. But is it that simple? In what political context does this interaction take place? Ideological? Purely transactional? Psychological? Who are the other players on each side? What women's rights organizations or party organizations may be involved on each side? In short, on what terrain of action and of meaning is each side operating?

An epochal incident in American civil rights history offered a real-life example of the interaction. The example of a single black woman refusing to go to the back of the bus electrified Americans. Here was 'individual efficacy' personified. But again, the situation was far more complex. Rosa Parks was by no means all alone. This was her second effort, not a sole act of courage out of the blue. She had long been considered as a possible test case. More important, she was part of a large group of activists that had been planning a strategic act for some time. Some of these were, or would become, famous, such as Martin Luther King, Jr. Others, perhaps more influential than the highly visible, were persons who received little publicity. Some of the key players were, in fact, wholly invisible, for tactical and other reasons. The bus boycott took place in the historic context of the national and international civil rights movements, the campaigns of the NAACP and many other organizations, judicial decisions such as *Brown*, battles in Congress, and/or state legislatures and city councils, lynchings, the deaths of civil rights workers in the South, the shift of black support from the old Abolitionist Republican party to the New Deal and LBJ Democratic Party, etc. So Rosa Parks was by no means alone. But this is not to undervalue the potential of a single courageous act. She maintained her ground – literally her seat – under immense direct pressure and intimidation. And she became in effect a moral leader in the nation and the world, for moral followers to seek to emulate. And many of those followers would become leaders.

The dramatic events in Montgomery and outside raised acute moral and ethical questions for participants including, one hopes, the segregationists as well as observers around the world. In the leadership literature today, the debate over the essence of leadership is largely a debate over what we think is the morally right way to lead. It is about how leaders *should* lead, and not so much about the jobs leaders actually do. Leaders have been doing the same kinds of things for a long time – they organize people, initiate change, arouse conflicts and settle them. Ethics concerns the morality of their goals and what they do and how they treat people in the course of achieving those goals.

On the causal impact of the broadest values, our group noted that the worldwide debate over principles will focus even more directly, over the decades ahead, on the mutually competing and reinforcing values of liberty and equality. How these values will be defined, how they will relate to one another in hierarchies of principles, how 'subvalues' of liberty such as privacy, for example, or freedom of innovation, will be protected under 1st Amendment free expression – these other issues must be dealt with. In response to the above, we also noted that the normative theory of leadership leaves the practical task of reconciliation to the leaders themselves. So in the midst of intense value conflict, what will serve as a moral constraint on the behavior of strong leaders? Can a leader be freed of constraint when he or she proposes to define the weightiest basic value? Allowing leaders that much freedom to make exceptions of their preferred key values would appear to be unjustified deviations from generally applicable moral requirements.

Values are not just static or integrated entities; they are very much in conflict, as the Montgomery bus episode dramatized. Conflict is another crucial aspect or element of leadership; some scholars indeed hold that leadership is simply conflict and hence conflict is the essence of leadership. The leadership–conflict relationship is not that simple. Conflict is not just interpersonal but *intra*personal. Many involved in the boycott had internal struggles along with their external battle. Some of the great American leaders had such internal conflicts – think of Lincoln agonizing over the political and human alternatives in overcoming slavery. Even more, there is conflict over the nature and need of conflict in a democratic society. Is progress toward the realization of 'higher' values achieved more surely and lastingly through consensual, step-by-step 'mutual satisficing,' or through confrontation, choosing of sides and hence clearly and even dramatically posed conflict? There was a school of sociology in the USA that described in exquisite detail the great balancing forces that conserved the harmonious equilibrium of a nation or community, and that studied how 'deviant tendencies' – sources of conflict – could be 'counteracted' and the system restored to that lovely equilibrium. This school of thought did not ignore disruption and dysfunction – it simply deprecated and marginalized them. Strong leadership, on the other hand, does not reject conflict – it thrives on it.

The functions of values and conflict cannot be separated from the causal role of power. We use the concept of power in two ways – humans empowering other humans, and the empowering of values in bringing about comprehensive change. The human empowerment, Joanne Ciulla (2004) wrote, gives people 'the confidence, freedom, and resources to act on their own judgments' and 'entails a distinct set of moral understandings and commitments between leaders and followers.' But she warns of 'bogus empowerment,' when leaders ignore 'the moral commitments of empowerment,' instead using the forms and language of empowerment to exploit followers more efficiently. Richard Couto examined (cf. Ciulla, 2004, p. 70) the differences among community-based organizations engaged in the exacting leadership task of forging coalitions of grassroots factions. He contrasts 'psycho-political empowerment that boosts people's self-esteem and mastery of their own lives,' as well as promoting democratic participation in actions for a common benefit, with 'psycho-symbolic empower-ment' that may elevate people's self-esteem and mastery of their own lives but leaves them politically powerless in an unchanged set of circumstances.

How about the role of power on a broader terrain, involving vast numbers of people? The bus boycott indicated the power of the single person, but only in the context of hundreds of supporters and fellow leaders. And, as noted, the boycott demonstrated the power of invisible leadership as well as visible, in an immediate context of supportive leaders and followers. Also, power takes many forms, for example in the impact of stories and storytelling. Another aspect: empowering leadership is not simply one-directional. Thus if leaders as initiators evoke positive motives like self-efficacy from followers, why should not the followers satisfy the self-directed motives of the leader, such as wanting to be heard, to have her ideas accepted, his special brand of leadership acknowledged? These various effects of empowerment need not diminish the role of leadership but rather enhance it.

It is in the linkage between the role of values and the function of power that leadership as action offers compelling historical explanations and at the same time provides an example of integrative possibilities in the study of leadership theory. Values invigorate leadership by helping to sustain the mobilization of leaders and deepen the empowerment of followers under conditions of competi-tion and conflict. Values strengthen leaders' capacity to reach out to wider publics and to gain support for still broader values (i.e., equality of opportunity as well as condition) and to empower leaders by providing a foundation for governing. Even more, by addressing basic questions of human nature, values help to clarify such questions as the relationship between liberty and equality, self-interest and altruism, individualism and collectivism.

Power is complex, despite all the simplistic popular accounts that impute vast and permanent authority and supremacy to various leaders and rulers. Power is not only quantitative, measured by dollars or guns or votes. It is qualitative and subjective, measured by leaders' and followers' wants and feelings and attitudes. Motives empower leadership, but leadership also empowers or at least legiti-mates motives. The various power relationships between leaders and followers, rulers and subjects, 'wielders' and 'targets,' reflect a parallelogram of dynamic forces: each has motivations, each has physical resources, whether gold or guns or merely their own bodies. And just as leadership can be carried out invisibly, so power can be exerted through inaction, as in the famous case of the Russian General Katuzov, who instead of marching his army out against the advancing Napoleon, stuck to his rear quarters and allowed the Emperor to be defeated largely by General Winter.

All the above ultimately leads to the transcending question of grand change – change that is intended, comprehensive, durable, and grounded in values. Each of these elements or aspects is crucial. We have not made sufficient progress to offer much to review here – the subject has been treated, rightly, as both the embodiment and the culmination of all the foregoing and much else perhaps bringing us closer to a more integrated conception of leadership.

As the search for a general theory of leadership continues, that theory will require a definition of leadership in action. We know that leadership is the mobilization, by activists, of followers, some of whom become leaders of the original activists. How this collective leadership is mobilized is tested by ethical values; what this leadership is mobilized for – its purposes or ends – by moral values. The interplay of these factors will be grounded in the economic, social, political, and cultural forces that our group has analyzed. These forces will lie at the heart of a general theory of leadership.

If I can summarize the general theory group's collective wisdom and offer our best thinking about the construct of leadership, we now see *leadership as an influence process, both visible and invisible, in a society inherited, constructed, and perceived as the interaction of persons in human (and inhuman) conditions of inequality – an interaction measured by ethical and moral values and by the degree of realization of intended, comprehensive, and durable change.*

Let me leave you with a challenge and a question. The amazing events that unfolded in Montgomery and the state and nation are that the people in action embraced every major aspect of leadership and integrated it: individual leadership, collective leadership, intra-group and inter-group conflict, conflict of strongly held values, power aspects, etc. – and ultimately produced a real change leading to more change. They made our country a better country.

If those activists could integrate the complex processes and elements of leadership in practice, in reality, should we not be able to do so in theory?

REFERENCES

Ciulla, J. (eds) (2004), *Ethics, the Heart of Leadership*, Westport, CT: Praeger, p. 59, 70.

Index